eBay Business the Smart Way

eBay Business the Smart Way

Maximize Your Profits on the Web's #1 Auction Site

Joseph T. Sinclair

AMACOM

American Management Association
New York • Atlanta • Boston • Chicago • Kansas City • San Francisco • Washington, D.C.
Brussels • Mexico City • Tokyo • Toronto

Special discounts on bulk quantities of AMACOM books are available to corporations, professional associations, and other organizations. For details, contact Special Sales Department, AMACOM, a division of American Management Association, 1601 Broadway, New York, NY 10019.
Tel.: 212-903-8316. Fax: 212-903-8083.
Web Site: www.amacombooks.org

This publication is designed to provide accurate and authoritative information in regard to the subject matter covered. It is sold with the understanding that the publisher is not engaged in rendering legal, accounting, or other professional service. If legal advice or other expert assistance is required, the services of a competent professional person should be sought.

Library of Congress Cataloging-in-Publication Data

Sinclair, Joseph T.
   eBay business the smart way : maximize your profits on the Web's #1 auction site / Joseph T. Sinclair
     p. cm.
   Includes index.
   ISBN 0-8144-7202-8
   1. eBay (Firm) 2. Internet auctions. 3. Auctions--Computer network resources. I. Title
HF5476.S478 2003
381'.17'02854678—dc21   2003004617
                                      CIP

Printing number
10 9 8 7 6 5 4 3 2 1

To my grandfather, Albert L. Hoener, Jr., and grandmother, Margaret Zoe Lorene Fellabaum Hoener, together the light of my life in my early years in Michigan

Contents

Acknowledgments

My thanks to Charlie Craft, real estate and business entrepreneur and ex-tax attorney, who brainstormed with me exactly what eBay business-people need to know about legal and business basics to get off to a good start. Thanks to my agent, Carole McClendon at Waterside Productions, who does a great job, and to Jacqueline Flynn and the folks at AMA-COM, including Mike Sivilli, who contributed to the book. The clever people at eBay continue to do a great job of creating a fabulous new marketplace and expanding it worldwide. Good work folks! And thanks to my wife Lani, daughter Brook, and son Tommy, who endured with grace the period of workaholic effort it takes to write a book. Well OK, with grace most of the time. Finally, hats off to the many eBay entrepreneurs who are setting the commercial trend for the new century, some of whom have contributed indirectly if not directly to this book. Thanks.

I

Introducing eBay Business

1

Introduction

This book focuses on selling on eBay as a profit-making enterprise for an individual, family, or small business. eBay is a dynamic new marketplace that's here to stay. With over 60 million registered members already, it continues to grow rapidly. Since the first edition of *eBay the Smart Way* in 1999, I have compared eBay to the stock and commodities exchanges when everyone else was comparing eBay to local flea markets. The fact is that today it is clear eBay will soon be as much a cornerstone of American business as the New York Stock Exchange. But more importantly, it is a democratic level playing field for individual entrepreneurs. eBay is no longer just for collectibles, garage sales, and flea markets. eBay accommodates the sale of both new merchandise and fixed-price items, and collectibles have shrunk to less than 20 percent of eBay's volume. In 2002, eBay's sales volume was $14.87 billion.

The following are some statistics from the first annual eBay Live! conference in June 2002.

eBay growth in registered users (first quarter of each year):

1998	4 million
1999	13 million
2000	30 million
2001	46 million

Number of monthly unique visitors in December 2002:

26 million

Average eBay customer:

Age	37
Household income	$63,000
Household size	3.1 people
Monthly visits to eBay	5.8
Minutes per visit	24.3

Distribution of participation across different regions of the US:

Lowest percent of norm	93
Highest percent of norm	108

This indicates very even distribution.

Composition of sales first quarter 2000:

> Collectibles over one-half
>
> Consumer goods about one-quarter
>
> Motors less than 5%

Composition of sales first quarter 2002:

> Collectibles less than 20%
>
> Consumer goods over one-half
>
> Motors almost one-quarter

Online marketplace share of merchandise sales:

eBay	12%
Amazon	12%
JC Penny	2%
Target	1%
K-Mart	1%
Walmart	1%

Sample annual sales growth on eBay:

Computers	54%
Jewelry	49%
Coins & stamps	38%

Additional statistics culled from my own eBay books show the number of items for sale (including the latest figure):

Jul 1999	2,400,000 items for sale in 1,600 categories
Jan 2001	5,000,000 items for sale in 4,000 categories
Feb 2003	12,000,000 items for sale in 18,000 categories

eBay Statistics

At one time, eBay published statistics on its home page. It cut back the volume of statistics and then finally quit publishing statistics on its home page altogether. Now it publishes statistics at its annual conference, and you can still find a few numbers in the company overview on the eBay website.

eBay Magazine published great statistics quite useful for eBay businesses. Unfortunately, *eBay Magazine* is now defunct. Statistics published by third parties about eBay are only estimates and are prone to error.

This book covers the business basics of selling on eBay, such as deciding the form of your business, getting assistance from people without hiring them as employees, avoiding undue risk and liability, borrowing money, and getting a sales tax license (very useful). Moreover, the book also shows you how to do inexpensively with Web services what formerly occupied several employees, such as inventory control, accounting, auction tracking, shipping, and customer service. Also included is practical information on finding inventory, being fee conscious, selling effectively on eBay, building your eBay reputation, creating your own storefront website, establishing merchant credit card status, and developing a strategy for profitability.

This book covers everything you need to know to get off to a quick but low-risk start selling merchandise on eBay. It's a timesaver that enables you to focus more on your particular retail business and less on researching the process of starting and operating a business.

The book also offers business buyers a few tips, such as how to buy equipment and even bulk supplies on eBay. Purchasing on eBay is a great way to cut your capital investment as well as reduce your operating expenses. But when all is said and done, this book is primarily for sellers (retailers) who want to dedicate themselves to a business on eBay.

How Many Full-Timers?

How many people are selling full time on eBay? The exact number is impossible to ascertain. It's likely in the tens of thousands, perhaps hundreds of thousands.

The number of eBay PowerSellers (people who sell over $1,000 each month) is one indication. Depending on the source, the estimates are 35,000 (last June before the sale volume requirement was lowered from $2,000 to $1,000) to 90,000 today. Even the number of a quarter-million has been alleged. But the eBay PowerSeller program is not so compelling for sellers that it captures everyone with high sales on eBay. Indeed, it may only capture a modest percentage. And many sellers sell a substantial portion of their goods to repeat buyers and bulk buyers in transactions that are not on eBay. On the other hand, $1,000 in monthly sales (the low end requirement to be an eBay PowerSeller) does not make a full-time career even with a 90 percent profit.

Consequently, it remains uncertain how many people sell full time on eBay. But the number is certainly growing, and there is no shortage of success stories.

The important thing to keep in mind is that eBay is still in its first decade. You can still get in on the ground floor. Look again at the statistics!

Who Should Read This Book?

If you're a casual eBay seller, this book probably won't amuse you, and you're better off with a basic eBay book. Indeed, this book assumes that you've already read a basic eBay book or otherwise learned most of the basics. You won't find many detailed step-by-step instructions here for doing your digital tasks. My other book, *eBay the Smart Way*, to be published in its third edition in the fall of 2003, has sold quite well, which I take to mean that it has been useful to many people.

It contains more step-by-step instruction. Naturally, this book builds on the basics covered in that book. I have tried not to repeat too much, although some ideas and information are so crucial to success that they bear repeating.

Changes

I completed this book in February 2003 at a time when the eBay website was changing almost daily. (eBay favors gradual changes rather than changes all at once.) Features that had been part of the eBay website for years were suddenly no longer available. A new look was coming online. In an attempt to keep up to date even beyond the printing press, I have created a website *http://bookcenter.com* to post significant changes that are of interest to readers.

In the past, readers have complained that I have provided erro-

neous information about eBay policies, rules, and other important things. In each case of consequence, my book was not in
error at the time it was written. But eBay changes. The policies
get more complex. The rules get stricter. And eBay devises
many new features, some of which replace the old. In my
opinion, this is a good trend. eBay is maturing as an institution.
But the changes make it necessary for you to review eBay policies and rules occasionally in order to keep up to date and to
stay alert for the introduction of new features. A book cannot
do that for you.

eBay's Place

I originally wrote a very extensive section attempting to prove a
point. When I read it, it seemed to be a well-reasoned but much
too lengthy sleeping pill. So, I will save you the somnolence and
simply state my point.

> When you have a product or service to sell, that's only half
> the story. The other half is marketing and selling.

Another way of stating this is that about 50 percent of the money
spent on any product or service represents the seller's cost of marketing and selling that product or service. This applies to manufacturers, wholesalers, retailers, publishers, attorneys, auto
transmission repair services, pest control services, and you name
it. Marketing and selling is a huge cost component in the cost of
doing business, any business. As Chapter 20 explains, it's no different for ecommerce websites. But it is different for eBay.

How Does eBay Fit In?

eBay provides inexpensive, efficient, and convenient marketing
and selling. Don't want to pay that traditional 50 percent for mar-

keting? eBay may be your economical answer. Let's look at several models.

1. **eBay Only Seller** You sell only on eBay. Your marketing cost is the fees you pay to eBay and the effort and money you spend on creating your auction ads. You have pinpointed your market. Only those who are interested in your product or service will look at your auctions. Those who look at your auctions (potential bidders) are exactly the people you want to reach. They are self-selected. And there is the greatest number possible of them because eBay is such a huge market, and in fact the largest market.

2. **Sell on eBay and Also on Your eCommerce Website** You have an ecommerce website where you sell your product or service and you also sell on eBay. Well, it generally costs just as much to market on the Web as it does off the Web. So, your ecommerce website probably won't save you marketing and selling expenses. But your sales on eBay will save you marketing expense for that portion of your sales that's on eBay. Thus, eBay can't reduce your marketing expense for all sales, but it can add to your sales with a minimal increase in overhead.

3. **Sell on eBay and Also Offline** You have a physical location where you sell your product, and you also sell on eBay. This is similar to operating an ecommerce website. You will save on your marketing expense only for that portion of your sales that are eBay sales. Consequently, eBay can't reduce your marketing and selling expense for all your sales, but it can add sales with little additional overhead.

The Great Equalizer

eBay is the great equalizer in that it puts you on an even playing field with other manufacturers, wholesalers, retailers, or even individuals. The cost of marketing is so low in the eBay electronic marketplace that you can potentially compete with anyone. In other words, you don't have to spend thousands of dollars on marketing, advertising, promotions, and salespeople to make sales on eBay. Anyone can potentially make sales on eBay. It's the new democratic marketplace. The big guys don't have an advantage. Abundant capital is not necessary for success. This situation presents a classic opportunity for those who want to work hard to build a business with sweat equity and a minimal investment.

The eBay Advantage

eBay provides you with a means of reducing your marketing costs to the point where you can potentially compete effectively with any competitors. You can beat the 50 percent marketing and selling cost rule for traditional manufacturing, wholesaling, retailing, and services business models. With the addition of just-in-time inventory control and short selling cycles (covered in Chapter 12), you can take advantage of a powerful business model.

You're in Business Now

Many people are so successful in person-to-person buying and selling on eBay that they decide to make a career out of it. That's great! They're off to a good start. Nonetheless, things change when one decides to stake one's future and one's income on an eBay business.

You're in business now. It's no longer a game, a pastime, a hobby, or a sideline. It's your new career. And it's a business not much different than any other business, offline or online.

You need to start thinking like a businessperson, particularly like a savvy retailer. Your focus needs to change from being self-centric to customer-centric. If your focus is customer-centric already, great! If not, you need to learn about customer service. You need to understand that some of eBay members' most cherished practices amount to poor customer service. You need to do better.

Customer Service

One bias of this book is that customer service is all-important. Why? Because it's the biggest trend in business today, both offline and online. It increases sales and retains customers. It's expected online where buyers can't talk face-to-face with sales clerks or fondle the merchandise. It's expected on eBay. And too many arrogant sellers on eBay think it's an impediment to profits; they set a poor example for you.

Customer service is many things. It's providing alternative means of payment. It's quick shipping. It's presenting an auction ad with complete information. It's answering questions in a timely manner. It's also many things online yet to be invented. It's whatever provides convenience to buyers and instills confidence in their purchase decisions. Customer service is your job.

But we're getting a little ahead of ourselves here. Before we can provide customer service, we need to find some customers. For many readers, the best way to get some customers is to find a selling niche on eBay.

Find Your Niche

Another bias of this book is that you need to find your niche. Selling anything and everything on eBay is an approach that works only for a few wheeling and dealing entrepreneurs. Most readers will find their retailing success in a niche (a specialty) that they can systematically exploit for sales. For some it will be an opportunistic niche where they can make money for a few months or a few years and then move on to another niche. For others it will be a niche where they can add value to the products they sell and stay in business indefinitely.

You need to decide what you want to do. This book will help you decide and then help you toward business success. I hope it will help you avoid jumping into activities that will contribute little to your business profit and will help you focus on those activities that will prove profitable.

If you're starting to get the idea that with new business models, customer service, and establishing a niche there might be a little more to starting an eBay business than meets the eye, you could be right. It's starting to look like work.

Work

Operating a business on eBay is work. In most cases, it's very hard work. I'm always amazed by those who think eBay is a pot of gold they just need to tap into and relax and enjoy the torrent of carats that comes gushing out. They've obviously never sold merchandise on eBay systematically with the intent to make worthwhile profits. If you think eBay is a working vacation, guess again.

What eBay offers is a well-proven opportunity to operate your own business profitably at home or even while you travel. It takes intelligent planning, finding a niche, mastering a series of learning curves ranging from business law to merchandise marketing, a home office, determination, persistence, some operating capital, and commitment, just to name a few of the ingredients for success. Don't underestimate the amount of work you will have to put in.

Books Can Help

This book can help. It condenses a lot of information into a reasonably small space and gives you leads to other information not included in these pages. Don't try to do it by yourself. Use this book or another like it. Also buy a basic eBay book such as *eBay the Smart Way* for reference. If you don't like my basic book, buy one like it. There's more to an eBay business than you think.

Will your labor be justified and lead to something worthwhile? The retail business is old and honorable in the US and can be financially rewarding as well as professionally fulfilling. Then too, your timing couldn't be better getting into retailing on this day, in this medium (the Web), and in this highly tuned online market we know as eBay.

State of Retail

The general state of retail today offline seems to be in decline. In many cases, retail clerks are paid minimum wages and not well trained. There are too few available to turn to conveniently for help. Often they can offer little help when a customer has a question about merchandise. Merchandise goes on the shelves without being marked with a price as if no one cares whether a frying pan costs $9 or $29. Notice, all these complaints are in regard to cus-

tomer service. Retail establishments that do provide good customer service are considered unique.

What an opportunity for online retailers! As a matter of fact, my
wife declared after last Christmas that for next Christmas she will
do all her shopping online. I'm ahead of her. I haven't been
Christmas shopping offline for five years and, in fact, bought her
Christmas present on eBay last year. In addition, most of what I
buy for my business and even personal use (except groceries) I buy
online. Over half of that I buy on eBay.

The Dark Side of Shopping

Did you see the Amazon.com television commercial during the
2002 Christmas season? Being originally from the Midwest, I
could appreciate it.

It shows a man walking searchingly in a parking lot on a dark
day with a few inches of snow on the ground. The man obviously cannot remember where he parked his car. He carries a
huge load of Christmas presents. One present drops into the
snow. He continues looking for his car without noticing the
missing present. Then the message of the television commercial pops up on the screen: *Amazon.com and you're done.*

Amazon.com in this television commercial represents not only
Amazon.com but all online shopping. Hence, you can see how
eBay enables you to compete with the malls.

eCommerce will experience steady upward growth in the years
ahead. That puts eBay, as well as you and your business, on a track
to success. This is where the action is in the new century.

So, why delay? Let's go ahead right now with your eBay aspirations and take action.

Call to Action

The prior section makes a good ending to this introductory chapter. Nonetheless, I would rather end the chapter with a call to action. You can't really know much until you step to the firing line and take a shot at eBay retailing. This is an essential step for an experienced seller as well as for a novice. You may decide based on your experience in this initial trial period that serious eBay retailing is not for you. Therefore, I don't advocate getting well set up to handle a lot of retail sales. That comes later.

Nonetheless, you have to be organized, and you have to handle your sales immediately and efficiently. Otherwise your reputation will suffer—from negative feedback—and your retailing experience will become a regrettable one.

This book leaves it to you to get organized for this initial experiment. There's no reason to learn and use anyone else's system for this trial period. Simply use a pen and paper system. Keep all your pen and paper records together in one place that you find handy to access. Your system should address the following:

- Inventory management

- Auction ad management

- Auction submittal management

- Follow-up management

- Payment management

- Fulfillment (shipping and handling) management

- Customer service management (e.g., customer communication management)

Later after your initial trial—should you decide to continue your eBay retailing—you will need to begin using an auction management service (see Chapter 17), whether eBay's or a third-party service such as Andale. But for the trial, put together your own system using the above list to guide you. Actually, creating your own system will help you choose a digital system later.

Volume

For a trustworthy retail experience (experiment), you have to do some volume selling. However, hold it to a low roar. Don't try to sell five pallets of baseball caps, one dozen per day, coming out of the chute. Keep your selling effort to something manageable given the auction management system you're using. This is just an experiment to determine whether it's worth your while to go further and invest the time, energy, and money to put your eBay retailing on an efficient digital system.

Try Dutch auctions as well as individual auctions. Every retailer should have experience with Dutch auctions and the confidence to use them when appropriate. Dutch auctions can be as few as two items or as many as a hundred (or more). All the items must be exactly the same.

The more volume you experience, the more likely it is that your provisional pen and paper auction management system will be overloaded. Don't let this happen. Volume can be a dangerous thing. If you lose track of what you're doing—very easy to do—your customer service will suffer, and you will surely get some negative feedback. Negative feedback will kill your business before it gets off the ground. In other words, instant success can ruin you. Take things slowly during your trial period.

What can you learn from your voluminous effort? The essential thing you need to learn is whether there's enough potential volume to sustain your proposed retail business on eBay.

Experiment

You should not get the idea from this book that you need to try selling one item once or twice and if it doesn't work, give up your effort. Rather, you need to experiment. If you don't get any sales, you have to change something:

Price eBay buyers typically look for bargains. If you can't sell at a price low enough to motivate buyers, you will have a lot of trouble being successful on eBay. That doesn't mean, however, that you need start with your lowest possible reserve price. Start high and work your way down. See what works.

Ad Copy The Web is an informational medium, which makes it more similar to mail order promotion than to magazine advertising. That is, you have to provide plenty of information to potential buyers. Try different approaches to writing the information. More is usually better. Photographs are a must, even when the only thing that it makes sense to photograph is the product's box.

Model When selling products, some product models (e.g., Sony TG50) are more popular than others even when they are practically identical. If you choose the wrong model, success may be out of reach. Experiment.

Shipping and Handling Arrangements It appears that some eBay sellers give away items at wholesale prices and make a profit on shipping and handling. This irritates buyers. Make your shipping and handling reasonable. Compare alternatives and offer a cost-effective (to buyers) method. Try including shipping and handling in the price (i.e., free shipping and handling).

Payment Methods A common mistake for retailers is to use a payment method that's convenient to themselves. Think of your customers instead. Use payment methods that make buying convenient for potential buyers. There are several popular ways to accept payment. I recommend that if you don't use all of them at least experiment with each of them until you find cause to reject any one of them.

If you get easy sales, you need to evaluate what you're doing:

Price If your sales go very well, you might want to try raising your price (reserve price) to find the point where sales drop off.

Sustainability If your sales go well, you have to ask yourself, Is this sales program sustainable? Can I get the products in the numbers I need from wholesalers and delivered on time? Can I continue to get the products at the wholesale price I need to be profitable? How easy will it be for someone to duplicate my sales effort?

It's a rare eBay business that is sustained by only one item. In most cases, but not all, there will be at least a small number of related items that you will sell in your eBay retailing business. You need to experiment with selling each one of them.

Unique Markets

Oddly enough each item, no matter how similar to another item, has its own market. For instance, there are two kinds of memory for digital cameras, CompactFlash cards and Smart-Media cards. When I purchased a memory module on eBay, I naturally bought the wrong kind for my new Fuji Fine Pix a few years back. I tried to return the CompactFlash card to the seller for an exchange. The seller refused and indicated that he sold only CompactFlash cards and could not make an exchange for a SmartMedia card. When I investigated further, I discovered that the seller monopolized the eBay sales of CompactFlash cards while another seller monopolized the eBay sales of

SmartMedia cards. The dynamics of these memory micromarkets were different enough to have different monopolies. Consequently, I bought a SmartMedia card from the other seller and sold my mispurchased CompactFlash card on eBay easily for a $10 loss.

What are the lessons for retailers here? The first lesson is that each item has its own market. Don't assume that similar items will produce the same sales results. You may have the market to yourself for one item and face an aggressive competitor for a similar item or even total disinterest from buyers for a similar item. The second lesson is that you will want to sell similar items to take advantage of eBay's potential. The person who sold me the CompactFlash card could have provided better customer service, not to mention making additional sales, if he could have provided me with an exchange.

Don't get carried away. If you have 225 items you want to sell, you don't have to experiment with each before deciding that eBay will be a good or bad venue for your retail business. Do some spot checks; that is, do some representative selling with a reasonable number of items. You will not get definitive results, but it's the best you can do under the circumstances without an unwieldy trial selling effort.

Price

eBay is like any other business. Price alone does not determine sales volume. Price and customer service are the primary determinants, but there are others. Experiment with a variety of things, not just price. For instance, changing the advertising copy in your auction ads may do wonders to improve your sales (see Chapter 8).

Let Your Brain Do the Walking

How often have you heard that someone started out selling one type of item with limited success but in the process discovered that selling a completely unrelated type of item was very profitable? That might happen to you on eBay. Keep an open mind. You may discover that the type of item you want to sell on eBay will not constitute a profitable business for a variety of reasons. Nonetheless, by putting yourself on the firing line, you may discover one or more niches that no one else has found or to which no one else is selling as well as you can (see Figure 1.1). Thus, it may pay off not to keep your brain in a straightjacket. Keep alert, and watch for opportunities. Find out what your competitors are doing. And research your markets well, both offline and online.

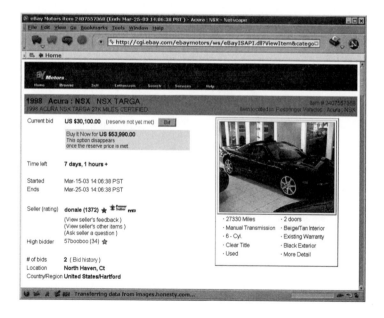

Figure 1.1   eBay Motors auction listing. ©1995-2003 eBay Inc.

There is another important consideration here. eBay provides a level playing field for everyone. That means that you can potentially compete effectively against major manufacturers and retailers, such as Sun Microsystems, now active on eBay. That's what makes eBay a fabulous opportunity. Without a huge capital investment, you can potentially compete as a retailer with the big retailers. However, that works two ways.

Suppose you have developed an eBay niche in which you sell snake-proof outdoor boots to people mostly in the southern states where poisonous snakes are populous. Your profit after all your expenses is 23 percent on monthly sales of $15,000. What if someone comes along who does all the things that you do and can buy from the same suppliers at the same wholesale prices but is willing to sell for only an 18 percent profit? You will soon have competition on eBay that may drive you out of business—or drive the profits so low that the boot business doesn't interest you any longer. How do you protect yourself against this?

This is really an age-old business problem, but it takes on a new dimension on eBay. If you are in a bricks and mortar business, you can see your competition coming. Your competitor has to rent a retail store (locally), start advertising, and spin up the business, a process that takes a fair amount of time. You will have adequate time to strategize and react to meet the competition. On eBay, your competition may appear instantly and become an effective competitor literally overnight.

The way to protect yourself is to realize that business on eBay can proceed at a faster pace than offline. You have to remain mentally attuned to your current retail situation, ready to react instantly to new competition. You also have to remain mentally attuned to potential new markets you can exploit when old ones go sour. Consequently, it's much more likely on eBay that you will end up selling something you've never dreamed of; it's also more likely your retail career on eBay may evolve through a series of different types of products rather than remaining with just one type of product indefinitely.

What is being said here? Simply, that right from the beginning you need to keep in mind how things are likely to evolve for you on eBay. Don't conduct just a few experiments in your trial retailing effort and call it quits if they fail. Experiment a lot until you find something that works. Then go after the profitable niche you have found. You are likely to be doing this again and again in your eBay retailing career.

What Do You Want to Do?

A trial selling period will often reveal to you what you want to do and what you don't want to do. For instance, some people don't mind doing the fulfillment chores such as packaging and shipping. It gives them a tangible sense of accomplishment. Others would rather do almost anything else than package products every day and deal with the Postal Service. Pay attention during your trial period. When you get into your full-fledged retailing operation, you're unlikely to have the time to do everything. Delegate the tasks you don't want to do to your spouse, your children, employees, or independent contractors.

Marketing Study

If you were to open a bricks and mortar retail store, you would want to do a marketing study first. That's the smart way to start a retail business. And marketing studies, usually done by an industry expert, tend to be expensive. For eBay, your trial selling period is your marketing study. In fact, it's the best of all marketing studies. It's an actual trial selling operation. And you can do it yourself.

You don't necessarily need an industry expert. What makes this possible and cost-effective is that eBay is a virtual market. It exists only online. It doesn't take a huge investment to operate in a virtual environment.

Take a hint from the market study concept. Conduct your trial sales as objectively (scientifically) as possible. Keep notes and records and accumulate statistics so that when you're ready to evaluate what you've done, you won't have to rely on your memory completely. Don't try to make your study complicated, but also don't make it so easy that you miss valuable market information.

To supplement what you've determined from your trial, try Andale's research function at the Andale website (*http://andale.com*). It's free and provides some useful statistics. Also try HammerTap's Deep Analysis (*http://hammertap.com*) for statistics about products and sellers on eBay in specific categories or keyword groupings. It will help.

When the Time Comes

You've completed your trial, and your selling has been successful. Now you're ready to commit yourself to a retail course of action on eBay that's profitable. This is not the time to keep the auction management system you have created, particularly if it's a pen and paper system as recommended above. Bite the bullet and subscribe to an auction management service (to be used via the Web). It's something of a learning curve and it's money out of your pocket, but it's about the only sensible ways to conduct eBay business. eBay offers its own auction management services, and third parties such as Andale also offer great auction management services.

Keep in touch after you've accomplished something substantial or unique in an eBay business, I'd like to hear from you. Email me at *jt@sinclair.com*. (Put EBAY READER in the subject line so I can find your email in the sea of daily SPAM.) Perhaps I'll be able to use your story (without revealing your trade secrets) in a future edition of this book.

Also, visit *bookcenter.com* for further information relevant to this book. This a website devoted to my eBay books.

Good luck with your eBay business!

II

Getting Started

2

Setting Yourself Up Legally

You don't think much about your legal form of business after you start selling on eBay until you start listening to your friends and relatives. "Be sure to incorporate." "A partnership is the best way to go." "Take advantage of special corporations to save tax." There's no end to this free advice. The fact is that you're probably better off just doing business yourself until you start acquiring a lot of employees and creditors. But let's get a general overview so that you know where you stand.

This chapter is for those who are beginning their eBay retailing businesses or who are small. Once you grow large, the issues regarding forms of business will be considerably different from what is outlined in this chapter.

Sole Proprietorship

You're the proprietor (owner) of your business. When you own it alone, you are the sole proprietor. Thus, the term "sole proprietorship" is used as the name for a one-person business. It's simple. The income belongs to you. The expenses are yours. The profit (or loss) is yours. You file income tax for your business under your own name.

Many people elect to be sole proprietors but do business under a special name, usually a name designed to attract business. This is normally called an *assumed name, fictitious name, alias*, or a *dba* (doing business as). To make it legal, you need to record (file) an assumed name affidavit (or whatever it's called in your state) in your county. This requires filling out a standard affidavit form available from the county, having it notarized, and publishing the affidavit in a local newspaper several times.

If sole proprietor John Harrison of Redding, California, operates a retail business selling boy's clothing on eBay under the name *Fontleroy Factory*, he needs to file an assumed name affidavit in Shasta County. The brand name he builds is Fontleroy Factory, not John Harrison. People will know his business as Fontleroy Factory, not as John Harrison. People will make out checks for purchases to Fontleroy Factory, not to John Harrison.

A bank will not allow John to deposit or cash the checks to Fontleroy Factory unless he opens an account under the name Fontleroy Factory. A bank will not allow him to open such an account without John providing the bank with a copy of his duly recorded assumed name affidavit.

Advantages of Filing

You and your name are official, and legal. Occasionally, someone or some company will ask you for a copy of your assumed name affidavit, and you have it ready to give to them. If you don't have it, you may be forced to get it before you can sell your business, borrow money, or get an account with a bank or a vendor (wholesaler). Assumed names are unique in each county. If someone else records your assumed name in your county before you do, you will have to switch to another name or get into a legal dispute.

Disadvantages of Filing

When you record and publish an assumed name affidavit, it's public information. Your city is likely to ask you to get a business license and perhaps pay a municipal tax. You will be inundated by vendors, who want to sell you everything for your business. You may even be visited by city inspectors responsible for regulating who knows what! And every time you change counties or change names, you will have to refile. How can you get around filing an assumed name affidavit?

First, choose a name that no one else is likely to use. For instance, John Harrison's choice, Fontleroy Factory, is not one that's likely to be chosen by someone else in Shasta County; that is, no one is likely to steal it. If you're worried about someone stealing it, trademark it.

Second, do an end run around the bank. Have a stamp made that states your assumed name (e.g., Fontleroy Factory). Endorse your incoming checks with that stamp. Then endorse the checks with another stamp that has your name, the words "For Deposit Only," and your personal bank account number. Deposit only via an ATM (automated teller machine). For instance, for John Harrison the first stamp would read, "Fontleroy Factory." The second stamp would read:

For Deposit Only
4879341807
John Harrison

When endorsing, you use the second stamp (second endorsement) below the first stamp (first endorsement). With this technique you do not need to open a separate business checking account. You can keep it simple. Or, even if you want to keep a separate bank account for your business (good idea for bookkeeping purposes), you can still open it under your own name.

Avoid Tellers

If you try using the two-stamp system for a deposit made through a teller, you may run into trouble, even though it's perfectly legal. Keep in mind also that every bank is different. Indeed, two branches in the same bank may operate a little differently. The two-stamp technique may not work everywhere.

If a vendor asks for the assumed name affidavit that you don't have (because you haven't filed it), stalling the request might work. They want to do business with you and may eventually forget about the assumed name affidavit.

Why Not to File

The prior subsection provided you several methods to avoid problems you will face by not filing an assumed name affidavit. I do not necessarily recommend that you don't file. You will do well to choose a business name that will promote your business, file an assumed name affidavit, get a business license from your city, and pay any municipal tax. (For an eBay business any municipal tax would normally be minimal.) That makes you legal and is the best practice. In fact, there may be some penalties in your state for not doing so.

The reality is, though, that many small businesses choose not to file assumed name affidavits. The following discussion indicates some reasons why.

Filing might be impractical where you are a one-person entrepreneur working at home who operates several businesses at once. For example, I know someone who operates about five home businesses (all Internet-related) each under an assumed name but has filed only one assumed-name affidavit.

If you attempt to get a business license, you may find that your home is not zoned properly for your business, and you face a potentially difficult situation. This is one of the primary reasons people fail to apply for a business license. There two considerations to keep in mind here.

First, regardless of the zoning, if your business poses no danger to the neighbors nor any detriment to the neighborhood, you might find it in your best interest to avoid getting a license. It's not difficult to feel justified that what you do in your own home is your own business.

Most residential zoning allows home businesses within certain guidelines. However, restrictive covenants (in your subdivision) may forbid home businesses even where the zoning law permits them.

Second, if your business is dangerous to neighbors, contributes to the deterioration of the neighborhood, or otherwise causes problems for neighbors, you may not be able to justify conducting your business at home. You need to find another location for your business.

Another reason to avoid filing an assumed name affidavit is that filing it seems to have little relevance to doing business on eBay. The laws governing how business is done were developed in the nineteenth and early twentieth centuries and seem a little curious now for online businesses. Certainly filing an assumed name affidavit in your county isn't going to put anyone outside your county on notice of your business, and 99.9 percent of your eBay customers and vendors are going to be outside of your county. Indeed, most of your customers will likely be outside of your state!

Your Own Name

Of course, if you do business in your own name, you do not have to file an assumed name affidavit. It's not a bad idea to operate under your own name for a while until you develop a complete eBay business strategy. At that point you need to come up with a business name and start building your brand. But until then, you won't have to worry about filing an assumed name affidavit.

Trademarks

The federal trademark statutes have little to do with filing assumed names. Filing an assumed name affidavit does not necessarily give your assumed name trademark protection nor does it protect you against someone outside your county who may have trademark rights to use the name exclusively. Read more about trademarks in Chapter 3.

Income Taxation

As a sole proprietor, you file your income tax return as a person. Your Social Security number is your tax identification number. Since you are not employed by anyone, and no one is withholding FICA from your income, you need to file quarterly tax returns and pay the estimated tax.

Partnership

A partnership without a partnership agreement is like an airplane with a weak airframe. You know that those wings are going to drop off sooner rather than later, and the plane is going to drop out of the sky like a stone. Just don't do it! Don't get entangled with someone else without a written partnership agreement.

Trust

On the other hand, some of the best business partnerships have no written agreement. They are based on the trust that each partner will be fair to the other. If trust proves to work well, it is usually not something that grows out of meeting someone and discussing your business aspirations with him. It builds over years based on some kind of business relationship between you and the other person. In other words, a long courtship is usually more durable than love at first sight.

Trust should be based not only on shared ideas and aspirations, but also on shared values and shared experience. In addition, partners should have complementary business skills. In a retail business, a person who has management skills and a person who has marketing skills may make good partners. However, a person who has marketing skills probably should not partner with a person who has similar skills.

Whether You Think So or Not

When you embark on an undefined business venture with someone else, you are partners whether you think so or not. You have a partnership without a written agreement. You may have a verbal agreement or an implied agreement, but such agreements are still legal. They're just much more foggy than written agreements.

Documents

You can have the longest and best partnership agreement ever written, but lack of trust will make your partnership business stressful and potentially unworkable. So, trust is important even when you use a written partnership agreement.

Most people will find themselves in a trust relationship with a potential business partner that is comfortable but not one of absolute trust. In such cases, a written partnership agreement will help hold the business together. If nothing else, it should clearly define the partnership relationship for most routine business purposes and enable the partners to do business in confidence. It should also cover special situations such as the death of a partner or the withdrawal of a partner from the partnership. It doesn't necessarily have to be long or complex.

Partnership agreements are normally drafted by an attorney who can also educate you regarding the legal and tax effects of operating a partnership. However, you may find the confidence to write your own agreement by using a book on partnerships such as one published by Nolo Press (see Resources section at end of chapter).

Responsibility

You are responsible for your partner. Suppose your partner gets in his car to do an errand for the partnership. He has an auto accident (his fault) in which the other driver is severely injured. The partnership is responsible.

Let's say the claim of the injured party is $300,000, and your partner's auto insurance covers only $100,000. The partnership is responsible for the remaining $200,000. If your partner can't (or won't) pay it, you will have to pay it.

Auto accidents are probably the most common liability risks for eBay retailing partnerships. Here are some questions to ask. Does your auto insurance cover business uses of an auto? Does your partner have such coverage? Do you have adequate coverage? Does your partner? Do you list your partner as a *named insured* on your policy? Does your partner do the same for you? The answer to all should be yes.

Insurance is useful to limit liability and keep things under control in a partnership, but it takes consultation with a business insurance agent to make intelligent use of insurance. Regardless of whether you use a written partnership agreement for your partnership, at the very least get proper and adequate insurance coverage. Otherwise you may have more liability than you anticipated.

Partnership Employees

When you become partners, you and your partner become employees of the partnership. The only way to avoid this arrangement is to have each partner be an independent contractor supplying services or products to the partnership under an arm's length written contract. This can be an awkward arrangement. But having employees also creates substantial concerns, as Chapter 3 explains in detail.

Avoiding Partnerships

One way to avoid becoming partners with someone inadvertently is to carefully define every business relationship you have with someone else. For instance, suppose you and a wholesaler decide to cooperate to create sales on eBay. You are going to carry on a vigorous eBay auctioning campaign, and the wholesaler is going to ship the inventory to you (stored in your garage), expecting no payment from you until after you sell the merchandise on eBay (no time period defined). This sounds more like a partnership than a traditional wholesaler-retailer relationship. What can you do to avoid an inadvertent (implied) partnership, as in this case?

Make sure the vendor sends you invoices for all inventory received. Have the purchase agreement briefly stated on the invoice. Typically a vendor wants payment within 30 days. Setting the payment period to 90 days might achieve the effect intended by the parties without leaving the payment period undefined. If not sold within 90 days, the right to send back the inventory within the next 30 days without obligation might also help achieve the effect intended without leaving the arrangement vague. With the agreement stated on the vendor's invoices and with the arrangements more specifically defined, it will be difficult for anyone to claim that you and the wholesaler are partners.

Define Your Relationship

It is especially important to define your legal relationship with people who will do some work for you. You don't want them to be partners inadvertently, and you may not want them to even be employees (see Chapter 3). Usually you can just define the relationship by signing a simple agreement and conducting business with paperwork that indicates a specific relationship such vendor-retailer or retailer-independent contractor.

Income Taxes

A partnership must file a tax return. It is just an information return, however, and a partnership pays no income tax. All the income passes through to the individual partners who declare the income on their personal income tax returns. Your partnership must have a federal Employer Identification Number (EIN).

Corporations

It seems to me that most people incorporate their business because they think it's impressive to have a corporation. After all, you get to be president. For business today, however, it probably matters a lot less than you think, at least as long as your business is small. If you are going to incorporate, you should have specific reasons for doing so.

The two primary reasons for incorporating are to limit your liability and to sell stock. It turns out that neither of these reasons is compelling for most small businesses.

Limited Liability

You need to be concerned with liability in regard to creditors. This is where being incorporated can help. You also need to be concerned with limited liability due to negligence.

Creditors

If your corporate business gets in trouble financially, you will not have personal liability to its creditors. The corporation owes the bills.

Many wholesalers and other vendors will not ask you to sign personally for inventory ordered, particularly for small orders. They will, however, rely on the corporation's credit rating to extend credit in the first place. If you don't have established business credit, you may have to make payment in advance. Some wholesalers will extend your corporation credit but not without your personal guarantee.

> If you make payment in advance for your inventory or if you have to personally guarantee payment for your inventory purchased on credit, you don't need the limited liability provided by a corporation.

Many small businesses borrow from a bank to raise the operating capital that they use to purchase inventory. Try having your corporation borrow money from your bank without you signing personally. Very unlikely.

Creditors

Do you really need protection from creditors as an eBay business? Keep in mind that if you operate properly on eBay, you get a quick turnover. That means you don't hold your inventory very long. Auctions are ten days at the most. Consequently, you don't need as much operating capital (or credit) as a traditional retailer that has to keep inventory on the shelves for many months before selling it. If the market for your products suddenly dries up, you shouldn't have six months of inventory in stock that you can't sell. Three or four weeks of inventory should be plenty for an eBay business. Thus, you face your lack of sales sooner, and your potential losses are much less.

This is not to say that as you grow you should ignore your liability to creditors. Rather it is to point out two considerations. First, you may not need as much protection against insolvency as traditional retailers as long as you stay small. Second, you can control your turnover rate easier than a traditional retailer, and you can certainly keep it higher than most traditional retailers. So long as you have a reasonable profit margin, it's hard to get insolvent on eBay due to the potentially high inventory turnover rate for an eBay business.

For Negligence

Liability for negligence is a different matter. If you injure another person in an auto accident (your fault) while driving on corporate business, both the corporation and you are liable for damages. So, there's no liability protection for you in this case. However, if an employee of your corporation causes an accident, the corporation will be liable, but you won't necessarily be personally liable.

As a small business, you are better off limiting your exposure to negligence liability with insurance rather than incorporating.

Selling Stock

Selling stock in your corporation to raise capital for your business is essentially illegal without a substantial disclosure statement written by an expensive securities attorney. That limits you to selling stock only to close friends and relatives who will not sue you in the case of a total loss (or report you to the US district attorney). Also consider that when you sell stock, you don't have to pay interest on the money raised, but you are selling an ownership interest in your business. If you can borrow money to get started instead of selling stock, you are probably better off, especially if the business is successful.

Disadvantages

When you incorporate, you have to file incorporation documents normally drafted by an attorney. In addition, you need to hold annual meetings and keep minutes usually drafted by an attorney. This can be more expensive than any benefits of incorporation are worth. Also, be aware of the state annual corporate fee. In some states the fee is nominal. In California, however, the fee is $1,000 per year. That would pay a lot of eBay fees.

You may be able to incorporate yourself and hold your own annual meetings (see Nolo Press in Resources below). However, the incorporation laws are different in every state, and you will need instructions for your specific state.

Income Taxes

A corporation pays income tax. If dividends are paid to stockholders, the individual stockholders pay income tax on the dividends. This is double taxation to be avoided at all costs. The way to avoid this is to take all the profit out of your corporation in expenses each year so that it doesn't show a profit for income tax purposes (has no net income). The most popular way to do this if you are a corporate employee is to pay yourself a bonus at the end of the year. If instead you are an independent contractor who contracts to do work for the corporation, you will have to figure out some other clever and legal way to pay yourself a bonus at the end of the year.

Subchapter S Corporation

The IRS does allow certain small corporations to elect to be taxed as partnerships, in effect. The corporate profit is not taxed but passes through to the stockholders.

Your corporation must have a Federal Employer Identification Number.

Hybrid Forms

In the last twenty years many states have passed statutes creating hybrid business forms that offer a combination of benefits from both partnerships and corporations. Some have even gone so far as to enable you to design your own form of business, in effect. You will probably want to wait until you have considerable business success behind you before you consider one of these legal forms of doing business, such as a limited liability company (LLC).

Virtual Businesses

A virtual business is not a legal form. It is essentially a business carried on by persons who are not in the same location and who communicate routinely by electronic means.

Virtual businesses predate the rise of the Internet. The inexpensive communication provided by the Internet (e.g., email), though, has made virtual business much more popular than ever. In additional, the Web provides a location for a virtual business. The business website is the business location.

For instance, an attorney who works in a home office and has a legal secretary in a home office two miles away is a virtual business. In the past, the attorney would communicate with the secretary via telephone, fax, and mail. Today they would most likely communicate by telephone, fax, email, and document file transfers via the Internet. The legal business might also have a website to give the law practice more substance. If you think this a bizarre example, you might be surprised to learn that there are thousands of attorneys with national practices (e.g., patent law) who do just this, usually living in resort places such as Hilton Head, Vail, or Sedona.

In any event, the idea of a virtual business should have a great deal of appeal to you. After all, you are already likely to be well tuned into the virtual world with your eBay business. One way to build your retailing organization is to have workers who work in their own locations. You don't have to pay the overhead for a physical location for anyone who works for you, and the routine communication via telephone or email is inexpensive. Indeed, the capability to attach digital documents to email messages makes virtual businesses very workable.

For instance, you might have a partner in Paris who identifies unusual French products likely to sell well in the American market on eBay. Your French partner arranges to buy wholesale in Paris, takes possession of the inventory, and ships items from Paris to your eBay auction winners. Or, you might have an independent contractor (person) storing your inventory in his garage. Each day you email him your eBay winning bidders, and he ships your products to the winners. There are thousands of possibilities.

Use Common Sense

Although virtual retail organizations might be a good idea, don't follow the virtual idea blindly. Sometimes a traditional business arrangement can work better and more inexpensively than a virtual one.

And Then You Grow

As mentioned in the opening of the chapter, this chapter is for beginners and eBay businesses that are small. Once you reach a certain size, things change. Partnerships, corporations, and other business forms do offer certain advantages for larger businesses. Some are tax advantages and some are operational advantages. When you find yourself thinking that the California corporation fees ($1,000 per year) seems like a pittance and you can see some solid benefits from incorporating, it might be time for you to start seriously considering a corporation for your eBay business.

Don't rush into a more complex business form, however. There are thousands of sole proprietors who have sales in the millions, make profits in the tens or hundreds of thousands of dollars, and who operate very simple businesses. They like it that way.

Why would anyone avoid becoming a large successful business (ripe to be incorporated) if they had the opportunity to do so in an eBay business? For one thing, risk normally increases with size. There's simply more at stake: more inventory, more overhead, more employees, more creditors, bigger loans, and more problems. For many people it's a better business strategy to stay small yet increase one's income by selling higher-priced goods or initiating more efficient operations.

Taxation

Most tax considerations for small business focus primarily on federal income taxation. The federal tax law is quite complicated. Each legal business form has different tax benefits and disadvantages. Most choices regarding business forms are heavily influenced by tax considerations usually discussed with a lawyer, certified public accountant (CPA), or other tax advisor. Even a basic discussion of tax law, however, is way beyond the scope of this book. Most opportunities for tax savings come once your business has grown to a substantial income and multiple employees. Until then, you won't miss much by remaining a sole proprietor.

In addition to federal income taxes, you also pay self-employment taxes (Social Security) as a sole proprietor. Also, don't forget state income taxes if your state has an income tax. But that's not the end. Consult a local CPA, lawyer, or other tax expert regarding taxes you need to pay.

Resources

A detailed discussion of business forms may be found in many of the books published by Nolo Press—for ordinary people, not attorneys. Visit the Nolo website at:

http://www.nolo.com

Nolo's *Small Business Start-Up Kit* is a good place to start. Nolo has books on a wide range of legal topics that will help you with whatever legal business form you choose. All of the books are downloadable as ebooks right from the website. It also offers legal kits for various small business matters. You can find Nolo Press books in most bookstores.

Commerce Clearing House (CCH), a legal publisher, offers a special website for small businesses at:

http://www.toolkit.cch.com

It's the Business Owner's Toolkit for nonlawyers and provides many downloadable legal forms you can use to get your business set up.

Another resource is the MyLawyer website which sells a set of legal documents for business and makes it easy to fill in the blanks. Check it out at:

http://www.mylawyer.com

FindLaw for Business provides legal articles covering a wide range of business topics and offers legal services as well. It includes an attorney directory. You can use it at:

http://biz.findlaw.com

At BusinessLaw you can get basic information for small businesses at a website sponsored by a variety of government agencies, including the Small Business Administration. It also provides links to useful legal resources. Go to:

http://www.businesslaw.gov

Useful basic books include the following:

Small Time Operator, Bernard B. Kamoroff, CPA, Bell Springs Publishing, Willits, California, 2002.

The Small Business Legal Guide, 2nd ed., Lynne Ann Frasier, Esq., Sourcebooks, Naperville, Illinois, 1998.

Conclusion

Everyone, every situation, every product, and every market is different. There is no right answer as to which business form to adopt for your eBay business. You might have a compelling reason to incorporate immediately even though your eBay business is small, has few creditors, and no employees. But most eBay retailers who have small businesses are probably best off remaining sole proprietors until their businesses grow large.

3

Business Details

The topics in this chapter are not an all-inclusive list of things you need to know to be in business for yourself. But the chapter does cover the basics and probably includes some things you didn't think of.

Sales Tax License

This is a license issued by your state to authorize you to collect sales tax on everything you sell in your state. With the license goes a periodic obligation to account for the funds you have collected and deposit the funds with the state. Some states may require a security deposit as a condition of issuing the license.

Other Names

A sales tax license goes by various names, such as resale license, sales tax certificate, seller's permit, or reseller's permit. Find out what it is in your state.

The license gives you the right to buy goods from wholesalers without paying sales tax. You collect the sales tax from the end user of the goods, your customer. Wholesalers will ask for your sales tax number (license number) when they sell you merchandise.

You only need to collect sales tax on items you sell to buyers inside your state. When you sell to a buyer out of state, they don't have to pay sales tax.

Do You Have Choice?

Can you sell on eBay without getting a sales tax license and without collecting sales tax? Sure. If you refuse to sell to anyone in your state, you don't need a sales tax license. But if you routinely sell to customers in your state, you will violate the law if you do not collect sales tax.

States Without Sales Tax

Alaska, Delaware, Montana, New Hampshire, and Oregon are the five states that do not have a sales tax.

Most people who do a garage sale on eBay just don't collect sales tax. In other words, those who sell stuff they've collected in their garage and thereafter quit selling don't bother to get a sales tax license. They may be violating the law (depending on exemptions), but they are not conducting an ongoing business.

Don't look at such examples of what you should or shouldn't do. If you operate an ongoing retail business on eBay, you must collect sales tax and pass it along to the state.

Report and Deposit on Time

Most small businesses that get into trouble with the state tax authorities do so because they did not file their periodic reports and make their periodic sales tax deposits. Don't let this happen to you. Once you get behind, it often becomes very difficult to catch up. File your reports on time as well as make your deposits on time. As you can imagine, having a sales tax license has a certain bureaucratic responsibility to it.

Your Passport to Success

Your sales tax license is your passport to the world of wholesaling. Wholesalers must collect sales tax on everything they sell unless they sell it for resale to a business holding a sales tax license. Consequently, wholesalers are always concerned that they deal with businesses (or people) holding sales tax licenses.

Employer Identification Number (EIN)

Wholesalers may also require your EIN if you're a partnership or corporation or your Social Security number (tax identification number) if you're a sole proprietor.

This provides you with a great benefit. When you get a sales tax license, you are de facto considered a legitimate retailer by wholesalers. This is an easy way to gain instant creditability. It doesn't mean that all wholesalers will do business with you, but many will.

Many trade shows require that you present your sales tax license to gain admission. Other trade shows give you preferential treatment if you present your sales tax license. The attitude of the trade shows is reflected throughout the business world. A sales tax license will open a lot of doors for you.

You might even consider putting your sales tax license number on your business card. If that doesn't appeal to you, use two sets of cards, one with the license number and one without. The same goes for stationery and other business documents you send to wholesalers.

Business License

Most municipalities will require that you get a business license, even for a home business. It's a way to identify a business and to collect any municipal taxes. Even the license fee itself may be a significant source of income for some municipalities. When you file an assumed name affidavit, it alerts municipal authorities that you have a business.

If you operate a business in a physical retail location in your locale, you will become knowledgeable about local taxation just by talking with other businesspeople. Sooner or later the municipal authorities will come to you if you do not get a business license and pay municipal taxes, if any.

If you sell only on eBay, operate out of your home, and don't attend Rotary Club meetings, you are not as likely to know or understand the byways of local business taxation. Municipal authorities are unlikely to find you, particularly if you do not file an assumed name affidavit or get a business license. Clearly, these local business considerations are irrelevant to you in doing business on eBay. Nonetheless, you are obligated by law to follow the municipal regulations and pay any municipal fees and taxes.

See the section on sole proprietorship in Chapter 2 for more information on conducting business at home.

State Use Tax

If you buy business assets (not for resale) out of state and do not pay sales tax to the state where you made the purchase, you probably owe your own state a use tax equivalent to your state's sales tax.

Regulations

Depending on what you sell, you may be required to meet local, state, or federal laws and regulations or obtain special licenses. The scope of such is so wide that it will take a book written for your state just to alert you to some of the laws and regulations you may have to follow. If you have any suspicion that you might need a special license, contact the proper governmental authority.

Employees

If you are successful selling on eBay, sooner or later you will need other people to work for you. Hiring employees subjects you to a huge set of new responsibilities. Just the paper work to do your payroll—even for one employee—is enough to discourage you. Be aware that employees cost more than their wages. You must contribute to their benefits, withhold taxes, and pay workers' compensation insurance.

For instance, suppose you hire a person (as an employee) to process eBay auction sales for you from his home. He slips in his home office, falls down, and severely injures his knee. It's your responsibility. He was injured on the job.

Or, suppose you want to fire an employee because you just caught a huge mistake he made, which will cost you a fortune. Can you do it? How can you do it? What are the employee's rights? (Yes, employees do have rights.) You take on a lot of potential liability when you hire employees. The employment or human relations (HR) laws are vast and complex. Small businesses are exempt from many of them, but they still provide insane complexities that will almost require a lawyer to sort out.

Be advised that hiring employees is a last resort that you should put off as long as possible. But what other choice do you have?

Independent Contractors

Until you are prosperous enough to take on the responsibilities of having employees, use independent contractors instead. What is an independent contractor? It's someone in business for himself who provides services to you.

Guidelines

When you have someone work for you as an independent contractor, the IRS becomes suspicious thinking you are trying to avoid paying withholding taxes. Therefore, there are guidelines that tell when a work provider is an employee or independent contractor. Some of the guidelines follow:

- Do you provide benefits to the worker in addition to payment?

- Do you provide on-the-job training?

- Does the worker use your tools and supplies?

- Does the worker follow a schedule set by you?

- Does the worker work on your premises?

- Do you tell the worker how to do the job rather what must be accomplished?

- Does the worker supervise your other workers?

- Can the worker quite at any time without liability?

- Does the worker get paid without submitting business invoices?

- Does the worker work only for you and no one else doing the same work?

If the answer to any of these questions is yes, you have a potential problem. See the IRS guidelines for further detail.

What's the worst that can happen? The IRS can and will claim your worker is an employee and collect income tax withholding payments going back to the date of the first work. The worker could get injured on the job, workers' compensation insurance wouldn't cover the injury, and you would be liable for the injury.

Tailor your worker relationships so that they meet the guidelines, keeping in mind that this matter needs further investigation and more detail than this book covers.

Always insist that independent contractors bill you with invoices that look business-like. It's best if they have a business name different from their own, too (e.g., Johnson Packaging Service instead of Robert G. Johnson). Independent contractors usually have their own business cards, stationery, equipment, tools, business bank accounts and the like.

Can You Help?

Can you set someone up as an independent contractor? Go lightly here. You can tell them how independent contractors operate. You can even tell them that you only work with independent contractors. But don't assist them to become independent contractors, and don't hire them on the condition that they become independent contractors. If you inspire someone to become an independent contractor to do work for you, encourage him to get other customers. Make referrals, if necessary, even to your competitors.

Contract

Always have a written contract with each independent contractor. It doesn't have to be complex or long, but it should show that you are contracting with the person to get something accomplished for a specific payment. It should not recite how or when the independent contractor shall do the work (although deadlines are permissible) or what he shall use to get the job done (although engineering specifications for quality in products and materials are permissible).

A true independent contractor is likely to get the work specified in the contract done. If not, you can bring a claim for damages. On the other hand, an employee can quit any time without liability.

Fulfillment Example

Suppose you contract with the guy down the street who has a big garage to do your fulfillment for you. He is to store your inventory, package your products, and ship the products to your customers. If he's an independent contractor, he can set up the garage and the fulfillment processes any way he desires, he can work when he wants, and he must buy his own packaging materials and equipment.

You can set quality (engineering) specifications for packaging, deadlines for shipping, and the means of communication (telephone, email), but you can't run the fulfillment business through him. You need to have a short written contract with him that shows the relationship between you and him.

If You Don't Have a Contract

Without a contract, you're inviting an eventual legal action. You might ask yourself, Who will ever question the independent relationship? Who will ever know? You and the other person are on good terms and have a complete understanding of the independent nature of the work relationship.

Unfortunately, it's always the other person who instigates the legal action. For example, the other person doesn't pay income taxes. The IRS eventually catches up with him. He says, "Oh, dear. I thought the eBay retailer (you) was withholding payroll taxes." Then the IRS comes after you. Yes, it happens a lot this way. Or, the other person gets injured while working but has no health or disability insurance. So, he applies for workers' compensation only to find that you have no workers' compensation insurance because you have no employees. Then, he sues you claiming to be an employee. Yes, this happens too.

Consequently, a contract is your best defense against an independent contractor being reclassified as an employee. But a contract by itself is not the sole determining factor. It's necessary also to make sure your practice follows the guidelines that determine the relationship.

Delegating

Here's a list of some things you might delegate to someone else (e.g., independent contractor):

- Fulfillment
- Bookkeeping
- Data entry
- Shooting photographs
- Creating auction ads
- Auction management
- Customer follow-up
- Customer service
- Web development (if you have a website)

And there are some things you probably will do better yourself when starting rather than delegate:

- Buying at wholesale
- Pricing
- Accounting (reviewing the books)

- Reporting (making business sense out of your accounting)
- Strategic planning
- Conflict management (handling irate customers)
- Customer service (certain aspects)
- Overall management

Insurance

Most traditional business entities are designed to rearrange liabilities to suit special business purposes. These are important considerations for large businesses. For small businesses, they are much less important. Yet, you have to deal with your business liabilities:

To creditors

To employees

To physically injured persons

To financially injured persons

To customers

The best way to get your liabilities under control is by purchasing insurance, not by agonizing over which business entity to use.

You should start by getting business coverage for your car (or truck). Should you have an accident while driving for your business, your insurance company may not cover you. Business coverage for automobiles shouldn't cost much more so long as you're not using your car a great deal for business.

The best thing for you to do is sit down with a business insurance agent and discuss what coverage you need for your business. Every business is different. If your insurance agent isn't familiar with business matters, you may need to find another. When you're in business, you're a bigger target with potentially more people gunning for you than when you're a private person. Insurance is your best protection.

Bank Account

The best practice is to run your business out of a bank account separate from your personal bank account. If you're a sole proprietor, it doesn't matter for tax purposes whether you do so or not, but a separate bank account makes your accounting easier. The bank will require an assumed name affidavit to open your business bank account. (See the section on sole proprietorship in Chapter 2 for a discussion of using a bank account in your name only, without providing an assumed-name affidavit.)

If you're a partnership, the partnership bank account should be separate from any of the partners and should probably require more than one signature on the checks. Because you have to answer to your partner, you cannot indiscriminately shift funds back and forth between your personal account and your partnership account.

If you are incorporated, the bank will require a corporate resolution to open a bank account. Because corporations are owned by and taxed separately from stockholders, you cannot indiscriminately shift funds back and forth between your personal account and your corporate account. It could be fatal for income tax purposes. This is an inconvenient disadvantage for a one-person business that's incorporated.

Tax Number

As a business, you need to get a tax number from the IRS and begin filing tax returns when due.

- If you are a sole proprietor, your tax number will be your Social Security number, and you will file your personal tax return as you normally do. In other words, your business is not a separate taxable entity.

- A partnership requires a federal Employer Identification Number and files an information tax return, while the individual partners each file a personal tax return.

- A corporation requires a federal Employer Identification Number and files a corporate tax return. Individual stockholders each file a personal tax return.

Don't put this off. Get set up to file your tax returns and pay your taxes regularly and on time. When you're an employee, filing a tax return is usually reasonably easy, straightforward, and done once a year. When you're running your own business, it's more complicated and takes more time, effort, and resources. And you need to do it quarterly (estimated tax). It's easy to put off this unpleasant chore. Almost every small business falls behind on their taxes sooner or later (not necessarily for the lack of money to pay the taxes). It can create very unpleasant situations with both the IRS and state taxing authorities.

Merchant Credit Card Account

If you want to accept credit cards for payment, you need to get a merchant credit card account. Unless you have good credit, this may be difficult to do. See Chapter 13 for more on merchant accounts and alternatives you might use.

Trademark

A trademark can be a graphic or a phrase or a name. You acquire the rights to it by using it. Ultimately the federal trademark regulations will govern, assuming you do business across the country (as you will with an eBay business). After using your trademark, you need to file a trademark application with the US Patent & Trademark Office ($375 fee). Getting a trademark is a long but worthwhile process. Being awarded a trademark will give you an exclusive right to use your graphic, phrase, or name within your industry and will help you protect your brand.

Don't use a trademark that someone else is using. Technically, you may be able to get the use of it (trademarks are awarded for specific industries), but it's not worth the risk of trademark violation. Instead, find a unique trademark. You can do a trademark search online at:

http://www.uspto.gov

Accounting

You can run your personal life out of a checkbook when you're an employee. When you're in business for yourself, you need something more. You should start using accounting software such as Intuit's Quicken or a comparable program. As you grow larger, you will want to graduate into using accounting software designed for business such as QuickBooks, Intuit's advanced accounting software intended for small businesses.

You will probably need an accountant or bookkeeper to help you get set up and understand accounting procedures. Learning to use accounting software will help you to understand accounting too.

You can't do everything forever when you become a successful eBay retailer. One of the first tasks usually delegated in a small business is the bookkeeping. That's something to keep in mind as you grow.

Accounting isn't just about money. It's about accounting for business assets, inventory, orders, customers, and the like. These should be integrated into your accounting of funds. It makes running a business easier, more efficient, and less expensive. Fortunately, inexpensive auction management software is available to do this; see Chapter 17.

Chart of Accounts

One of your first accounting tasks is to set up a chart of accounts. Your bookkeeper or accountant can do this for you. You might even be able to find a chart of accounts to fit your business somewhere on the Web and use it as your own. Each business has a unique chart of accounts.

Manual Accounting

You can keep your books manually. That was done for a long time before computers came along. It seems like it's less expensive. After all, Quicken or comparable programs cost almost $50 and take time to learn how to use.

Don't fall into the trap of thinking this way. Accounting software will save you a huge amount of time and effort worth considerably more than the small amount you pay for the software. It will also provide you with a certain amount of accounting coaching (usually provided in the software documentation) for which you would otherwise have to pay a bookkeeper or accountant or buy a book.

Branding

For the purposes of most beginning eBay businesses, branding is the same as marketing. It is the marketing process of building a brand. This comes up in this chapter because it requires some practical ground work to be done (regarding names) on the front end rather than down the road.

What Brand?

Branding takes resources and focus. You don't have the time and resources in a starting business to brand your items (assuming they're unbranded) unless you have just a few products. Consequently, most eBay businesses will attempt to brand their business name; and that makes sense.

What Is Branding?

Branding is what you do to promote your business name. If you can promote your name well enough to gain recognition from your customers, you have established a brand. Here are some ideas for building your brand:

1. Know the market.

2. Keep your products and your sales effort up to date.

3. Provide outstanding value.

4. Use customer service to generate customer loyalty.

5. Pursue excellence.

6. Build brand recognition through advertising (online and offline), public relations, and marketing.

7. Leverage your marketing via eBay.

eBay is quite conscious of eBay businesses needing to build their brands and gives them every opportunity to do so on eBay.

Brand Action

What can you do to create your brand? You certainly can't do as much as national companies, which build national brands with millions of dollars in advertising and promotion. You probably can't even get your customers on eBay to remember your brand. But if you can get your customers to recognize your brand when they see it as they're looking on eBay to buy the type of merchandise you sell, you've done about as much as you can do. How do you accomplish that?

Remember?

Your customers won't remember your brand on eBay unless you're selling items that people need to buy on a regular basis. People are bombarded with thousands of brand names every day. In other words, they won't look for your brand when they need an item. However, when a customer returns to buy another item of the same kind later, you want them to at least remember your brand when they see it as they go through the list of eBay items. That is, you want them to recognize it.

Simple Name

Pick a simple assumed name. Would you buy a beverage named *Carmel-Colored Sucrose Carbonated Water* from the Carmel-Colored Sucrose Water Bottling and Processing Corporation? Would you buy a *Coca-Cola*? Even *Coca-Cola* is not simple enough. Would you buy a *Coke*? Keep it simple.

The name should be understandable so customers can recognize it; that is, remember it when they see it. If your brand is *Elechron*, who's going to recognize it? If it's *ElegantClocks*, it's at least understandable.

If you are selling in a niche, the name should address the niche. For example, if you're selling nice clocks, a name like *Elegant-Clocks* gets right to the point. A name like *Sathutral Trading Company* doesn't say anything about what you're selling.

The name should be easy to spell and pronounce. No one is going to have trouble with *ElegantClocks*. But how do you spell or pronounce *Elechron* or *Sathutral*?

If you're not selling in a niche but sell anything you can get at wholesale, use a name that reflects that fact. How about *Auction Emporium*? Certainly *eBay Emporium* would be better, but you would get a letter from eBay's attorney suggesting strongly that you not use the word "eBay" in your name.

Uniform

Keep your name uniform throughout your business operation. Your name should be the same for your domain name, website, eBay ID, AOL ID, MSN ID, Yahoo ID, eBay Store, email, letterhead, telephone directory, all documents, and everything else. Don't be sloppy and operate under more than one name. And do put your name (brand) on everything.

Now You Know

Now you know why the discussion of branding goes in this early chapter. One of the first things you do when you start a business is chose a name. It's important that you choose a name that's available as a domain name and as an eBay ID, one that hasn't yet been trademarked. If you do business on

AOL, Yahoo, or MSN, your name needs to be available for those portals as well. It's a lot of work to figure out a name that works these days. The brand starts here.

Logo

Don't worry about getting a logo and all the other trappings of a national brand. You don't have the resources to make a logo stick. Just use your business name consistently. If you insist on having a logo, just use a specific typeface to make it.

Remember that *Coca-Cola* and *Coke* are just typeface logos. The *Coca-Cola* is a little bit fancy. The *Coke* is plain and straightforward. You can easily make a typeface logo.

You can use a typeface in an image editor to create a logo. You can make the typeface any color with any color background (or a transparent background) and give your name a drop-shadow or some other simple enhancement.

ElegantClocks

Building Your Brand

Once you have chosen a name, how do you make it stick? Remember, making it stick on eBay means making customers recognize your brand when they see it.

Advertising

Advertising is the traditional means of building a brand. You can't afford the advertising dollars (millions) it takes to build a brand off the Web. On the Web, the primary way to advertise is to put banners on other websites directing potential customers to your website. This is expensive too. The only way to find out if it's cost effective is to try it. But without your own website to which to direct potential customers, banner advertising doesn't make much sense.

Cross-Selling

Use the Andale Gallery (see Chapters 17 and 19) and other cross-selling techniques to build your brand and your sales. This is an excellent technique and one readily available. It works best when the items are related. If the items are not related, cross-selling is not likely to work well. For instance, when you're selling leatherworking products, cross-selling to stereo speakers isn't going to be very productive.

Speaking of Leatherworking Products

Tandy (leatherworking products) evolved into Radio Shack (electronic merchandise), but that happened over a long period a long time ago when both leatherwork and home electronics were considered hobbies.

Continuous Visibility

You have to have continuous visibility to have a brand. If you go to buy soft drinks in a supermarket and Coke isn't on the shelves, the Coke brand is seriously diminished. For your eBay business, you need to have plenty of auctions going all the time. You have to have high visibility on eBay. If you're not there, bidders can't recognize you.

Customer Service

And the winning brand builder is! Our old friend customer service! This is the best way to build your brand. This is where your focus needs to be. Without good customer service, you can't build a brand on eBay. With good customer service you can build a brand over an extended period. It takes a while, but it boosts sales.

Don't confuse good sales with building a brand. A brand is about plenty of repeat sales and referrals. It is your customers coming back again and again and telling their friends and relatives about you. Good customer service is a major component of effective branding.

If All Else Fails

If all else fails, read the manual. That is, read a book on branding. Branding is a hot topic in business today as well as a hot topic in online business. There are lots of current books on branding.

Resources

SCORE (*www.score.org*) is a non-profit association, affiliated with the US Small Business Administration, which provides extensive free business counseling to small businesses. This is a great resource that will cost you only your time. Use it.

American Small Businesses Association (ASBA at *http://wwwasbaonline.com*) is a professional organization for small businesses.

4

Equipment, Supplies, and Space

Don't get carried away with buying a lot of equipment and supplies to start your eBay business. You may not need very much, but you will need some basics. This chapter covers the basics but isn't intended to be a definitive guide to building the office infrastructure for your business. It will help you set priorities, and priorities are useful when you have limited start-up capital.

71

Hardware

You need a normal PC (or Mac) computer, nothing fancy. Business software (word processor, spreadsheet, database, accounting) works just as well on a slow computer as a fast one. Webpage editing software doesn't require a speedy computer either. A faster computer is nice to have for editing digital photographs, but you generally don't need a lot of speed for managing eBay auction photographs.

Computer

What you do need is a computer that will run an up-to-date operating system such as Windows 98 (or later) so that you can use up-to-date software. A 300 MHz PC will provide enough speed for Windows 98, but you may need more speed for some of the more recent operating systems such as Windows XP.

You also need basic peripherals such as a printer and possibly a scanner. One important item is USB capability (not available in Windows 95). A USB (Universal Serial Bus) connector is the latest greatest way to hook up devices to computers. When you start using a digital camera, you will almost certainly need a USB connector (port) in your computer in order to get the digital photographs from the camera onto your hard disk.

If you are starting from scratch, you can purchase adequate computer equipment for under $200 used. New equipment will cost you closer to $700. Of course, you can spend much more.

Backup

Backup is nice when you're having fun with your computer. Unless you're creating and storing a lot of valuable personal records, however, backup is not absolutely essential. Yet, when you operate a business on eBay, backup is absolutely essential. Record keeping is not only a necessary task but is the core of competent customer service. Without the protection of a reliable backup, any malfunction in your computer system becomes a nightmare that threatens to destroy your business.

There are two levels of backup. The first is a backup medium onsite (e.g., a CD made by a CD recorder). The second is a backup medium offsite. The first will protect against the failure of hardware and software. The second will protect against fire or theft. Make your backups regularly and then take them offsite to a safe place.

Easy Backup

The easiest and perhaps best backup today is a USB 2.0 external case with an IDE hard disk. The case costs about $40. A new hard disk can cost as little as $45 depending on size. Connect the external hard disk to your computer using a USB 2.0 cable. Use a program like Norton's Ghost to back up your computer hard disk completely onto your external hard disk. Disconnect the USB cable for the external hard disk and store the external hard disk offsite.

I use a very small USB 2.0 external case (more narrow than a CD) with a 20 GB laptop hard disk. (Laptop hard disks cost a little more, but they're smaller.) I make a complete backup of my computer hard disk in about a half-hour (12 GB). Then I take the external (backup) hard disk offsite to a safe place. I happen to have a special requirement for smallness regarding storage. A larger case with a normal size hard drive is just as handy and a little bit less expensive.

A data CD made by a CD recorder (CD-R) makes a good backup for data. Keep your software and data (e.g., documents and other work products) separate. Back up only the data. You can always reinstall programs from the original software CDs to replace corrupted software. Backing up your data is the more crucial chore.

You can buy a CD-R for as little as $60. Make sure you get CD recording software bundled with it. If you buy the software separately, it may cost more than the CD-R. The blank CDs cost as little as 30 cents each.

Software

Hardware is inexpensive today. Software tends to be expensive. Be prudent in what you buy. Don't assume you will need something until you actually have a specific need for it. For instance, do you really need Microsoft Office (about $300 – a current business standard)? When you look at the overall picture for your eBay business, perhaps you don't need it. For instance, your use of an auction management service (covered in Chapters 16 and 17) may mean you will never need to use Microsoft Office.

Buying Software

It is easy to say that you will need a word processor, a spreadsheet, a database manager, and an accounting program, at a minimum, to run an eBay business. But that may not be true. You may need a word processor, but an auction management service (which you certainly do need) may provide the functions for which you would otherwise need spreadsheet, database, and accounting programs.

You should always keep in mind, too, that software is not an expense. It is an expense saver. It enables you to do something much more efficiently and inexpensively than doing it without the software. If it doesn't, there's no point to using the software. Therefore, the three questions to ask yourself before buying software are:

1. Does the work need to be done?

2. Does the software do the work more efficiently and less expensively?

3. Is it true that I presently own no other software that can do this work?

If you can answer all three with a yes, then buy the software. You won't save money by not buying it. One thing is certain, however. You shouldn't buy any software until after you have decided which auction management service you will use (see Chapter 17).

Free Software

You will need a Web browser and an email program. It's handy to have a webpage authoring program too. Web browsers are free from both Microsoft and Netscape. Microsoft used to give away Outlook Express (email) and FrontPage Express (webpage authoring) free until it monopolized the browser market. Now it no longer does. But you can still get comparable programs with the free Netscape browser.

Download the Netscape 7.0 (or greater) browser from Netscape's website (*http://www.netscape.com*). It comes with a good email program and a great webpage authoring program, Composer, all free.

Bundled Software

Bundled software is free software that comes packaged with hardware. For instance, most scanners and digital cameras come bundled with image editing software. If you're taking pictures with a film camera and don't have a scanner, you may need to find free image editing software somewhere else. For a great free image editor, try IrfanView:

> *http://www.irfanview.com*

You need the image editing software to edit and improve your auction photographs.

Internet Access

You can get dial-up Internet access as low as $8 per month, although a more standard price is $20 per month. Every time you need to get online for email or to surf the Web, you must dial up and connect first. The top speed is about 56 Kb per second. (A more expensive ISDN dial-up line runs at 128 Kb second.) This is OK if you can't afford more.

A better deal is a DSL telephone line with a top speed of 1,500 Kb per second (1.5 Mb per second). Some DSL vendors provide the line only at a lower speed. The typical price for a DSL line is $50 per month. The nice thing about DSL besides being faster is that it is connected 24 hours per day. You do not have to dial up. Consequently, DSL is recommended. It will save you a lot of time and make your online work seem easier.

Other Internet Access

Your television cable company may be able to provide Internet access to you. The speed and cost of the service is comparable to DSL, but it comes over your televison cable rather than a telephone line.

You can also get satellite Internet service that's fast and full-time. Unfortunately, it's more expensive than the other alternatives, but the prices are coming down.

You connect a network cable (Cat 5e) from a DSL/cable modem to the network interface card (NIC) in your computer. The modem is provided free by your Internet Service Provider (ISP), the company that provides your access line. A NIC costs about $10-$35.

Don't despair if you can't get a broadband DSL, cable, or satellite Internet connection. A dial-up connection works just fine, but it will slow you down a little.

Home Router

Don't use a DSL or cable line without a 4-port home router ($50-$90). You will have no protection against hackers, an intolerable situation, particularly for a business. You connect a network cable (Cat 5e) from your DSL/cable modem to your home router. You connect another network cable from one of the ports in your home router to your computer NIC. You can connect up to four computers to the Internet this way. They can all have high speed access to the Internet at the same time.

If you buy a home router with a built-in print server, you can connect a printer to the router. Four computers can use the printer at the same time too.

Long Distance Service

Want to pay for your DSL or cable line with long distance telephone savings? There's a way. Use a voice-over-IP (VoIP) telephone service. Try Vonage at:

http://vonage.com

First, you have to have DSL or cable Internet service. Second, you need a home router. Third, you need a black box (Cisco ATA-186), which Vonage provides free. You connect a network cable (Cat 5e) from a port in your home router to the black box. You connect a normal telephone wire from the black box to any normal telephone. Voila! You have VoIP telephone service.

Compare Vonage's rates to any long distance service. If you have much long distance usage at all, you may be able to save enough on your long distance bill to pay for your DSL or cable Internet service.

How does Vonage work? As the book goes to press, I've been using it for about a year and am quite pleased. Occasionally, I have a connection that breaks up a little, but otherwise it's comparable to normal telephone service. You can use it for local, regional, or long distance calling. My wife went to Singapore on business for two weeks in 2002. I talked with her almost every day for six cents per minute (overseas long distance has a surcharge), and the connection sounded like she was on a telephone in the next room.

Incidentally, Vonage provides full telephone services (e.g., voice messages, call waiting) for no additional charges.

I'm sure Vonage will have some competitors, but I have yet to find a company that provides an identical service for a consumer price.

Vonage for Your eBay Business?

If your eBay business requires that you talk with your customers via the phone a lot, Vonage is a good deal for you. They offer unlimited long distance service for $40 per month (residential line).

Business Machines

Don't go wild buying business machines you don't need. Times are changing. For instance, you may not need a fax machine these days. You can send and receive faxes through your computer. For some people that's more convenient, for others less convenient, than a fax machine. If you don't use fax very much, however, you can stand the inconvenience. (I have managed to cut my fax usage to about one sent and two received a month.) Likewise, if you don't need copies often, don't buy a copier. Use a cheap scanner instead. It's slow but bearable if you don't use it often.

Your computer is your most inexpensive means of doing anything in business. A computer and printer are basic to business life. Attempt to do everything digitally with your computer system. That means a paperless office—easily achievable today. It will save you a ton of money in the long run.

On the other hand, if you have frequent use for a fax machine or a copier, buy one. Make your home office easy to work in. There is no standard set of devices you need. Tailor your office machines to your work style.

Basic List

A basic list of business machines for an eBay business looks something like this:

1. Computer (with monitor, keyboard, mouse, and speakers)

2. Computer printer.

3. Telephone modem if using dial-up service, or a NIC if using DSL/cable.

4. Home router (if using DSL/cable) with print server.

5. Fax machine (optional) if you really need one for something.

6. Copier (optional) if you really will use one regularly.

7. Scanner (optional) if you need one for a copier substitute or for scanning color film prints.

Inexpensive Combo

HP, Canon, and other manufacturers now offer combination printer-copier-scanner-fax machines for as little as $200. One of these can serve all of your needs in one purchase.

Fulfillment Equipment

Don't hesitate to buy strange machines for the packaging and shipping room so long as they save time and energy and don't cost too much. This is a separate consideration from setting up an office because every fulfillment operation is different. See Chapter 12 for more information.

Office Furniture

You may be spending more time in front of your computer now that you're an eBay business. Make sure your furniture is comfortable and ergonomic. Otherwise you may develop health problems such as carpal tunnel syndrome. Try these resources for more information on ergonomics:

http://www.ergo-2000.com

http://ergo.human.cornell.edu/ergoguide.html

http://www.osha.gov/SLTC/computerworkstations_ecat

http://www.safecomputing.com

http://www.ergostoreonline.com

Ergonomic furniture doesn't have to be expensive. A table and chair are recommended below. An ergonomic chair should be a top priority.

On the Move

One potential benefit of an eBay business is that you can do business from anywhere you can get a connection to the Internet. But it's tough to find ergonomic furniture even in the best hotels, motels, and resorts. I take along a small folding table with a 25-inch height and a folding chair (with a cushion) matched to the table. I can use my computer for long periods comfortably—and safely.

Office Supplies

You're in business now. Buy your office supplies in bulk because you will be using more of them. When you run out of printer paper, you will have to drive to the office supply store to get more, an unforgivable waste of time. Buy printer paper by the carton (10 reams), not by the ream (500 sheets). Ah, maybe that's a poor example because we're striving for the paperless office. But you get the idea. Buying in bulk is usually significantly less expensive than buying one at a time.

Most office supplies are made to fuel the flow of paper. With minimal use of paper, you will need fewer office supplies.

Office Premises

You can have a home office almost anywhere you can be comfortable. Typically home offices are in a spare bedroom, a study, or a basement room. The room must have adequate lighting so you don't go blind and adequate electricity so you can feed your computer and other electronic devices.

Watch out for windows and lights. If they're in your line of vision (in front of you), they can cause eyestrain. If they're behind you, they can cause an unwelcome glare on the screen of your monitor, which will also cause eyestrain. You need to be careful to position your monitor ergonomically in regard to the lights and windows in the room. This is the primary consideration in the placement of your desk or table.

The availability of telephone and cable outlets should not be the primary factor in picking a room. You can run a telephone line or cable around the outside of your house at a modest expense to get to the room you want to use. An office should be comfortable and ergonomic. Let those two factors be your guide.

Storage, Packing, and Shipping

You will need a place to store your inventory and do your packing and shipping. First, it's the spare bedroom. Then it's the garage. Finally, it's out the door to somewhere else. There are a number of possibilities:

1. A relative's, friend's, or neighbor's garage might work well.

2. In an outside office, usually the space will be too expensive for storage. Though, if the office space is cheap, it might make sense for storage.

3. Mini-storage is inexpensive, but access is inconvenient. It's generally not an appropriate place for a packaging and shipping operation.

4. A commercial warehouse might work well if the rent is reasonable.

5. An office-warehouse building is a good bet if you can afford the rent.

6. An old building with low rent is perhaps your best bet.

If you are storing a lot of inventory—even though you shouldn't be for an eBay business—you can save rent by separating the storage from the packaging and shipping. Storage space is inexpensive. Work space for packaging and shipping requires lighting, electricity, and open floor space and tends to be more expensive. Thus, you might do your packaging and shipping and a small amount of storage in your garage but store the remainder of your inventory in a nearby mini-storage unit.

Tax Deduction

Many business gurus advise you to declare your home office a business expense and take an income tax deduction (depreciation) for it. This is one of the overrated benefits of being in business for yourself. For the little bit of tax relief, you will have to do a significant amount of extra record keeping. Also, rumor has it that a home office deduction triggers an IRS audit. This may not be true, but if you do get audited, a home office deduction will make the audit more complicated.

Same Home in San Francisco and Oklahoma City

East Bay (San Francisco Bay Area)

Improvements	$130,000
Land	$300,000
Home Value	$430,000

Oklahoma City

Improvements	$100,000
Land	$40,000
Home Value	$140,000

Suppose the office you use is 10 percent of the area of the home, and you will depreciate the value of the improvements over 30 years.

East Bay: $13,000 ÷ 30 = a $433 expense each year

OKC: $10,000 ÷ 30 = a $333 expense each year

At a tax rate of 28 percent, how much tax do you save?

East Bay: $433 × .28 = $121 tax saving each year

OKC: $333 × .28 = $93 tax saving each year

On the other hand, if you have a creative accountant and are willing to keep meticulous records, you can milk a considerable number of deductions out of your home office. But don't take the deductions unless you're willing to record the minute details necessary to support the deductions.

If you use your car for business, you can deduct the mileage used for business at about $0.36 per mile (2002). Again, you must keep careful records to do so. (Also, make sure you have added your business use on your auto insurance policy.)

The point about tax deductions is that there is much misinformation and rumor all around us. Learn something about basic income taxation or consult an accountant.

Inexpensive Home Office

Here are eight ways to set up a home office inexpensively:

Desk Buy a folding table (particle board) at an office supply store. They come in different sizes, give you considerable flexibility, and cost between $30 and $50. The tables are durable enough for personal use. The tabletops are not durable enough for careless or heavy-duty use, but you can buy folding tables with durable Formica tops for about 50 percent more if needed. For extensive typing you need the tabletop to be about 25 inches high. Most tables and desks are about 29 inches high. Cut 4 inches off the steel legs to get the table down to secretarial height. Put your monitor, keyboard, and mouse on the table.

Office Chair This is not a place to save money. Your health depends on a chair that will support your back well. Fortunately, today you can buy such a chair for as little as $80 at an office supply store. Make sure it has an adjustable height.

Out of Town

I fly to visit the in-laws in another city for about 10 days at Christmas. I was in the habit of using a laptop computer (terrible keyboard) at desktop height (29 inches) to work there. It wasn't much fun, and I didn't get much done. On the last trip, I purchased a small folding table at a local office supply store, cut 4 inches off the legs, and cut away part of the steel support underneath to make room for my legs. I took along an old laptop plus a good keyboard and used my father-in-law's adjustable desk chair. The work I was able to get done far surpassed my expectations—and I had fun working as I do at home where my office is set up ergonomically. (I left the table at the in-laws' for the next visit.)

Office Supplies Buy office supplies in bulk to save money. You need more office supplies for a business than you do for personal use.

Files You can purchase plastic cartons that will hold hanging files. They are more flexible and less expensive than filing cabinets. Remember, however, you want to operate as digitally as possible and keep the paperwork down to a minimum.

Business Cards Buy inexpensive business cards wherever you can find them. As a virtual business, you won't use them much, so don't invest a fortune in them. Or, you can make your own elegant business cards with heavy paper stock (acid free), a word processor (or desktop publishing program), a laser printer, and a paper cutter.

Computer You probably don't need the latest computer (see the Hardware section above). Your priorities should be elsewhere.

Printer You can buy an up-to-date inkjet printer for under

$100 new, albeit a slow one. However, you'll do better to opt for a used laser printer for under $150.

Communications Broadband via a DSL telephone line or a television cable is about $50 per month. This will make your use of the Web and an auction management service much more efficient. Broadband will also support voice-over-IP telephone service (see Vonage in the Long Distance Service section above) that will save you considerable money on long distance and even in-state telephone calls. You can also use it for local calling.

On the Road

Can you work well on the road? There are those who will disagree, but in my opinion you can't work very well with a laptop computer on just any tabletop with just any chair. The information below outlines my formula for inexpensive, efficient mobility with a motor home, van, SUV, or even a car.

1. Use an old computer, not necessarily a laptop. You can even use your normal office computer provided you leave an up-to-date backup of your hard disk at home.

2. Use a flat panel active matrix LCD screen (if you don't use a laptop). You can buy a 14-inch model now for under $200 (if you can find one). Don't use a normal monitor (CRT); it's too heavy and far too cumbersome to cart around.

3. Buy a small sturdy folding table with a 25-inch height. You can probably get one locally for about $30. Costco seems to sell a lot of small tables made by Lifetime (*http://www.lifetime.com*). If you cannot find one locally, try Midg-ett (*http://www.midg-ett.com*) for good quality at about $50. I use a Midg-ett folding table that's 18 x 32 inches.

4. Get a folding chair. Steel card table chairs are fine. Buy a specific cushion to make your chair just the right height in regard to your portable table. An office chair is too cumbersome to cart around.

5. You need a dial-up account from an ISP that offers local access telephone numbers everywhere nationally. Make sure your computer has a modem. The alternative for the more serious traveler is satellite broadband Internet service (the type than doesn't need a separate upstream line) with a small dish. Such service is now available at a reasonable price. You can even buy special dish mounts made just for RVs. Look at a Budget Satellite System RV mounting system (*http://www.ideamaster.com/budget/rvmount.htm*).

6. Naturally, you need to farm out your fulfillment to an independent contractor. For most eBay businesses, a mobile fulfillment operation would be much too cumbersome to operate and too susceptible to a sizeable loss through theft.

This traveling idea may seem a little frivolous when you're just trying to start your eBay business. Keep in mind, however, that one of the great advantages of being in a virtual business is that you can travel and still work. The other consideration is that when you do travel, you need to keep up on your auction management. You can't be out of touch for long periods and still expect to deliver good customer service—and get positive feedback.

A Lot of Resort Rooms

I have a friend who operates a lucrative one-man digital business online. He invested in a motor home at a cost of about $85,000 with special tables and fittings for all his computer equipment just so he doesn't have to stay at home.

My special setup (folding table and chair plus LCD screen and old computer) is worth less than $500 and doesn't take up much room in my Trooper (SUV). I can work as easily and efficiently as my friend can on the road. When I leave my Trooper at a trailhead for six days and go backpacking, I don't have to worry about expensive computer equipment being stolen.

It's nice to have a motor home, particularly for long-term trips, but you don't need one to put your show on the road. And $85,000 buys a lot of resort rooms.

5

Finding Inventory

At the first national eBay conference in Anaheim, California, in 2002, the word going around the convention center among the attendees was that auction management software makes an eBay business easy to run. The only tough problem remaining is finding some inventory to sell. I believe that shows a lot of insight. The auction management software (see Chapters 16 and 17) does make an eBay business a no-brainer. Finding a product niche and the inventory to fill it is where you need to focus your effort, if you haven't found a niche already.

Keep in mind while you read through this chapter that the word "manufacturer" is used to mean any company that creates something (e.g., from automobiles to fruit cakes to software) for sale.

This chapter contains ideas for acquiring inventory, explained one at a time in no particular order of priority. However, my favorite is the trade show.

Basics

Before going down the list, it's useful to go over some basics that keep things in perspective and increase your chances of success.

Playing the Field

The ideal niche to find will be one in which the products sell well on eBay at a profit and you have an exclusive on obtaining the supply. That's a long shot. Consequently, your experience is likely to be finding niches that prove profitable for a while and then get too crowded or otherwise decline. Then it's on to something else.

For that reason as you look ahead to a career as an eBay businessperson, it pays to be nimble. If you can find something to sell temporarily that has a high likelihood of success (profit), don't pass up the opportunity. In the future a good percentage of the opportunities for selling on eBay will be temporary ones. Be prepared to move quickly and try new ideas. (See Chapter 23 for more information on developing a strategy for your new eBay business.)

Knowing the Market

If you don't know the market for the goods you buy to sell on eBay, you will be unsuccessful before you even start. Buy low and sell high is how it's done in retail. There are no short cuts. Do your homework. Research eBay sales data thoroughly before you start buying inventory. Where no sales data exists, you need to make estimates by analogy using eBay data for similar products. If no data exists, do some test auctions. Don't commit a lot of resources to building inventory until you're certain of the eBay market.

Sales Tax License

Having your sales tax license will give you more creditability with the people you approach to acquire inventory. You will want to get it before you go out knocking on doors.

Drop Shipping

A wholesaler's or manufacturer's willingness and capability to do drop shipping can save you the headache and cost of storing and shipping products.

The List

Here's the list. It's not an all-inclusive list, but it will get you off to a good start thinking about where you might find some inventory to sell.

Trade Shows

Trade shows are great places to search for eBay inventory for many reasons:

- Some are open to the public.

- Most are open to those with a sales tax license.

- They are a place for new products to be unveiled.

- They are a place to get detailed information on products and hands-on assessments of products.

- They are a place to get information on an industry, or in some cases multiple industries.

- They include small manufacturers and producers that might be difficult to find otherwise.

- Large trade shows, particularly regional and national trade shows, have a large variety of products.

- They are places to get good deals such as product introductions or closeouts.

- They are places to negotiate good deals.

- They are places to make valuable contacts.

It's difficult to find the time to go to trade shows, even ones in your own city. But they're worth it. Trade shows make a great place to start your trek to find products you can sell profitably on eBay.

What Trade Shows?

Local trade shows can be interesting and informative. They are usually a mixture of retailers and distributors. The chances of finding wholesale sources of inventory at local shows, though, are not as great as at the regional and national trade shows.

Exhibitors at the regional and national trade shows are mostly wholesalers. They provide your best shot at making a connection with a supplier of inventory. Such trade shows are often quite large and make a fertile ground for finding products.

Food Show

In one day at one regional food trade show in 1994 that I attended with my food entrepreneur clients, we were able to get about two dozen unique gourmet food products from different companies. I put these in an online catalog for my clients that became the first gourmet food store on the Web. Some of the products were new at the time and have proven so successful since that they eventually migrated into the supermarkets.

Finding Trade Shows

Some trade show websites where you can find trade show schedules follow:

- Computer Digital Expo Las Vegas, *http://www.internettradeshowlist.com*

- Trade Show Center, *http://www.globalsources.com/TRADE SHW/TRDSHFRM.HTM*

- Trade Show Plaza, *http://www.tradeshowplaza.com*

- Tradeshow Week, *http://www.tradeshowweek.com*

- TSNN.com, *http://www.tsnn.com*

A Tradeshow Week directory search for Food & Beverage shows in the United States (2nd half of 2002) at *http://www.tradeshowweek.com* yielded the following (strictly an example):

ACF Chef Forum/American Culinary Federation (Las Vegas)

AFD Beverage Journal Holiday Show/Associated Food Dealers Beverage Journal Holiday Show (Livonia)

Atlantic City Gourmet Food & Gift Show (Atlantic City)

Bar Essentials Expo Great Lakes (Chicago)

Bar Essentials Expo New York (New York)

Chicago Pizza Expo (Chicago)

Coffee Fest Atlantic City (Atlantic City)

Coffee Fest Seattle (Seattle)

Dallas National Gourmet Food Show (Dallas)

Expo Comida Latina (Los Angeles)

Florida Fiery Foods Show

InterBev®/International Beverage Industry Exhibition & Congress (Atlanta)

International Fancy Food & Confection Show® (New York)

International Kosher Food Trade Show (Secaucus)

Mid-Atlantic Food, Beverage, & Lodging Expo (Timonium)

Missouri Grocers Association Annual Convention & Food Trade Show (Osage Beach)

NAMA National Expo/National Automatic Merchandising Association National Expo (Atlanta)

Natural Products Expo East (Washington)

Northeast Pizza Expo (Atlantic City)

Ohio Grocers Association Annual Convention & Trade Show (Columbus)

Private Label Trade Show (Rosemont)

SOHO Expo (Orlando)

South Carolina Foodservice Expo (Myrtle Beach)

Western Food Industry Expo (Las Vegas)

A list of permanent trade buildings follows:

- 225 Fifth Avenue, *http://www.225-fifth.com* (home furnishings)

- AmericasMart, *http://www.americasmart.com* (general merchandise)

- California Market Center, *http://www.californiamarketcenter.com* (fashion, gifts, and home decor)

- Charlotte Merchandise Mart, *http://www.charlottemerchmart.com* (general merchandise – see Figure 5.1)

Figure 5.1   Charlotte Merchandise Mart.

- Chicago Merchandise Mart, *http://www.mmart.com* (clothing, gifts, and home accessories)

- Columbus Marketplace, *http://www.columbusgiftmart.com* (gifts, garden, and home accessories)

- Dallas Market Center, *http://www.dallasmarketcenter.com* (general merchandise)

- Denver Merchandise Mart, *http://www.denvermart.com* (gifts, clothing, and interior design)

- International Home Furnishings Center, *http://www.ihfc.com* (home furnishings)

- KC Gift Mart, *http://www.kcgiftmart.com* (gifts, gourmet food and implements, and home accessories)

- Kitchen Bath Building Design Center, *http://www.kitchen-bathcenter.com* (kitchen and bath furnishings and decor)

- LA Mart, *http://www.mmart.com/lamart* (designer home furnishings and decor)

- Michigan Gift Mart, *http://www.michigangiftmart.com* (gifts)

- Minneapolis Gift Mart, *http://www.mplsgiftmart.com* (gifts)

- New Mart, *http://www.newmart.net* (designer clothes)

- New York Merchandise Mart, *http://www.41madison.com* (home accessories)

- Pacific Design Center, *http://www.pacificdesigncenter.com* (home decor and accessories)

- Ronald Reagan Building and International Trade Center, *http://www.itcdc.com*. See Figure 5.2 for the building website where you can get information.

Figure 5.2   Ronald Reagan Building and International Trade Center, Washington, DC.

- San Francisco Gift Center and Jewelry Mart, *http://www.gcjm.com* (gifts, jewelry, fashion)

- Seattle Gift Center, *http://www.seattlegiftcenter.com* (gifts)

- The Center, *http://www.thegiftcenter.com* (gifts and decorative accessories)

How to Work a Trade Show

In the old days, having a corporation and other legal signs of business identity might have given you the credibility you needed to get wholesalers to take you seriously. That's been so overdone that I don't think it works well any longer. What you need is a story and the capability to conduct yourself in a business-like manner.

Your Story

Your story needs to be well thought out ahead of time—and it should be honest. If you are just starting your eBay business, don't hide it. Everyone will eventually figure it out anyway. Let people know. On the other hand, also tell people about the serious steps you have taken to get your eBay business off the ground. Mention what distinguishes you from an eBay hobbyist. Everyone loves a good story. Make yours personal, honest, interesting, and short. You will get some unexpected help from folks.

Business-Like Appearance

Dress in appropriate business clothes. In some parts of the country that means a suit or dress. In other parts of the country casual clothes are acceptable for business. Take a lot of business cards along to hand out. Most industries float on business cards. Be confident. Your confidence attracts people's attention.

Be friendly but stick to the point. Sure, small talk is great, but turn the conversation to the business at hand, which is: selling products at retail. That's what the wholesalers are there for, and that's what you're there for. Visit every booth and listen carefully. You can never learn too much, and you can't learn when you're doing the talking. Note on the back of each business card you collect something to remind you of the individual. Even take notes on important conversations. This is no picnic. This is your eBay business life.

Who's in Charge?

Most of the time, you're in charge. Most wholesalers want you as a customer. Nonetheless, some are fussy about to whom they sell. Such wholesalers often have good reason to be fussy. They have great products in high demand, and they want to protect their successful retailer customers by not diluting the market too much. If you're interested in their products, you're going to have to talk them into taking you on as a retailer. Your best technique here is to ask probing questions, then listen. Listen a lot. You can often figure out a way to become one of their retailers even if it takes a few days or a few weeks.

Trade Organizations

Every industry has trade organizations. If you commit to selling products in a certain industry, join the leading trade organization, particularly if it has a local chapter. Attend meetings. Serve on a committee. It's a great way to make contacts that will lead to some profitable inventory.

Craftspeople and Artists

It's my observation that many craftspeople and artists create very attractive products. Some of these people will sell on eBay or otherwise market their products. For many, marketing is an anathema. They just don't like it. If you can buy their products at wholesale prices, you may be able to make a profit selling such products on eBay.

Craftspeople

Some craftspeople make things that have more aesthetic value than practical value. These people are more like artists (covered below). Still, most craftspeople make practical things that people can use. Many craft products are cleverly designed and highly desirable. For instance, a handmade wrought-iron BBQ grill may be much more attractive than a manufactured BBQ grill you buy in a store. And there are plenty of people who will pay a lot for it to get something unique for their outdoor BBQ parties.

The craftsperson who makes such a BBQ grill has a huge marketing problem. She needs to reach upper income people who can afford and are likely to buy such an outdoor appliance. Such potential customers might be scarce at local shows and other small-scale venues. It makes sense to try selling such a product on eBay.

It seems to me that a huge untapped market exists here. There are unique craft items that have the potential to do really well on eBay, but you don't see a great deal of them. What you do see on eBay is a lot of run-of-the-mill craft items. If you can find unique craft items and purchase them wholesale, you may be able to make some profit.

List Carefully

Although the natural place to list crafts seems to be in the various crafts section of eBay, for many craft items you will do better to list them where they otherwise belong. For instance, a wrought-iron BBQ grill might be listed under Kitchen Appliances or perhaps even under a garden category.

You can find a schedule of art and craft shows at:

http://www.artandcraftshows.net

http://dir.yahoo.com/Arts/Events/Festivals

http://directory.google.com/Top/Arts/Visual_Arts/Resources/Events

Attend a show and find artists or craftspersons who don't intend to market their work on eBay. Buy from them at wholesale and sell their products on eBay.

Artists

Art is perhaps more difficult to sell than craftwork, because often each piece is unique, and customers' tastes are widely varied. A large selection of art products probably makes a better marketing milieu than a one-at-a-time eBay auction offering. Nonetheless, there is a lot of potential here to sell art that has proven popular in other markets such as local art shows or even art galleries. And don't forget the eBay Gallery where you can place your auctions to be searched via photographs rather than titles.

If you can't buy the art you want at wholesale—many artists are touchy about "wholesale" prices—try selling it on consignment. Your risk is less because you don't have to buy the art, but your profit will be smaller.

Your Business Library

Your local library is likely to have a wealth of information relevant to finding inventory. Even better, if your library system has a business library, try that. You may want to familiarize yourself with the SIC (Standard Industrial Classification) system recently replaced with the NAICS (North American Industry Classification System). Using SIC or NAICS codes may help you identify wholesalers more easily.

Many of the directories and other resources are expensive books or expensive online services. You will probably not be motivated to buy them yourself. However, they are available at most libraries and provide a handy way for you to look up a wholesaler that you've heard about. Or, you can use them to find wholesalers that are potential suppliers of inventory you want to sell on eBay. A few examples of the printed references usually found in the reference section of the library follow.

The Gale Group (*http://www.gale.com*), Farmington Hills, MI, publishes a number of directories that may help you track down manufacturers or distributors (see Figure 5.3). Among them are:

American Wholesalers and Distributors Directory

Dun & Bradstreet/Gale Industry Reference Handbooks

Small Business Sourcebook

Ward's Business Directory of US Private and Public Companies

Gale also publishes information and data on its website.

Figure 5.3   Gale Group website. ©2003 The Gale Group, Inc.

Harris Infosource (*http://harrisinfo.com*), Twinsburg, OH, publishes many directories that may help you identify manufacturers and wholesalers:

[State]: All Businesses (one for each state)

Complete Guide to NAICS

National Wholesalers and Distributors (also regional editions)

Harris also publishes on CDs and on its website.

Hoover's (*http://www.hoovers.com*), Austin, TX, publishes several directories you will find useful for tracking down companies:

Hoover's Handbooks

Hoover's MasterList of Major US Companies

Hoover's also publishes on its website.

McGraw Hill, Charlottesville, VA, publishes a standard reference for US corporations:

Standard & Poor's Register

Thomas Regional (*http://www.thomasregional.com*), New York, publishes business resources (see Figure 5.4) including:

Thomas Register of American Manufacturers

Figure 5.4   **Thomas Regional industrial website. ©2003 Thomas Regional Directory Co.**

The *Register* is the definitive directory for industrial companies. Thomas is also a great Web resource for finding industrial product suppliers. You will want to take a thorough look at the Thomas website. Publishing products are also available on CDs and DVDs.

Small Manufacturers

Small manufacturers often have a big marketing problem. They just don't have the marketing horsepower to promote and sell their products effectively, even to distributors. The result is that they get less market share than their products justify.

You can probably find some of these manufacturers in your own community. You may be able to sell their products profitably on eBay. The products should be unique and not directly competitive with similar top brand products. Or, the products should sell at a price point favorable to consumers.

The question then becomes, What is your community? Naturally, your municipal locale may have some small manufacturers with products that interest you. But you may belong to a state or national community (e.g., a trade association), too, through which you can identify small manufacturers with products that have potential for selling on eBay.

Wholesale

Buying at wholesale and selling for a profit at retail is the name of the game. If you can identify and do business with some reliable distributors, you can turn such relationships into a powerful eBay business. Just because you're getting something at wholesale, however, doesn't mean you're getting it cheap enough to make a profit selling it. Some distributors charge higher prices than discount stores, making it difficult for you to sell on eBay profitably.

Usually you can buy in minimal quantities from distributors. If the wholesaler is a manufacturer, you may be required to buy in large quantities. This is something to keep in mind when choosing a vendor.

When dealing with wholesalers, always treat them well and in a business-like manner. Some may become your creditors, and a little prior good will goes a long way if you should hit a rough spot financially. Look at the terms of sale carefully. Pay on time. This is often difficult because you will likely deal with numerous wholesalers and thus have numerous different payment arrangements.

Vendor Financing

Once you become established with a wholesaler, the wholesaler may finance your business. By extending 15, 30, or 60-day credit, a wholesaler is, in effect, providing you with free operating capital. Because you can potentially turn over inventory quickly on eBay, wholesaler financing can be a major funding source for your retailing business.

In some businesses, you need equipment to facilitate selling. For instance, if you sell trophies and awards, you may need an engraving machine. Your trophy wholesaler might provide you with an engraving machine free if you do enough business. More likely, your wholesaler will lease you an engraving machine. Getting a lease for a needed machine is the same, for all practical purposes, as getting a loan to buy the machine. It gets you off to a good start without having to get a business loan. Leasing specialized equipment from your vendors is a time-honored means of getting a business off the ground.

Special Mail-Order Wholesale

There are special mail-order distributors geared toward those looking for a home business. They are often something of a scam. However, if an offering is legitimate and provides you real opportunities for profit, it's likely to be appropriate for eBay selling as well as for mail-order.

Government Surplus

Government surplus conjures up visions of Army-Navy WWII gas masks. The fact is that federal government surplus is not tied to the military, and there is surplus at every level of government from federal to municipal. The surplus could be new merchandise and supplies as well old, used, or damaged goods.

Governmental agencies sell their surplus at special sales or auctions after public notice. Read the newspapers and get on mailing lists to learn about surplus sales activity in your locale. If you can buy surplus at low prices, you may be able to sell on eBay for a profit.

You might be able to put the following phone book to use published by Omnigraphics, Detroit, MI, available at libraries:

Government Phone Book USA

Closeouts

There is a closeout industry that buys surplus merchandise from large retailers, wholesalers, and even the government in bulk for pennies on the dollar and resells it in bulk to other retailers for a few more pennies on the dollar. Some closeout vendors sell goods by the warehouse pallet (4 ft × 4 ft wooden base piled about 7 feet high with goods), some by the truckload. This is a competitive industry that like any other industry requires a lot of hard work for success. Many closeout companies have gone to the Web to sell their goods in bulk to wannabe businesspeople who think they can sell the goods profitably online, in many cases on eBay. Some closeout companies are even selling on eBay themselves.

This is a big business that covers liquidations, returns, job lots, overstocks, salvage, unclaimed freight, and pallet merchandise. There are closeout shows, newspapers, and magazines.

Is this a potential source of inventory for your eBay business? Sure. Do you have to be careful? Yes. In fact, your chances of success in playing the closeout game are perhaps less than for most other sources of acquiring saleable inventory.

Nonetheless, there is another closeout game to play, a local one. You can buy your closeouts directly at any level of commitment with which you feel comfortable. For instance, you can make a deal with a local linen shop that you will buy its grossly overstocked towels. You buy the inventory for a good price and sell it at a profitable markup on eBay. Sounds easy. But it's a lot of work to line up a variety of small retailers, negotiate good purchase prices, cart the inventory away to store it, and sell it one item at a time on eBay. Then too, always keep in mind that the products closed out are generally goods that didn't sell as well as expected.

Below are some closeout companies and organizations you can investigate:

- American Merchandise Liquidators, *http://amlinc.com*

- American Science & Surplus, *http://www.sciplus.com*

- AmeriSurplus, *http://amerisurplus.com*

- Closeout, *http://www.closeout.com*

- Closeout Central, *http://www.closeoutcentral.com*

- Closeout Heaven, *http://www.closeoutheaven.com*

- CloseOutNow, *http://www.closeoutnow.com*

- CloseoutServices, *http://www.closeoutservices.com*

- Closeout Warehouse, *http://www.thecloseoutwarehouse.com (see Figure 5.5)*

- Commodity Surplus, *http://www.commoditysurplus.com*

Figure 5.5   Closeout Warehouse, a closeout website, one of many.

- Computer & Electronic Surplus, *http://www.73.com*

- Discount Warehouse, *http://www.closeouts.digiscape.net*

- Government Liquidation, *http://www.govliquidation.com*

- Lee Howard's Business Inventory Closeout Sources Directory, *http://www.chambec.com/closeout.html*

- Liquidation, *http://www.liquidation.com* (see Figure 5.6)

- Liquidation Connection, *http://www.liquidationconnection.com*

- Maverick Enterprises, *http://amaverickent.com*

- MUSA, *http://www.merchandiseusa.com*

- My Web Wholesaler, *http://mywebwholesaler.com*

- Overstock B2B, *http://www.overstockb2b.com*

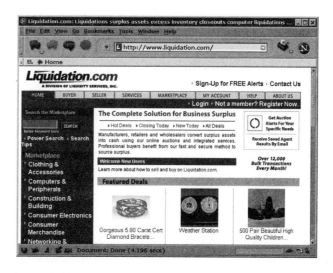

Figure 5.6   Liquidation.com, a closeout website. © 1994-2003 Liquidity Services, Inc.

- RetailExchange, *http://retailexchange.com*
- RLC Trading, *http://rlctrading.com*, where you can find an online tutorial on closeouts, *http://rlctrading.com/101.htm*
- RO-EL On-Line, *http://www.ro-el.com*
- Jane's Closeout Marketplace, *http://www.janesdeals.com*
- Salvage Closeouts, *http://www.salvagecloseouts.com*
- Sav-On-Closeouts, *http://www.sav-on-closeouts.com*
- Sell 2 All, *http://www.sell2all.com*
- Surplus Net, *http://surplus.net*
- TDW Closeouts, *http://www.tdwcloseouts.com*
- Tradeout, *http://www.tradeout.com*
- uBid, *http://www.ubid.com*
- Wholesale Central, *http://wholesalecentral.com*

Special Products

Special products are those you see on television selling for $19.95 that you can't get in the stores. Find out where you can buy these products at wholesale and sell them on eBay. People have already seen them on television.

The special products you see on television have been culled from a larger number of candidates. Some enjoy wildly successful sales. If you can get such inventory at wholesale and promote it, you may have a winner on eBay.

There are thousands of products available from inventors or small companies that may have sales potential on eBay. Find them and try selling them.

Special Manufacturing

You can have something manufactured yourself and sell it on eBay. It could be a product that you or a friend invented. More likely it will be a custom-made version of an existing product. Special T-shirts, mugs, and the like made to commemorate an event (e.g., World Series) make a good example. Any customized mass-produced product has a special potential for selling on eBay. Many manufacturers are set up to make small runs of custom products.

Manufacturers

Some manufacturers don't use distributors but sell direct to retailers. Others sell to both distributors and retailers. As a retailer you may be able to get inventory for a lower wholesale price by buying direct from the manufacturer.

Expect to be required to purchase in large quantities when you buy directly from a manufacturer. If holding large quantities of inventory for extended periods doesn't fit into your eBay business model—and it shouldn't—you may have to settle for buying smaller quantities from distributors at higher wholesale prices.

Remanufacturing

Remanufacturing is a large industry. Many states prohibit reselling goods returned on warranty (or for other reasons) as new, even after being fixed. Consequently, such goods go through a remanufacturing process. Quality is usually high and wholesale prices are lower. Remanufactured goods, particularly from major brands, enjoy healthy sales. Yet, retailers don't like to sell such goods because they compete with the new merchandise on the shelves.

This provides an opportunity to sell these goods on eBay. Find a source of remanufactured goods, and sell the goods on eBay. Remanufactured goods such as camcorders have sold well on eBay at solid prices.

Retail Excess Inventory

Your local retail stores are good sources of inventory for selling on eBay. They will have some excess inventory every season. Get to know the managers of the stores from which you would like to buy merchandise. Then keep in touch. When surplus at one of the stores becomes available, negotiate the best price you can, and be ready to buy with cash if necessary.

Off-Season

Buy off-season and sell the next season. Everyone in the Great Lakes area knows that the best time to buy a boat at a bargain price is in October and the best time to sell one for top price is in May. This phenomenon applies to all sorts of merchandise. If you buy it in the off-season, you can sell it profitably in the next season.

Unfortunately, this requires holding the merchandise for six months or more. This doesn't fit in very well in the ideal eBay business model, where quick turnover in merchandise is the name of the game. Whether this makes sense is determined by such factors as the certainty of selling profitably in the on-season, the amount of profit to be made, the amount of time the merchandise must be stored, the amount of storage space required, and the amount of money (working capital) to be tied up while the merchandise stays in storage.

Picking

A picker is one who goes to sources of inventory and picks among the offerings to find something worth selling. For instance, pickers go to garage sales looking for antiques. When a picker finds an antique, she buys it and immediately sells it to an antique dealer. The dealer then sells it to the public. As you can imagine, antique pickers now are going straight to eBay to sell instead of selling to antique stores.

Where can you pick? Garage sales and estate sales are obvious places. You can also go picking at second-hand stores, Goodwill stores, Salvation Army stores, going-out-of-business sales, flea markets, swaps, exchanges, antique shows, trade shows, and the like.

Don't get the idea that picking is for antiques only. It's for anything that will sell. Your best shot at making a profit is to specialize in picking items with which you are familiar. You have to know the markets for the types of items you are picking. Otherwise you may get burned.

One problem with picking is that sellers often have a better understanding of the value of what they're selling then they did just a few years ago. Why? They look up prices on eBay. So, picking generally isn't as profitable as it used to be, but it remains a solid means of finding inventory.

Retail Picking

A special type of picking is retail picking, and many eBay sellers practice it. It is simply going to ordinary retail stores, particularly discount stores, and picking merchandise selling at a deep discount that can be sold for a profit on eBay.

For example, many people frequent outlet stores looking for nice clothes, buy such clothes, and sell them on eBay. These people must understand the clothing market quite well in order to be continually successful on eBay, but this is a fairly common eBay business.

Designer Clothes

A woman I met at the annual eBay conference is a loan closer. She's an expert on designer clothes. She buys designer clothes at outlet malls at bargain prices. She then sells them on eBay for a profit. I asked her why she didn't quit her job as a loan closer and work on eBay full time. She told me that she couldn't handle any more business. I asked her why she didn't use one of the auction management services to organize her efforts more efficiently. She said that's why she was attending the conference. She wanted to find out about the services that are available to enable her to rev up her eBay business and quit her job.

Keep in mind, too, that you can pick at retail stores such as dollar stores (everything is for sale at $1), discount club stores, discount stores, and other retailers that sell at a deep discount. Many of these stores buy closeouts of prime merchandise and sell it at unusually deep discount prices. The closeout merchandise is only available while the supply lasts. It may be profitable to visit regularly and watch for this type of merchandising, buy some merchandise, and sell it on eBay.

At a Discount Store Near You

Costco seems to get a lot of closeouts on electronic items. In early 2002, I saw a huge stack of DVD players for $59 at Costco. I believe those could have been sold easily on eBay for $90 at that time. It was many months before I saw a low price close to that again at Costco or anywhere else. I finally bought one at Costco for $69 about six months later.

Local Sources

Don't overlook local sources. If you're picking, you have to go to local sources or else travel out of town. But there are potential local sources for every category in this chapter. Local retailers may have overordered, resulting in excess inventory that you may be able to buy cheaply and sell profitably on eBay. A local craftsperson may have a product that you can make into a hot item on eBay.

Find out what every local manufacturer makes. Become familiar with local craft organizations and shows. Become familiar with local artists. Ask around about local inventors. There may be something made locally you can sell.

Packages

Put a package together and sell it. At least one person on eBay sells a home network wiring kit. He puts 500 feet of Cat 5e network wire together with a crimping tool, a punchdown tool, RJ-45 modular plugs, and jacks and sells it. There's a certain synergy going on here. He gives people the components they need with one-stop shopping and is successful on eBay selling at a higher price than he could get selling the components separately.

It's easy to put together kits using your expertise regarding certain merchandise even if you have to buy some of the components at retail. If the kit sells well on eBay, then focus on getting all the components of the kit from wholesale sources to maximize your profit. Then, ramp up your sales.

Partnerships

There are still a huge number of people who are computer illiterate and who may never come to use computers. Find one who is a retailer and partner with her to sell her merchandise on eBay. You do all the digital work. She supplies the inventory. You divide the profits fairly. This is a good way for a retailer with a physical store to increase sales without additional fixed-cost overhead. It's a good way for you to be in business on eBay without financing a lot of inventory.

Classified Ads

Looking through the classified ads section of your newspaper may reveal some opportunities to buy low locally and sell high on eBay. This is particularly true if you're selling in a niche. You need to check only one portion of the classifieds, not the entire classifieds section.

Consignment

Consignment sales offer you a lot of possibilities. You provide a service of selling retailers' merchandise on eBay, and the retailers pay your fees. You don't have any money tied up in inventory, and if any items don't sell, you're not stuck with them.

There are a number of things to keep in mind:

1. Use a written consignment agreement.

2. Make sure each retailer understands all the fees and other costs to be paid in addition to your consignment fee. If you pay all such fees and costs, you will have to charge a higher consignment fee.

3. Reserve the right to refuse an item due to an unreasonably high price or for other reasons. Help retailers set realistic prices.

4. Consignment for an eBay business doesn't necessarily mean you have to take possession of the goods. Make a judgment as to who will store and ship the item. It's great if the retailer will store and ship. However, you need to have assurance that the retailer will ship promptly and will not sell the item in the shop before the auction is over. It's your eBay reputation that's at stake. It's safest to store and ship an item yourself, and it provides a more complete service to a retailer.

5. Reach an agreement with each retailer about guarantees to buyers. You need to be able to provide good customer service (e.g., guarantees), but you can't be liable for the cost of fulfilling such guarantees.

6. Handle the item as if it were your own merchandise. Create good auction ads, take good photographs, and communicate with buyers. Even though none of the inventory is yours, you are still building your brand.

This is a business that will require you to go out and find clients. Consequently, you will have a marketing burden that you don't have with most eBay businesses. However, there are plenty of retailers digitally challenged (computer illiterate), and there always will be. You're most likely to find them locally where you can talk with them and discuss their needs. Some will need you only once a year or once a season to handle excess inventory. Others will have an ongoing need for you to sell their merchandise. This can be a tough business, handling items from retailers one at a time. Rather, you want to find clients who give you ongoing repeat business in significant volume.

Approach local artists or craftspeople about selling their works on consignment. Many art galleries have this type of arrangement with such people.

What do you charge? That depends on the scope of your service to a specific retailer. Talk with other people in your community doing consignment sales. Look at what auction houses charge and what services they perform. Find out what other eBay businesses are charging by hanging out in the various eBay communities and asking questions about consignment sales.

Local Auctions

Local auctions are a proven means of acquiring inventory to be sold at a profit on eBay. Unfortunately, eBay now has such an effect on local markets that auctioneers are using eBay to appraise goods and set minimum auction prices. The good deals at auctions aren't as plentiful as they used to be. In fact, the good deals at auctions were never automatic. You have always had to know market values well to find a good deal at any auction. Many items are auctioned off at prices above market value.

There are still good deals to be found at auctions for those who know market values well, but the pickings are often fewer and farther between these days. Liquidation auctions are a good bet. Estate auctions (or estate sales) can be productive, too, if you do well at garage sales. Look routinely for auctions advertised in the newspaper. Identify some local auctioneers and get on their mailing lists.

eBay

eBay itself can be a source of inventory for your eBay business. There are several approaches:

1. Buy at wholesale in quantity on eBay. Sell at retail one item at a time on eBay. There are plenty of wholesalers and close-out companies selling on eBay.

2. Go picking on eBay just as you would locally. You will spot bargains that provide profit opportunities. Buy an item on eBay and then immediately sell it on eBay.

3. Look for mishandled merchandise. Mishandled on eBay means auctioned with lack of competence. This can happen because an item is placed in the wrong category, is misspelled, has a poor title or auction ad, lacks a photograph, or a dozen other reasons. The result is that the item does not get bid up, and you can buy it at a bargain price. This happens much more than you might think. Then, sell it competently on eBay.

4. Refurbish or repair broken or defective items. Such items sell cheap on eBay (assuming the defects are properly disclosed). Buy an item on eBay. Repair it. Sell it on eBay.

5. Invent your own approach. With 12 million items for auction each week, there will always be plenty of anomalies in the marketplace with which to do something profitable.

The trick to buying on eBay in order to get inventory is to make good use of the eBay search engine.

Go for It!

There's enough in this chapter to keep you brainstorming or buying for a while. Go for it! What's the primary problem in getting an eBay business started? It's the inventory. Finding something to sell. That's the tough job. The rest is just busy work.

6

Borrowing Money

You need money (capital) for three things when starting a business:

Equipment The equipment (and fixtures) you need to do business.

Inventory The merchandise you sell.

Other Operating Capital The funds you need for overhead such as space (real estate), utilities (electricity, telephone,

Internet service, auction management service, etc.), employee wages (or independent contractors), transportation (using your vehicle for business), services (bookkeeping), and the like.

You are undoubtedly paying for some of these things now, such as a computer, space, utilities, and transportation. Nonetheless, you will need money for the remainder.

Savings

Most people can get a good start with their business on eBay with a modest amount of savings. After all, an eBay business is not as money demanding (capital intensive) as starting a business in a physical location where you need inventory that takes time to turn over, store fixtures, employees, and other extensive and expensive overhead. Make a plan to get your business started on your savings and save yourself the trouble of trying to raise money.

Credit Cards

Credit card credit has become a means of borrowing large amounts of money today, even for people of modest means. It may not be wise for you to use this method. First, because this type of credit can be extraordinarily expensive, it should be a last resort, particularly if you need a large amount of money. Second, it is too easy to get in over your head charging on credit cards. No one will ask any questions until you default. (Often a relative or a banker asking probing questions before loaning you money can be a good thing.) Then too, the huge amount of interest and the unconscionable late and over-limit charges can bankrupt even a millionaire.

If you do use credit card credit, plan such use so that you avoid any future financial crises, and end your dependence on credit cards as soon as possible.

However, if you charge inventory on your credit card and turn it over (sell it) before you are obligated to pay back the money (usually the next month), credit card financing can be a real benefit.

Time Your Purchases

Time your inventory purchases so that you get more than a full month of an interest-free loan. For example, suppose your credit card closing date is the 25th of the month. You typically get a statement a week later on the 2nd of the next month, and you have until the 20th of that month to pay off the amount owed before it starts accumulating interest. Buy all your inventory on the 26th and charge it on your credit card. You won't have to pay it until the 20th of the month after next.

In other words, suppose you buy your inventory on the 26th of March (the day after the account closes for the month). You don't get billed until the statement that comes May 2nd, and you have until May 20th to pay without accumulating interest. That's 54 days of credit. With an eBay business, you ought to be able to turn over your inventory, get paid by your customers, and pay your credit card balance in less than 54 days, thus obtaining interest-free financing for your inventory.

Check the terms of your credit card agreement to determine how you can work the system to obtain the longest period of interest-free financing. Terms are different for each credit card issuer, and the scheme outlined above may not work for you.

If you can't do what is suggested here, do what is suggested above; that is, avoid using credit card credit. It's nice if you can get 54 days of free credit, but if you can't make it work, seek a source of financing less expensive than credit cards. For long-term financing, credit card interest will bury you.

Relatives

A time-honored means of getting money to start your business is to borrow from relatives or close friends. You don't need much to start an eBay business, so restrict your method of getting money to borrowing only. Don't give away a share of the business to anyone in order to raise money.

Angels

Angels are people who seek to make loans to (at high interest rates) or buy ownership interests in start-up or immature businesses. This is a type of venture capital and an early step toward raising money through a venture capital firm. Such an investment is normally for a significant amount of money and is well beyond the amount the average eBay start-up business needs. Nonetheless, you may need angel financing someday to expand your eBay business after it becomes well established and continues to expand.

Bank

Banks are good sources of funds because they charge reasonable interest rates and in some cases may be able to give you some assistance with your business. They can also tailor commercial loans and payback plans to fit your needs. Ultimately, as your eBay business expands and needs more operating capital than you can provide, a bank may be your best source of money.

Business Plan

If you are a start-up eBay business, you need a well thought out business plan before going to a banker. It doesn't have to be fancy, and you don't have to pay someone $2,000 to write it, but it needs to explain the nature of your business, why you need to borrow money, and how you're going to pay the money back. Numbers (estimates of income and expenses) are an important part of a business plan.

Operating Statement

It's normally easier to borrow money after you have been operating for a while, if your business is successful. You still need something that resembles a business plan, but an operating statement (an accounting of your operations) is important too. Consequently, it's important to keep good bookkeeping records, which you will need to create an operating statement.

Net Worth Statement (Collateral)

A banker is not likely to loan you money without collateral. Consequently, your banker will be looking for assets to be used as collateral. Your net worth statement lists your assets and liabilities and gives your banker an idea of what might be used for collateral. The bank has a standard form for this statement, and you should use that form.

Occasionally a banker may loan you money without collateral (referred to as "on your signature"). That sometimes happens when you have a large bank account balance, borrow a relatively small amount of money, and have a long history of good credit with the bank.

Borrowing Dilemma

The borrowing dilemma is simply that if you are successful and growing, you will be likely to need increasing amounts of money from your bank to increase your operating capital. If you always need more and more money, when do you pay it back? Theoretically, you would never pay it back (until you quit growing) because as soon as you paid it back you would need to borrow more. Unfortunately, bankers don't see it this way. They want to see a payback.

An easy way to show a payback is to borrow on a long term. Your loan payments will normally be monthly. Thus, if you borrow $30,000 amortized over 7 years at 8 percent interest, your monthly payments will be $467.59 per month. If at the end of a year you go back to your banker to borrow an additional $25,000 to finance your eBay business expansion, you will already have paid back $3,331 of the original loan (i.e., $2,279 interest and $3,331 principal). Your banker will be happy.

It's the short-term borrowing that's a little more ambiguous. Typically you will borrow quarterly (every three months). At the end of the quarter your banker will expect you to pay interest for three months plus reduce the principal by a reasonable percentage. Thus, if you borrow $20,000 at 9 percent interest, at the end of three months you might be expected to pay interest of $1,800 plus make a payment of $3,000 for the reduction of principal. The loan would then be rolled over. That is, you would receive another three-month loan of $17,000 ($20,000 - $3,000 = $17,000) at the then-current interest rate.

The trouble here is that you need another loan of $24,000, not $17,000, because your business is expanding. Assuming your banker approves this additional amount, you will be paying $4,800 interest and principal and will immediately receive an additional

$7,000 as the loan is rolled over at the increased amount. Does it make sense for you to pay $4,800 and immediately receive an additional $7,000 from the bank? Why not have the bank just advance you $2,200, the difference between the new loan ($24,000) and the old loan ($20,000) less interest ($1,800)?

The answer is that bankers like to be paid back. It's evidence that you have the capability to pay back the loan even if you have a legitimate need to borrow more and more money as your business expands. This is the dance. Pay attention to it. Always pay back your loan as per agreement. It will make your banker happy, even though she may immediately loan you an increased amount of money.

Keep in mind that you are at risk when you borrow in the short term. At the end of any quarter, the bank can decide not to loan you any money at all and may call the loan; that is, you will have to repay the full amount of the loan.

Different Loans

Normally when you borrow for buying equipment and fixtures, you borrow long-term. This makes sense on the theory that your equipment will last a long time and can even be used as collateral until it substantially depreciates.

When you borrow to buy inventory and cover other operating expenditures, you borrow short-term. This makes sense on the theory that your financial needs for operations depends on day-to-day variables such as seasonal sales. Typically, your inventory will be part of your collateral.

Compensating Balances

For every dollar deposited in a bank account, the bank can lend a certain number of dollars and charge interest to borrowers to earn money. The Federal Reserve controls the ratio, in effect, by mechanisms that you can read about in books on economics or banking. For instance, let's say the current ratio is .9:1, and the current commercial interest rate is 7 percent. That means that for every $1,000 deposited in a bank account, the bank can loan $900 to borrowers and charge 7 percent interest on the $900. (The ratio may be higher or lower depending on a number of factors beyond the scope of this book.)

Suffice it to say that bank deposits are important to bankers. One of the first things your banker is going to want to know is how much money you will keep in your business bank account. If you are required to keep a certain amount of money in your bank account as a condition of getting a loan, it is called a compensating balance arrangement. For instance, if you borrow $30,000 but are required to keep no less than $5,000 on deposit at all times, that's a compensating balance.

Regardless of whether your banker makes a compensating balance mandatory in your loan agreement, she will still monitor your business bank account balance and will undoubtedly encourage you to keep your balance as high as possible.

This presents three realities to you. First, your large account balances at another bank will entice a banker to loan you money because she will require you to move such balances to her bank. Second, you will probably not get the loan unless you move the balances to her bank. Third, the higher the balances, the easier it will be to get a loan.

Timing

When do you borrow money? First, when you don't need it. Bankers love to loan money to people who don't need it. It's the joke of the business world, but it's true. The time for you to borrow is when you don't need the money and can pay it back without any financial strain. Second, borrow early in the initial phase of your business. Don't wait until you need a lot of money to borrow some. Start borrowing early to build your track record of repayment on time. When you need to borrow a lot, it will be easier.

What amount should you borrow? Start with a small amount. Bankers are eager to get new customers. Even if they have a minimum loan limit, they may waive it and loan you less just to cultivate your business.

Something to note is that a small bank is much more likely to loan you a small amount of money than a large bank or a branch of a large bank. Indeed, a large bank may not be interested in your business at all until you grow into a substantial small business.

SBA Loans

The Small Business Administration (SBA) guarantees bank loans to small businesses. What does this mean to you? It means that you may be able to get a loan because the SBA guarantees it whereas otherwise the bank would not make the loan to you. This, however, can be a little misleading. The bank will not lower its underwriting (lending) requirements just because the SBA will guarantee payment on the loan.

First, the SBA has to approve the loan and will not do so unless the bank uses sound underwriting practices. Second, for the bank it often takes effort to collect on an SBA guarantee just as it does to foreclose on collateral. Consequently, don't assume that it will be easy to get an SBA-guaranteed loan.

Trust

Always be straight with your banker. It's the only way to build a lasting relationship. Make sure you're the one to give your banker any bad news about your business. She should never hear it first from someone else. An early communication of bad news is better than a late one. Indeed, your banker can often help you work through a financial crisis. Keep in mind too that any false statement to a bank may be a violation of state or federal law.

On the other hand, never trust your bank. Your banker doesn't loan you the money, the bank does. Assuming you can trust your banker, it still doesn't mean you can trust the bank. The bank can decide to call your short-term loan (require repayment in full at the end of the current term, normally one quarter) at any time for reasons in many cases that have nothing with you or your credit record. The exception is a long-term loan agreement; but a bank might attempt to call a long-term loan, too, based on some technical breach of the loan agreement.

If the survival of your eBay business requires short-term bank financing, you are at the mercy of the bank. This is not a good situation to be in. You may be required to pay back the loan for your business before you can replace it from another source. Failure to pay off the loan immediately could put you out of business.

What defenses do you have against a bank? First, cultivate contacts with bankers at other banks. If your eBay business is a financially sound one with a good track record, you may be able to borrow from another bank reasonably quickly should your lending bank cut you off. Second, run your business so that you can survive should you lose your source of loaned funds. You may have to cut back the scope of your eBay business activities temporarily until you can find another source of money, but at least you won't be bankrupt.

Feedback

There are many bankers familiar with eBay today. If your banker understands eBay, the first thing she will do when you attempt to borrow money is to check your feedback record. This is yet another reason to ensure that you maintain an excellent eBay reputation.

Other Lending Sources

Some of the other sources of money for your business are obvious but not always recognized as sources of capital.

Lease

When it comes to investments for equipment, your wholesalers or suppliers may be able to help you by leasing you equipment related to what they sell you. This is often an easy source of business capital.

Except for legal differences (mostly irrelevant to financing), a lease is virtually identical to a loan. That is, lease payments are just like loan payments. You don't have to pay for the equipment up front. You make monthly payments over a certain number of years.

For instance, a supplier of packing materials might lease you a shrink-wrapping machine for your fulfillment operation. That's probably only between $1,000 and $2,000, but it reduces the amount you will have to otherwise borrow. Sometimes there's not even a credit check, particularly if you've done business with the supplier before and paid your bills on time.

Always ask what the interest rate is on a lease. The interest can be calculated, and your best protection against paying high interest is to know what the interest is in the first place.

Shrink Wrap

With a shrink wrapper, you place a packaged item inside a plastic bag made from doubled-over wrapping, seal it, and apply heat. The heat shrinks the bag tightly around the package. Not only does the shrink wrap protect the item, but it gives the package a attractive commercial appearance.

Sometimes a supplier might even loan you equipment at no cost just to encourage you to order more supplies. It's smart business to ask your wholesalers and suppliers if they will lease you or loan you the equipment you need.

Vendor Credit

You don't have to borrow money from the bank if you can get it from your wholesalers and suppliers. If they provide you with goods and services on credit, it's just like loaning you the money to buy your goods and services up front. The big question is, What is the length of the period you can keep this money? The answer is, whatever is offered or whatever you can negotiate. Here are some possibilities:

Cash Discount Terms

The presumption is that the payment is due 30 days after the reference date. The expression indicates the discount for prepayment within a specified period.

½ % 10 A half-percent discount if paid onthe 10th day after the reference date.

1% EOM A 1% discount if paid by the end of the month.

2% EOM 10 A 2% discount if paid on 10th of the following month.

2% 10th & 25th A 2% discount if paid on the 25th of the month for invoices issued in the first half of month and 2% discount if paid on the 10th of the next month for invoices issued in the second half of the month.

Net Terms

There is no discount. The terms are for payment.

Net Payment due upon receipt of invoice.

Net 10 Payment due on the 10th day after the reference date.

Net EOM Payment due at end of month.

Net EOM 10 Payment due on 10th of the month after the reference date.

Net 30 Payment due on the 30th day after the reference date.

Net 10th & 25th Payment due on the 25th of the month for invoices issued in the first half of month and due on the 10th of the next month for invoices issued in the second half of the month.

Compound Terms

These expressions are a combination of discounts and terms for payment.

1% 10 Net 30 A 1% disocunt if paid on the 10th day after the reference date; payment due on the 30th day after the reference date.

2% 10 Net 60   A 2% discount if paid on the 10th day after the reference date; payment due on the 60th day after the reference date.

Clearly, if you have a physical location where you sell off the shelves, most wholesale purchasing terms do not permit you enough time to turn over all of the merchandise before you have to pay for it. On eBay, however, the sales periods are relatively short (the longest auction is ten days). If you plan properly and obtain favorable terms of payment, you can turn over all of your inventory before having to pay for it. This is just like a free loan for operating capital.

Check Out Rates

Go to Bankrate.com to check out loan rates and get other information for small businesses (*http://www.bankrate.com*).

III

Business As Usual

7

Selling on eBay

The way you sell on eBay is via auctions (except for eBay Stores). Even eBay's fixed-price selling takes place through the eBay auctions. Therefore, the auctions and the auction regulations will be among your ongoing concerns.

Types of Auctions

You use the different types of eBay auctions for different purposes. This gives you some flexibility. You don't have to conform to only one means of selling all the time.

Normal

The normal eBay auction is a silent auction with a certain time of termination (exactly 3, 5, 7, or 10 days later to the second from the time it's entered) and a minimum bid. It is for one item only. Where do you set your minimum bid? Depends on with whom you talk.

If you set your minimum bid low, it will attract inexperienced bidders, but it won't necessarily impress experienced bidders. If you set it a little below market value, you'll eliminate all but serious bidders. If you set it over market value, you won't get any bidders.

Reserve

eBay allows you to set a reserve. It's really a secret minimum bid. Unless the bidding meets or exceeds the reserve, you don't have to sell the item.

The auction is marked as a reserve auction. As soon as the bidding meets or exceeds the reserve, the auction shows the reserve as having been met. Some bidders will not bid on a reserved auction. They don't know whether the seller is reasonable about pricing, and they don't want to waste their time to find out.

It's a little crazy to have a minimum bid and a reserve, really two minimum bids. Be careful how you handle these. If you set your minimum bid low, it doesn't tell serious bidders anything except that you want to suck in the amateurs. If you set your minimum bid high but still somewhat below market value, it's a signal that you are a reasonable seller and that your reserve is probably only a little higher.

I have seen some sellers reveal their reserve. That makes no sense. You might as well use the normal auction format and use one minimum bid.

Dutch

This is an auction of multiple identical items. Bidders specify how many of the identical items they are bidding on and bid in the normal way. The highest bidders for the items win the auction. However, everyone pays only the bid of the lowest winning bidder.

The seller sets a minimum bid but no reserve is allowed. Is this a strange auction, or what? Nah, it's not that strange. Let's look at two ways you can use a Dutch auction. Suppose your Dutch auction will normally sell 15 items at the minimum bid you set or a little higher. If you want to get a significantly higher price, try offering only 10 items at a time instead of 15. You have reduced the supply.

If you want to sell at a fixed price (the minimum bid price), offer 30 items at a time. You have increased the supply to the point where the price will not get bid up.

This latter technique is a good one for selling multiple identical items at a fixed price without using the eBay *Buy It Now* device. In fact, sellers used it for this long before *Buy It Now* was instituted.

Private

Since anyone can bid at a private auction, what makes it private? Simply, the identity of the bidders is not shown. Even the seller only knows the winning bidder's identity.

Restricted Access

This is an auction that restricts participants. For instance, auctions for Adult Erotica are restricted to those who have *proven* that they are 18 years old or older. This is not a separate type of auction.

Fixed Price

Fixed prices are relatively new to eBay. The *Buy It Now* price is posted in the auction listing until someone makes a bid. Then the *Buy It Now* fixed price disappears and is no longer available.

Fixed pricing has become popular. It gives eBay the flavor of a Web mall, a huge Web mall. It especially appeals to buyers who look for a good price but need an item immediately. A buyer may need an item immediately for a specific purpose, or she may need to buy it immediately because she doesn't have the time to keep looking or to come back tomorrow.

In any event, the *Buy It Now* device gives you one more way to induce people to buy. If you don't think you want to use *Buy It Now*, you might consider at least experimenting with it.

Fixed-Price History

Flint and Palmers, a London haberdashery, made history in the latter half of the 18th century by opening its door one morning with every item in the shop marked with a price. Prior to that customers bargained for every purchase. "Business at Flint and

Palmers was brisk due to the low prices and the elimination of time wasted on bargaining, and Mr. Flint became wealthy. When other shopkeepers observed his success and growing fortune, they too began pricing their goods." (*Old London Bridge*, Patricia Pierce, Headline, London, 2001)

The fixed price is not a type of auction. It is an add-on to an auction. Be aware that when you use it with a reserve auction, it may confuse bidders. Why? It's like a minimum bid. An auction with three minimum bids, in effect, is bound to be a little confusing. You will want to keep your reserve below the fixed price. It may unnecessarily irritate bidders if it's higher.

Listing an Auction

Listing an auction (offering an item for sale) is easy. You simply fill in the listing information in the eBay listing form. Voila! The auction is published immediately.

Posting

To list an auction go to Seller on the eBay navigation bar. Log in, and you're ready to enter information (see Figure 7.1). Make sure you enter complete information. The Web is an informational medium. You get only one chance. You can make corrections or add more information later, but such is simply added to the auction ad and does not replace what's already there. It's easy to post one auction ad or even a few action ads. But for bulk ads, you will want to use Turbo Lister.

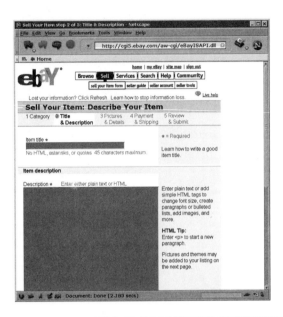

Figure 7.1   Auction ad entry form. ©1995-2003 eBay Inc.

Category

The placement in a category is extremely important. You need to find out where other similar items are being sold on eBay. It may not be self-evident. It may take a little research on your behalf. If you miss the proper category, your chances shrink of selling your item or getting top price for it.

Suppose you go to water toys and find that five water guns similar to the one you want to sell are listed. If you list your water gun there, however, you may not sell it easily. Under squirt guns, dozens of water guns are listed, and that's apparently where most bidders go to look for water guns.

Pricing

If the price isn't right, you're wasting your time on eBay. Read Chapter 10. Information on minimum bids and reserves are presented earlier in this chapter.

Auction Title

The auction title needs to contain keywords that will help potential bidders find the item. It should be straightforward and contain no eBay abbreviations or any other abbreviations (see Figure 7.2). The object here is to have your item get found, not to market it.

Old Beveled Glass Gold Filagre Jewelry Box
Item # 2622972365

Figure 7.2   Auction title.

eBay Abbreviations

Few buyers or sellers today will understand eBay abbreviations. eBay is now so large that most auction participants aren't active members of the eBay community. Don't use eBay abbreviations unless you want to give up part of your market.

It's also essential that the title be easily readable. That means it should adhere to typesetting (typography) rules (see Chapter 8). All caps, bold type, abbreviations, and the like all impair reading. When a potential bidder is skimming the auction list, she may miss any titles that aren't readable.

This idea runs in the face of the common wisdom that a seller should make the title stand out. Don't fall for it. (Be conscious of your auction skimming the next time you look for something on eBay. Observe what you notice easily, what's hard to decipher, and what's irritating. You'll see what I mean about good typesetting.)

Often the flawed attempt to stand out with poor typesetting is an amateur attempt at marketing. Why would you put a Ford pickup truck in all caps? The gal looking for a Ford pickup is going to be interested in your auction ad no matter how the title is typeset. In fact, she is more likely to read the title if it is typeset in a readable manner, not all caps. Do you really think that someone looking for a Dodge van is going to look at a Ford pickup because the title is in all caps and then buy it? Never happen.

The title is your opportunity to have your item get found. It is not a marketing opportunity. Your auction ad is your marketing and selling opportunity.

However, for impulse items that buyers are not looking for, a title made up of hype will sell well. Nonetheless, most items don't fall into the impluse category.

Auction Ad

The listing information goes at the top of the listing webpage in standard eBay format. Below is the auction ad, your opportunity to make a sale. Below that is the standard eBay bidding form. In other words, you enter the auction ad, your chance to be creative. The remainder of the listing webpage is in standard eBay format out of your control.

Common Mistakes

Mistakes in your listing will cost you money either in lower bids or no bids.

1. Spelling mistakes can place your item out of the loop; that is, bidders can't find it because you spelled its name or some

crucial bit of information incorrectly. Use a spell checker and otherwise be careful.

2. A poorly worded title can have the same effect as a misspelling. Include all the key words that bidders will look for.

3. Placement in the wrong category can make your item invisible to all potential buyers. Take the time to make sure the listing category is right.

4. Mistiming can be a bummer too. Your auction should end when potential bidders are at home; that is, evenings and weekends. I was criticized in a book review as being so simpleminded as to mention this in *eBay the Smart Way*. Yet anyone can find plenty of auctions ending at 2AM any morning. It's a rare auction that should end at 2AM.

I have purchased merchandise at great prices because of every mistake mentioned above. This is not theory. Sellers make these mistakes every day and make less money than they would have had they been more careful.

Optional Listing Features

For an additional fee, you can get some extras for your listing:

Home Page Featured Your listing rotates through the home page (not guaranteed) and appears in the special Featured Items section.

Featured Plus! Your listing appears in the Featured Items section at the head of the first page in its category. Your listing also appears in the main list for the category. In other words, it appears twice.

Highlight Your listing appears highlighted to draw attention to itself.

Bold Your listing appears bold to draw attention to itself.

Gallery Your listing and photograph appear in a listing where bidders shop by pictures (photographs) instead of by words.

Gallery Featured Your listing (photograph) appears in the Featured Items section at the head of the first page in its category in the Gallery.

List in Two Categories You list in two categories just to make sure you have the primary categorizations for the item covered.

10-Day Duration Extend your auction to 10 days.

Buy It Now For fixed price listings.

Gift Service Tags the item as being recommended for a gift.

Are they worth it? Generally, no! You have to have a hot item to make paying extra for special treatment cost-effective. eBay is going into contortions trying to squeeze extra revenue out of you. Indeed, who visits the featured page? I never have. Who visits the Featured Items section of each category? Many bidders skip it because they know the item will be in the general list, and they don't want to see the item twice.

Bidders can read a plain title much easier than a bold or highlighted title. Bidders like to skim, and bold and highlight get in the way. Why pay extra for it? The Gallery is great for some items, useless for most. The Gallery Featured is much the same as the normal listing Featured Plus: not worth it.

Listing in two categories makes good sense for some items but no sense for most items. This is worth the money where it is necessary. Extending your auctions to ten days makes sense for most items. (See Daniel Reeves' paper, cited in the beginning of Chapter 24, which indicates that longer auctions get significantly higher prices.) Do it particularly for items that are difficult to sell. Paying for a fixed-price presentation is another way to sell, and it makes a lot of sense. Experiment with it. The Gift Service is a little dubious as a cost-effective technique for selling.

Rather than accept my candid comments, however, you need to experiment with your items to see what works and what doesn't. Every item is different. When you sell in quantity, the considerations are different too.

Relisting

If your item doesn't sell, you can relist it free. Take advantage of this eBay policy.

Listing Fees

You pay a non-refundable insertion fee to list an item. If the item sells, you pay a final value fee. If the item doesn't sell, you can relist once free. Check the listing fees on eBay. They change from time to time. Note that the fees for real estate and eBay Motors are different than normal items.

(Extra fees are charged for the optional listing features covered above.)

Master Lister

The Master Lister was a means of entering multiple auctions at once to save time. It has been replaced by Turbo Lister.

Turbo Lister

This is eBay's newest means of entering listings in bulk. Finally, eBay got it right. You can export data from a database in comma delimited form (or other delimited form) and import it into Turbo Lister offline. Then you go online, and Turbo Lister enters your auctions. This makes integrating a database into your eBay operation simple and straightforward. eBay should have offered this a long time ago, but Turbo Lister didn't come on the scene until 2002.

Almost every database, even those in software not labeled as a database, can export its data via a delimited file. For instance, the auction management services use databases to account for everything. Some can upload auctions in bulk via Turbo Lister. Others have their own program for entering auctions in bulk. A database is the key to eBay happiness.

Turbo Lister enables you to integrate other applications you want to use into your eBay operations easily. This is a particularly important feature for retailers operating a physical location with typical retailing software. They may not want to switch software just to accommodate eBay auctions. They can use their normal software to export delimited data on products into Turbo Lister for automated auction postings. This can be a simple process, but I recommend that you get a database expert to help you with this if you fall into the category of someone with a physical location who wants to stick with your normal retailing software.

But that's not the whole story. Turbo Lister is also a good program to use without data from other applications. You can work on your auction listings in a table format like a database table or a spreadsheet. This is far more efficient than using an entry form.

Taboo Items

You can't sell everything on eBay. Certain items are prohibited either by law or by eBay policy. In addition, certain items are not advisable except in certain circumstances.

Prohibited

eBay doesn't prohibit selling every item prohibited by every state, but it does prohibit many items which the federal government or the states prohibit. For instance, not surprisingly eBay prohibits the sale of body parts. A sample list of other items prohibited and restricted follows:

Academic software

Alcohol

Animals and wildlife products

Anti-circumvention policy

Artifacts

Authenticity disclaimers

Autographed items

Batteries

Beta software

Bootleg recordings

Brand name misuse

Catalog and URL sales

Catalytic converters and test pipes

Comparison policy

Copyrights

Compilation and informational media

Contracts and tickets

Counterfeit currency and stamps

Counterfeit items

Credit cards

Downloadable media

Drugs & drug paraphernalia

Electronics equipment

Embargoed goods and goods from prohibited countries

Event tickets

Faces, names and signatures

Firearms, ammunition, replicas, and militaria

Fireworks

Food

Freon and other refrigerants

Games software: Sony, Sega, and Nintendo

Government IDs and licenses

Hazardous, restricted, and perishable items

Human parts and remains

Image or description theft

Importation of goods into the United States

International trading - buyers

International trading - sellers

Lockpicking devices

Lottery tickets

Mailing lists and personal information

For mature audiences

Medical devices

Misleading titles

Mod chips

Movie prints

OEM software

Offensive material

Pesticides

Plants and seeds

Police-related items

Postage meters

Pre-sale listings

Prescription drugs and devices

Promotional items

Real estate

Recalled items

Recordable media

Replica and counterfeit items

Satellite and cable TV descramblers

Slot machines

Stocks and other securities

Stolen property

Surveillance equipment

Tobacco

Trademarks

Travel

Unauthorized copies

Used clothing

Warranties

Weapons & knives

Wine

Note that the list grows as people push the eBay rules. Check an up-to-date list before you commit yourself to a major selling effort.

Note also that some of the items on the list are perfectly legal, such as alcoholic beverages. However, such items are heavily regulated and taxed. Since eBay feels that it cannot ensure that buyers and sellers follow such regulations, it simply prohibits the items.

eBay itself prohibits many items as a matter of policy. This makes many people angry. Nonetheless, eBay can do it. For instance, eBay doesn't allow spam lists or spam software to be auctioned. Although legal, eBay likely feels that such lists and software are not healthy for the Internet community. In many cases, eBay doesn't allow something to be sold, probably just because it is worried about potential liability. It's simply a business decision.

Restricted

Some items are not absolutely prohibited but are what eBay terms "questionable." A sample list follows:

Food

Autographed things

Artifacts

Hazardous materials

Used clothing

These are items that may cause problems. Food may spoil in transit. Autographs may be forgeries. Artifacts may be stolen from protected archeology sites. Hazardous materials require special packing and shipping. Used clothing should be clean.

If you can solve the potential problems, you can sell the items on eBay. Food needs to be shipped by a means that preserves it properly. Autographs and artifacts need to be authenticated. Hazardous materials need to be packed and shipped safely. And used clothing needs to be thoroughly cleaned.

The Effect of the Taboo

Most reasonable people reading these two lists will immediately understand why most items are prohibited. eBay is more reasonable than arbitrary. Out of thousands of categories of items being auctioned every week, the prohibition of a few dozen items does not seem to be particularly smothering. The taboo has little effect on eBay's income and is otherwise inconsequential except to those who would like to deal in the forbidden merchandise.

You need to carefully check the list before you commit yourself to selling a particular set of items. You will want to make sure that your items are not included.

Illicit Practices

In addition to product taboos, you will want to avoid illicit practices. Some violate eBay rules, and you can get suspended from eBay for violating such rules. Keep in mind that eBay can keep track of its members better today than it did in the past and will continue to improve in this regard.

Some illicit practices are criminal violations. You don't want to end up defending yourself in criminal court. Auctions are not games. They have legal status.

The list of offenses that follows is my version. Don't take my word for it. For further up-to-date information, study eBay's SafeHarbor (Rules & Safety) on the eBay site map.

General Offenses

To get warmed up, we start with some general rules you don't want to violate.

Shill Bidding Using a second eBay ID to bid and raise the level of bidding on your own auction. Also, using another person to do the same.

Extortion Threatening to leave unjustified negative feedback when another eBay member doesn't do what you want them to do.

Feedback Accumulating feedback to a negative 4 (positive and negative combined) results in an automatic suspension.

Criminal You are not exempt from criminal violations on eBay. Every state has laws governing auctions as well as theft and fraud.

Selling Offenses

These are of particular interest to those who make a business of selling on eBay.

Fee Avoidance Avoiding the payment of fees by manipulating the eBay system.

Auction Interception Misrepresenting that you're the seller (when you're not) to collect payment from a winning bidder.

Non-Performance Not sending the auction item to the winning bidder.

Soliciting Off-site Sales Using member contact information to sell any listed item outside of eBay. This is a tightening up of prior prohibitions.

Identity Offenses

You had better be who you say you are and be 18 years old or older too.

Misrepresentation Misrepresenting who you are. This also may be criminal fraud in many states.

Invalid Email Address Using a defunct or invalid email address.

Under Age Participating on eBay if you are under 18 years old. The laws regarding financial responsibility make it legally impractical for eBay to permit the participation of minors.

Miscellaneous

You sometimes wonder what abhorrent behavior prompted the making of these rules.

Interference Interfering with eBay online operations. Don't abuse the eBay system. Follow the guidelines.

Spamming Sending email to other eBay members unsolicited. This prevents you from stealing the bidders from another auction as well as from bothering other eBay members.

Threatening Threatening harm to another eBay member.

Contact Information Taking another eBay member's information and making it public.

Vulgar Language Hateful, sexual, racist, or obscene language is not permitted in eBay public areas.

Bidding Offenses

Some of these are offenses you might see as a seller. Don't be shy about reporting offenses to eBay.

Bid Siphoning Offering the same merchandise by email to bidders in a current auction at a lower price.

Auction Interference Keeping the bidding low in an auction by communicating with the other bidders so as to reduce the number of bidders.

Bid Manipulation Manipulating the bids to find out the current high bid or using a second eBay ID to raise the number of bids above 30, which puts the item in the HOT category.

Nonpayment Not paying for an item for which you are the winning bidder.

Persistent Bidding Bidding after a seller tells you to stop. The seller has the right to refuse bidders.

Bid Shielding Bidding up an auction with a second eBay ID to prevent other bidders from bidding; and then retracting your high bid leaving your lower bid made with your first eBay ID as the winning bid.

Your Marketplace

Many of the rules against these offenses have been prompted by naughty neo-post-adolescents who are not mature enough to realize that ecommerce is not a game. Nonetheless, there are enough mature bad actors participating in eBay, too, who are in it for ill-gotten gains. Consequently, you need to be cautious.

eBay is your market, your community, and your business. It's your responsibility to help keep it an honest and healthy marketplace. It's your duty as a responsible member to report any illicit practices to eBay or to an appropriate law enforcement authority.

What's eBay doing about illicit practices? They have tightened up the sign-up process for new members and the tracking of bad-acting members. They have hired an ex-federal district attorney to head up their investigation and enforcement department. And they continually institute new policies and use digital technology to attempt to minimize illicit behavior on eBay.

eBay claims that only 0.003 percent of all eBay auctions experience illicit activities. That's a pretty good record, although it is difficult to estimate how many claims go unreported.

Review the Rules

As the book went to press, eBay was in the middle of changing its website and updating its rules. Therefore, don't rely on this

chapter for a current summary of the rules. Please review the
rules as published on eBay to bring yourself up to date.

Passive Endeavor

Auctioning is a passive endeavor. You put up your auction. You
don't do anything. Then when it's over, you start dealing with the
winning bidder. Occasionally, you may communicate with bidders
during an auction, should they need additional information about
something. You don't need an auctioning strategy. You just need to
wait until it's over. The bidders do all the work.

This view points out that you need to do all your work before the
auction starts, because after it starts, you cannot do anything.
What do you need to do for a successful auction?

1. Set your target price intelligently.

2. Devise a strategy for setting the minimum bid, the reserve,
    and the *Buy It Now* price.

3. Create an attractive auction ad overflowing with informa-
    tion about the item and include a photograph.

4. Stand ready to communicate with bidders promptly, if neces-
    sary.

5. Stand ready to promptly follow up immediately after the
    close of the auction.

And that does it. If you do numbers 1 and 3 with skill, doing number 2 imperfectly probably won't matter much.

The Heart of the Matter

It's appropriate to end this chapter with encouragement to pay attention to your auction ads (the middle part of the eBay listing). Again, the Web is an informational medium. Include plenty of information on the item you're trying to sell. There's no practical limit. Information sells. The auction ad is the heart of eBay selling. Chapter 8 provides details on how to create effective auction ads.

8

Auction Details

Selling effectively on eBay is a matter of managing the details. To some degree you can automate your eBay procedures with an auction management service. Even so, you need to manage the details in setting up such automation.

Advertising

Your auction ad is your key not only to selling in the first place but to getting the maximum bid you can get for an item. The fact that your item sells profitably is almost meaningless if it would have sold much more profitably had you advertised more effectively.

Certainly advertising is an art well beyond the scope of this book. However, eBay advertising gives you an advantage over other forms of advertising such as display ads in newspapers and magazines. Volume of information matters; hype doesn't.

Complete Information

The Internet is an informational medium, not a hype medium. Website visitors' expectations are different from newspaper and magazine readers' expectations. Space in newspapers and magazines is expensive. You have to keep things short to stay within a reasonable advertising budget. You're forced to use hype to catch the reader's attention. You don't have enough space to inform a reader. Readers expect hype.

On the Web in an eBay auction ad you have all the room you need to tell the story of the item being sold. Space is not at a premium. Website visitors expect to be informed about the item.

Think about it. A potential bidder cannot see, hear, feel, taste, or smell the item offered in an auction as he can in a store. He cannot casually talk with a sales clerk as he can in a store. Therefore, he seeks a substitute. A good substitute is plenty of information (text) and something to look at (photograph) in an auction ad. The information has to describe the item completely, going even so far as to list the product specifications and features in detail. A photograph is effective even if it's just a photograph of the box in which the item is packaged.

Easy to Read

The information must be easy to read. Text is easiest to read in a column with normal size serif type and normal writing style. For instance, text in one huge paragraph as wide as the webpage is almost unreadable, and you will lose a percentage of your prospective bidders with such an ad. In contrast, if you divide up the text into multiple paragraphs, set it in a column (using the HTML TABLE markup), and make the type large enough, every reader will be able to read your ad easily.

Type

The normal size for type is from 10 to 13 points. The browser default is 12 points. Set text in a column that's 9 to 11 words wide (a table about 450 pixels wide). This is optimal for reading at the default type size. Make sure the color of the type contrasts with the color of the background. Low contrast makes reading difficult. Black type on a pastel color (white is a little harsh on the eyes) makes a good combination.

Typesetting Guidelines

By following a few simple guidelines, you can make your text look professional.

Italic

Use italics for *emphasis* and for customary uses, such as for book titles (see Figure 8.1).

We had started out of Mexican Hat about 3:30 PM. By the time we started down the trail off the mesa, it was about 6:00 in the evening. The shuttle of vehicles between the trailheads at Slickhorn Canyon and East Slickhorn Canyon is about four or five miles, and you can make good time driving it in good weather. We carried *ten gallons* of water in each vehicle (five in each of two containers) as recommended in my pamphlet Desert Hiking Essentials.

Figure 8.1   Proper use of italics.

Bold

Use bold for headings, headlines, and even for warnings. But do not use bold for emphasis. It makes reading more difficult (see Figures 8.2 and 8.3).

We had started out of Mexican Hat about 3:30 PM. By the time we started down the trail off the mesa, it was about 6:00 in the evening. The shuttle of vehicles between the trailheads at Slickhorn Canyon and East Slickhorn Canyon is about four or five miles, and you can make good time driving it in good weather. We carried **ten gallons** of water in each vehicle (five in each of two containers) as recommended in my pamphlet Desert Hiking Essentials.

Figure 8.2   Improper use of bold.

Warning: Never start a trek into a canyon where water sources are unknown without taking enough water to last two days with a comfortable margin.

Figure 8.3   Proper use of bold.

Bold Italic

Use only as a substitute for bold.

All Caps

Don't use "all caps" (text made up entirely of capital letters). It's difficult to read. All caps is an old typewriting technique, no longer necessary. And don't use all caps for headings or headlines either (see Figure 8.4).

WE HAD STARTED OUT OF MEXICAN HAT ABOUT 3:30 PM. BY THE TIME WE STARTED DOWN THE TRAIL OFF THE MESA, IT WAS ABOUT 6:00 IN THE EVENING. THE SHUTTLE OF VEHICLES BETWEEN THE TRAILHEADS AT SLICKHORN CANYON AND EAST SLICKHORN CANYON IS ABOUT FOUR OR FIVE MILES, AND YOU CAN MAKE GOOD TIME DRIVING IT IN GOOD WEATHER. WE CARRIED TEN GALLONS OF WATER IN EACH VEHICLE (FIVE IN EACH OF TWO CONTAINERS) AS RECOMMENDED IN MY PAMPHLET DESERT HIKING ESSENTIALS.

Figure 8.4   **All caps are difficult to read.**

Superscripts and Subscripts

HTML supports superscripts and subscripts. Use them when appropriate.

Bullets

HTML supports bulleted lists. Use these to dress up your text and make it look professional (see Figure 8.5).

You will need the following 7.5 minute topographical maps for the Slickhorn trek.

- Slickhorn Canyon East
- Slickhorn Canyon West
- Pollys Pasture

You can obtain these maps at your nearest US Geological Survey office.

Figure 8.5   **Bullets are handy to use, particularly for advertising.**

Numbers

HTML supports numbered lists. Readers find numbered lists useful and readable (see Figure 8.6).

You will need the following three 7.5 minute topographical maps for the Slickhorn trek.

1. Slickhorn Canyon East
2. Slickhorn Canyon West
3. Pollys Pasture

You can obtain these maps at your nearest US Geological Survey office.

Figure 8.6   Numbered lists are handy too.

Border

To create boxed text, use borders. Use boxes for special instructions or sidebars. You create boxed text by putting the text inside a one-cell table with the border showing (see Figure 8.7).

You will need the following three 7.5 minute topographical maps for the Slickhorn trek.

1. Slickhorn Canyon East
2. Slickhorn Canyon West
3. Pollys Pasture

You can obtain these maps at your nearest US Geological Survey office.

Figure 8.7   A border around text draws attention to it.

Type Size

One sees a lot of small text used on the Web. It looks neat, but it's hard to read. Use the browser default size (12 points) instead. If you use type much larger than 12 points, people will also have trouble reading it easily.

Rules

Use rules (straight horizontal lines) to divide your auction ad into sections if appropriate. Using headings is better, but sometimes rules are OK too.

Underlines

Don't use underlines in Web pages. An underline signals a link. This will confuse your buyers.

Flush Left

Keep the text flush left (lined up on the left side). If you use flush right, the text will be difficult to read. If you center all the text, it will be uncomfortable to read (see Figures 8.8 and 8.9).

We had started out of Mexican Hat about 3:30 PM. By the time we started down the trail off the mesa, it was about 6:00 in the evening. The shuttle of vehicles between the trailheads at Slickhorn Canyon and East Slickhorn Canyon is about four or five miles, and you can make good time driving it in good weather. We carried *ten gallons* of water in each vehicle (five in each of two containers) as recommended in my pamphlet Desert Hiking Essentials.

Figure 8.8   **Flush right text is difficult to read.**

We had started out of Mexican Hat about 3:30 PM. By the time we started down the trail off the mesa, it was about 6:00 in the evening. The shuttle of vehicles between the trailheads at Slickhorn Canyon and East Slickhorn Canyon is about four or five miles, and you can make good time driving it in good weather. We carried *ten gallons* of water in each vehicle (five in each of two containers) as recommended in my pamphlet Desert Hiking Essentials.

Figure 8.9   Centered text is difficult to read too.

Creating Efficiencies

The fact that information in volume sells items has two realities. First, it's easier and less expensive to provide effective written information than effective hype. Just supply the facts, all the facts. Second, a volume of readable information takes time and effort to produce. What can you do to reduce the workload? After all, you have a lot of items to sell, and you can only do so much for each.

Templates

Use a template for your auction ads. It doesn't have to be fancy. It should place the text in a readable column. You don't have to reinvent each new auction ad. You merely fill in the template with information, and the ad is ready to upload to eBay. Auction management services provide a variety of nicely designed templates for you to use.

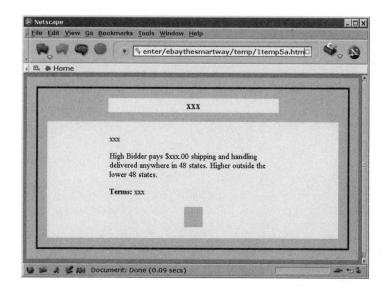

Figure 8.10   Auction ad template.

Links

Use links to manufacturers' websites for additional information. This is permitted by eBay and is a good way to provide potential bidders with features, specifications, and even narratives on products. Be sure to check the link to make sure that it works.

Manufacturer's Information

If you can't link to a manufacturer's website, try to find the manufacturer's information in digital form. Then copy and paste it into your ad. Likewise, you can save and paste a manufacturer's logo into your ad.

You Are Liable

I recommend these two processes with some reservations. First, using a manufacturer's information without permission is a copyright infringement. Second, using a manufacturer's logo without permission is a trademark violation. You are liable if you do either. However, out of the millions of auctions on eBay each week, a significant percentage of the auction ads do include either a manufacturer's information or a trademark or both. Few, if any, of the sellers obtain permission to use either. As a practical matter, it seems a safe and even a reasonable practice until a manufacturer complains.

If you can't find a manufacturer's information in a digital format, you might scan an advertising brochure or a product package and put it in your ad as a photograph. The ad will take somewhat longer to download, but it's better than nothing.

Boilerplate

Boilerplate refers to text in a contract or document that is used over and over again in similar contracts or documents. In other words, it's the part you don't have to rewrite. You need to use boilerplate in your auction ad. What should it include?

Marketing Information

Always use your eBay auction ads to market your eBay business. It's a great opportunity you can't afford to miss. Promote your website first. You can't include a link to it (eBay outlawed that a while back), but you can publish your URL and even talk about your website (in the text).

Promote your business. Tell about your history, your success, and what you sell. Surprisingly, bidders want to know more about you.

Information increases their comfort level with you. They will read about you. Don't overdo it, but do something.

Some of the auction management services automatically provide a display menu with a few of your other auctions on it for inclusion in your auction ad (at the end) in order to boost overall sales via cross-selling. eBay links in the head of the auction listing do the same thing. This works as long as the other auction items are similar or relevant. Otherwise the items may not interest buyers. But it shows that with a little imagination you can use your auction ad for something beyond just selling one item.

A Thin Line

If you promote your website in your auction ad, you are walking a thin line. Check with eBay rules to see what is permissible and what is not.

Arrangements

There are a few things you have to tell bidders in every auction ad. How they can pay for the item. That's a constant. How the item will be shipped. That's probably a constant, too, except in the case where the winning bidder wants faster shipping. And how much the shipping will cost. That's a variable, but the wording can be a constant except for the exact amount, which will change with each item.

This is a good place to tell bidders anything else you want them to know in regard to how they can do business with you. Some sellers include elaborate rules in their boilerplate, and they expect bidders to follow such rules. Each time they get burned by another winning bidder in a new way, they add another rule.

It makes sense to me to have several simple guidelines for the people you are about to do business with. After all, it's your auction, and you're expected to take the lead in making the business arrangements. An extensive set of rules, however, is a little too enthusiastic. What will happen is that winning bidders will ignore them, and that may lead to a genuine misunderstanding that you may interpret to be a total violation of your rules.

The rules may even turn bidders away offended by your arrogance, although that prediction depends on someone reading your rules, which is unlikely. So, if you're one of those people who thinks you can pull off a perfect transaction through rule making, lighten up and do a heavy edit on your list of rules.

Like Products

If each item you sell is unique, then you will have a lot of work to do to make each auction ad on a custom basis. On the other hand, if you sell the same products over and over again, you can reuse your auction ads with little, if any, adjustment.

Auction Title

Your auction title needs to be straightforward, be readable, contain key words, and follow typesetting guidelines. This requires a little research. Find out what other sellers are using as titles in auction ads for the same or similar items. This will give you some ideas for keywords.

Don't use all caps, bold, or other gimmicks in the auction title. Don't pay extra for bold or highlighting. Make it readable according to typesetting guidelines.

For standard consumer items, just stating the facts is enough:

Sony DCR-TRV22 Mini DV digital camcorder, new

This is a good title. For unfamiliar merchandise, you need to provide maximum descriptive information on one line.

For a few rare items, particularly impulse purchase items, you have to use a little hype. But as soon as you do, you risk losing your credibility. All things considered, experiment to see what works.

Placement

You must put your ad in the right place—in the right eBay subcategory—to be found by potential bidders. Unfortunately, this is not always self-evident. Often you have to do an analysis to determine the proper subcategory. Indeed, your item may be appropriate for several subcategories. If you don't pay adequate attention to placement, your eBay business will suffer. You have to advertise your products where people can easily find them. Unfortunately, there's no automatic way to make this decision.

Timing

Don't lose a lot of sleep over what is the best timing. Common sense dictates that people are most likely to visit eBay when they are at home and awake. You will want to make sure that the end of your auction (exactly 3, 5, 7, or 10 days from the commencement of your auction) falls during the evening (but not too late) or on a weekend. Some items may have a special time that's best to sell, but most items sell best when people are at home. See timetable in Table 8.1.

Table 8.1   eBay Time and US, Japan, and Britain Time Zones

Japan	Hawaii	eBay	Pacific	Mountain	Central	Eastern	Britain
5:00	10:00	**0:00**	**12:00**	1:00	2:00	3:00	8:00
6:00	11:00	1:00	1:00	2:00	3:00	4:00	9:00
7:00	**12:00**	2:00	2:00	3:00	4:00	5:00	10:00
8:00	1:00	3:00	3:00	4:00	5:00	6:00	11:00
9:00	2:00	4:00	4:00	5:00	6:00	7:00	**12:00**
10:00	3:00	5:00	5:00	6:00	7:00	8:00	1:00
11:00	4:00	6:00	6:00	7:00	8:00	9:00	2:00
12:00	5:00	7:00	7:00	8:00	9:00	10:00	3:00
1:00	6:00	8:00	8:00	9:00	10:00	11:00	4:00
2:00	7:00	9:00	9:00	10:00	11:00	**12:00**	5:00
3:00	8:00	10:00	10:00	11:00	**12:00**	1:00	6:00
4:00	9:00	11:00	11:00	**12:00**	1:00	2:00	7:00
5:00	10:00	**12:00**	**12:00**	1:00	2:00	3:00	8:00
6:00	11:00	13:00	1:00	2:00	3:00	4:00	9:00
7:00	**12:00**	14:00	2:00	3:00	4:00	5:00	10:00
8:00	1:00	15:00	3:00	4:00	5:00	6:00	11:00
9:00	2:00	16:00	4:00	5:00	6:00	7:00	**12:00**
10:00	3:00	17:00	5:00	6:00	7:00	8:00	1:00
11:00	4:00	18:00	6:00	7:00	8:00	9:00	2:00
12:00	5:00	19:00	7:00	8:00	9:00	10:00	3:00
1:00	6:00	20:00	8:00	9:00	10:00	11:00	4:00
2:00	7:00	21:00	9:00	10:00	11:00	**12:00**	5:00
3:00	8:00	22:00	10:00	11:00	**12:00**	1:00	6:00
4:00	9:00	23:00	11:00	**12:00**	1:00	2:00	7:00

Theoretically, if a buyer uses proxy bidding, the timing of the end of the auction is irrelevant. Many potential bidders who use proxy bidding, however, feel more comfortable bidding if they can conveniently attend the end of the auction—even if it turns out that they don't attend. Many do not rely on proxy bidding. And many look forward to bidding in the final minutes of the auction. That makes timing important.

Remember, the auction must be a convenience for buyers, not sellers. If you're a workaholic seller and post auction ads in the middle of the night, you're going to lose potential bidders.

Valuation

Valuation is another important key to success on eBay. This is a simple concept. You appraise an item before you auction it. That is, you estimate the sales price based on research. The adverse consequences are drastic if you don't.

One consequence might be that you end up selling the item for much less than its current market value. In other words, you cheat yourself because you didn't know enough to set a reserve price high enough. Another consequence might be that you ask too much for the item (minimum price or reserve price), and no one will bid on it. You waste time, energy, and money.

See Chapter 10 on Pricing for a more complete discussion of this crucial topic.

Linking

As mentioned, you can't link to your website from an auction ad. You do have a link to your eBay Store (if you have one), a red price tag by your eBay ID in the auction listing. That's great, particularly if you don't have a website. Unfortunately, a link to an eBay Store with dissimilar or irrelevant items may not be very fruitful in generating extra profits.

About Me

In your auction ad, you have a link to your *About Me* entry at eBay by your eBay ID in the auction listing. Don't overlook *About Me*. It's a great opportunity to tell your story, which will help sell your merchandise (see Figure 8.11). It's only one page, but you can make that page as long as you want to. Think of it as your one-page brochure website on eBay.

Give some background information on yourself and your eBay business. Say something about your business philosophy. Brag about the unique character of your business, if it has one. If not, brag about something else. But don't use a lot of hype. You have plenty of room. Just state the facts, especially when you're bragging; that is, provide a lot of information.

Tell people who you are and where you are. Include photographs of yourself and even of your home office or warehouse. As you materialize through your webpage, people will trust you more and look favorably on doing business with you.

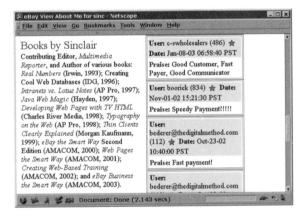

Figure 8.11   The author plugs his books on his *About Me* webpage.

You need to know a little HTML to do a generous *About Me* webpage, but it's worth the effort. (See the webpage authoring and HTML tutorials in Appendices 5 and 6.)

You can have a link to your website in your *About Me* presentation. This is your chance to promote your ecommerce off eBay while on eBay.

Where the Work Is

This is where the work is. As mentioned in Chapter 7, your job is to prepare well for the auction. There's not much you can do after it starts. The seller's strategy is to do things rationally before the auction is commenced.

And now to close this chapter with an eloquently written auction ad, I give you the productive ad Bob Kitchner (Dangerous Threads) has written and used.

> A Beautiful Piece of Leather! Cut in our own shop from Thick #1 Belt Grade 7/8 ounce Domestic Hides tanned in Tullahoma, Tennessee, this belt will outlast you! The leather, called "Tomahawk", was specially developed for us: it is chrome tanned for heat and shrinkage resistance, then veg retanned with quebracho and wattle tree extracts to fill in the grain and give it plumpness and a smooth texture. Then it is dyed and wet-stuffed with fat liquors to give the leather a fine, supple "hand". Ain't no cheapie import... Sturdy Antiqued Buckle cast in Rhode Island. (Fastened with snaps; you can change buckles if you want to). Color: "Tobacco", a rich shade of medium brown. Width: 1 1/4.

9

Photographs

Elsewhere this book cheerleads the use of photographs in auction ads. Photographs really do help sell. Omission is often fatal to auctioning success, leading to either a lower winning bid, a final bid below the reserve, or even a lack of bids. If you want to conduct a business on eBay, plan on using a photograph, or several photographs, in every auction ad.

Taking Photographs

This isn't a book about photography, but I've provided some basics for photographing auction items.

The Pros

There are not only photographers who specialize in photographing merchandise, but many of them even specialize in certain types of merchandise (e.g., cars, office machines, clothes). Don't be disappointed if you can't duplicate their quality. That's what they do all day, every day using thousands of dollars of equipment. But you can routinely take acceptable photographs by following a few basic guidelines.

Follow the guidelines, experiment, and devote some resources to equipment that enables you to take attractive pictures.

Equipment Quality

Your goal is to present a sharp picture of the auction item you want to sell. Although an image editor can do a lot to enhance a photograph, it can't work miracles. You have to use a camera that has at least minimal quality.

Avoid plastic lenses. Glass lenses are generally better quality, but glass by itself is not a guarantee of quality. Stick with brand name cameras. There's plenty of competition in the camera business, and there are some great brands. It's not difficult to find good quality at a reasonable price.

Beyond the lens, the quality is in the light metering and the focus mechanism. If you have to worry about light metering, you're going to spend more time taking photographs than you should. Get a camera that has good light metering. Focusing is a little different. You can focus a camera easily, quickly, and accurately if it has a manual focus mechanism. Many fixed-focus cameras are perfectly adequate also. But if the camera has automatic focusing, make sure it's good quality. In addition, your camera should have reasonable close-up capability. You should be able to take a picture that's as close as two feet away (see Figure 9,1).

Figure 9.1   Close-up photograph.

If you need to photograph small things such as diamond rings, you need special close-up capability. This requires a special lens or the addition of a special lens mounted over the existing lens. Consult an expert before you buy a camera if you need this capability. Otherwise, you may pay more than you need to.

Many other camera features are not essential but can provide convenience, particularly for mass production work. For instance, many cameras have zoom lenses. Although not necessary for high quality photographs, zooming can save time. It's also nice to be able to operate a digital camera or a flash unit with an AC adapter instead of batteries. It saves money and provides convenience. Your eBay photography studio will certainly have an electrical outlet nearby.

You can get a good film camera for under $70. Indeed, today you can get a good digital camera for about $100.

Flash

Normally you take photographs of merchandise close up with a flash. To keep the flash from overpowering the photographs with glare, it's best to use a diffuser over the flash, something translucent but not transparent such as a white plastic bag. Use a one-color plain cloth for the background. A plain bed sheet spread over the back and seat of a chair or taped on the wall and floor makes a good studio.

Lights

Unless you want to spend a lot of money, you cannot count on your flash being effective at a distance of more than about eight feet. One way to take better photographs indoors is to use photo floodlights for large objects such as furniture. But such floodlights are also good for photographing almost anything indoors, even close up. They help reduce the glare of the flash.

A pair of economy photo floodlights with stands costs about $100 but will save you many wasted photographs. Why do they come in pairs (or threes)? You need to set them at angles on each side of the auction item. In other words, using photo floodlights straight on is not very effective. You can use a third light effectively to backlight large bulky items (see Figure 9.2).

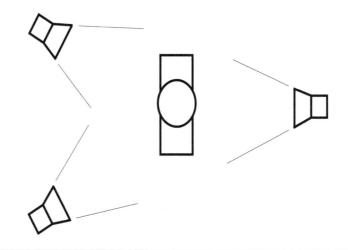

Figure 9.2   Lights set to photograph subject.

Inexpensive Lights

Try using Halogen lights for flood lights. You can get them at a home and garden store such as Home Depot for as little as $8 each.

Outside

Outside, try to take your photographs on a sunny day or at least a bright overcast day. If you take your photographs on a dull overcast day, they will be dull photographs.

Make sure the sun is coming from behind you over your shoulder as you photograph your auction items. And work around where your shadow falls. For instance, that means that you have to move a car three times to photograph it. You start on the left side with the sun coming from behind over your shoulder. Then you reposition the car to photograph the rear with the sun coming from behind over your shoulder, and so forth.

Some photographers say that bright sunlight causes shadows that are too harsh, and a bright overcast day provides better photographs. That may be true, but you can have the sun and soft shadows too. Use photo floodlights outdoors to fill in the shadows caused by strong sunlight. That's what the pros do.

Take care also to present a background that does not distract from the auction item. A sense of marketing helps too. For instance, a photograph of a car in a pleasant residential setting is preferable to a photograph of the same car on a used car lot.

Tripod

A tripod is the mark of a professional and is essential to photographing eBay items indoors and outdoors. Make sure you always use one.

Display Props

Not all auction items are displayed properly lying on a bed sheet set in a chair. Spend a little imagination and money on props to help display certain items better. You can get ideas from traditional retailers and in mail-order catalogs.

Mannequins

Find an old mannequin somewhere and buy it. Use it to display clothes or other items worn on the human body (e.g., jewelry). You can also use mannequin parts to display certain items (e.g., arm and hand to display a glove).

Display Stands

There are hundreds of different kinds of display stands and racks. Some are worth buying if you have a specialty niche. Most can be duplicated with materials such as coat hangers, 2×4s, duct tape, clamps, and the like. Be creative.

Fabrics

You can achieve the plain studio background look with bed sheets as suggested earlier. This is appropriate for many auction items, but some items need a little extra pizzazz. For instance, velvet and satin can give a look of elegance to appropriate items. Always use solid colors. Printed or multicolored fabrics are too busy and will detract from the item being photographed.

Film

You can use a normal film camera to take photographs of merchandise for your auction ads. This works well. You have the film developed. Then the next step depends on the method you use to digitize the photographs.

Print Scanning

One method is scanning. Normally you will use a home flatbed scanner, which you can buy for between $50 and $250. The difference in the price of scanners is usually based on features, not necessarily on resolution quality. You need to have prints (glossy not matte) made when you get your film developed. You then scan the prints on the scanner.

Another scanning method is one you probably won't use. You can have the prints scanned professionally. A camera shop or service bureau will scan your prints on an expensive high quality scanner for a considerable fee. Few auction ads require this high level of quality.

A scan produces a digital image file that you can edit with an image editor and use in your auction ad.

Film Scanning

You can also scan your film negatives or positives (slides) on a film scanner. Prints are not required. Film scanners cost considerably more than home scanners. Even though they produce higher quality in general, they may not provide enough more usable quality for the Web to justify their additional expense.

Kodak Picture CD

An easy method is simply to order a Kodak Picture CD instead of prints at your local photofinisher (see Figure 9.3). This service is widely available, reasonably inexpensive, and high quality. You transfer the images from your CD player to your hard disk for image editing.

Figure 9.3   Kodak Picture CD.

Kodak Photo CD

This method is almost identical to Kodak Picture CD except that you get each photograph in five or six different sizes, each a high quality image. Although the Kodak CD service has been available since the early 1990s, Photo CD has become a specialty service for serious photographers. Those selling artwork on eBay may want to consider using Photo CD for special purposes. The extra expense is not justified for most eBay auction ads, so stick with Kodak Picture CD.

Digital Camera

The most convenient and least expensive (over the long run) method for taking auction ad photographs is to use a digital camera. Although you can take some good pictures with 1-megapixel cameras, a 2-megapixel camera will give you professional quality for eBay use. Today 2-megapixel cameras are inexpensive.

Digital cameras usually take sharp close-up shots and do not require a close-up lens except for very small items. In general, it seems easier to take good photographs with a digital camera. Thus, buying and using a digital camera is money well spent and is almost essential to anyone serious about their eBay business.

Highest Quality

Most digital cameras give you a choice of quality settings for your photographs. The higher the quality, the more memory used. Using lower quality enables you to take more photographs at one time. Always use the highest quality photograph setting on your digital camera for auction ad photographs. If you need to shoot more pictures at one time, buy more memory for your camera.

Removable memory is highly desirable because it enables you to upgrade the size of your memory to take more photographs at one time. Most digital cameras now use SmartMedia cards (small and thin) or Compact Flash cards (small but thicker).

Cameras typically come with 8 MB cards (about 10 photographs) or 16 MB cards (about 20 photographs), but you can use 128 MB cards (about 160 photographs) in most cameras.

One of the features to look for in a digital camera (see Figure 9.4) is the means of getting the image out of the camera and onto your hard drive. The most popular means is a USB cable and the use of software that comes bundled with the camera. You plug the small fitting at one end of the USB cable into your camera and the large fitting at the other end into a USB port in your computer. The photographs (image files) show up as a separate disk on your folder tree populated with numbered image files. Older digital cameras use other connections such serial or Firewire cables.

Figure 9.4   Inexpensive, good quality digital camera.

You can also remove SmartCards or Compact Flash cards from your digital camera and put them in a card reader connected to your computer via a USB cable. Your computer will see the card reader as a separate disk populated with image files.

Software, Too

Don't assume that because you have the proper connections between your digital camera and your computer you can make a transfer. The capability to transfer requires special software too. This isn't a problem when you buy a digital camera new. The camera invariably comes with the requisite software to make the connection work. If you buy a used digital camera, however, make sure that you get the software with it to make the camera-computer connection work.

Image Editing

Image editing software runs from $40 (wide variety) to Adobe Photoshop at about $700. You need only a few features of an image editor, so don't buy image editing software unless you want to spend a lot of time doctoring images. Use the image editor that comes with your digital camera or your scanner.

You will need only four features:

Cropping The capability to cut a small photograph out of a larger photograph.

Brightness Adjustment The capability to change the brightness of a photograph.

Sharpness Adjustment The capability to make the resolution of the photograph appear sharper.

Resizing The capability to reduce the size of the photograph.

You should take care to get the best photographs possible by learning how to use your camera. The four features above will enable you to use your image editor to make acceptable auction ad photographs.

Remedial Image Editing

You can use advanced image editing software to make good photographs out of bad. But you have to ask yourself, Is this the best use of my time? In most cases, it probably isn't. Image editors are not the easiest programs to learn, and remedial image editing takes a lot of time. You're better off learning how to take good pictures in the first place.

Cropping

Cropping is the first step in your image editing. Use the cropping rectangle tool to outline that portion of a photograph you want to use. Then crop it out of the photograph (see Figures 9.5 and 9.6). Everything outside the outlined rectangle will disappear. If the cropped image looks right, use Save As to save it as a new image.

Image File Management

When using image files, start with an original, but after cropping save as a new file. Then continue your editing. This procedure preserves the original. Should you get carried away with your editing and end up with something awful, you can always go back to the original file and start over.

Until digital editing made it easy to crop photographs, you had to be very careful to frame a good picture before you clicked the shutter of your camera. Today you can be more careless with your framing. The thing to remember is that your eBay auction ad photograph should include everything in the image needed to sell the auction item, but nothing more. Crop away the excess portion that contributes nothing to selling the item.

Cropping is fun. It gives you ultimate framing control over your photographs. Try it.

Figure 9.5   Original photograph.

Figure 9.6   Cropped photograph.

Free Image Editor

One image editor that's free does a pretty good job. Try Irfan-View. It does everything you need, and you can download it from: *http://wwww.irfanview.com*.

Brightness

Brightness and sharpness adjustments require some experimenting. You can find a certain adjustment that will work for most of your photographs. Use such an adjustment keeping in mind that some photographs will require special editing.

I've found that making most photographs a little darker works well (but only with a corresponding boost in sharpness). I use an adjustment between -5 and -10 as my standard for brightness.

Sharpness

Almost every photograph looks better with a little digital sharpening. Making your photographs sharper will also make them brighter, an undesirable side effect. Consequently, you can darken your photographs a little, with the brightness adjustment as mentioned earlier, to offset the lightening effect of sharpening.

I usually boost the sharpness of photographs with an adjustment factor of $+15$ to $+30$. This, combined with the brightness adjustment mentioned earlier, substantially improves the look of about 80 percent of my photographs. The remaining 20 percent require custom adjustments.

All in One

Some digital editing software now has one adjustment control to adjust your photographs. It includes both brightness and sharpness, and possibly gamma (another type of brightness). Some controls are proprietary and also make other adjust- ments at the same time. You will have to be the judge of whether such an adjustment control is right for you. I have found all-in-one adjustment controls to be very useful.

Resizing

Your final editing step is to resize the photograph to the size that you need. You can't go larger. If you do, the image will grow fuzzy and finally start showing the pixels. However, you can always go smaller. Since most digitized photographs are quite large, you will almost always need to resize them to the smaller size appropriate for display in your auction ads.

Larger photographs require larger digital files, which take longer to download. Potential bidders don't like long downloads. So, keep your photographs no larger than the size you need to display. Usually 300 pixels wide is the maximum needed for eBay ads. If you want to show special details or show art work, you can use a width up to 700 pixels.

It's Your Call

Everyone takes photographs differently, uses different equipment, and edits differently. The guidelines in this chapter are just that: guidelines. They are not hard and fast rules. You need to experi- ment and put together a photographic procedure that suits your capabilities, satisfies your aesthetic judgment, works efficiently, fits your budget, and produces photographs of reasonable quality. And that's all.

Image Services

Your photographs can be uploaded to anywhere (any address) on the Web, and then you can use them in your auction ads. What's the best place for them? It's probably on the Web storage space provided to you by your Internet Service Provider (ISP). When you get dial-up or DSL service, your ISP usually provides you with Web space to put up a website. If you don't use all of that space for your website, you can use it to store your photographs for your auction ads. It's easy to upload the photograph files to your website via File Transfer Protocol (FTP).

Use an FTP program like WS_FTP Pro (see Figure 9.7). The program will show your folder tree on the left and your website's folder tree on the right. It's quite simple to transfer an image file from a folder on your computer to a folder on your website. In fact, you can upload multiple image files in one upload making it fast and efficient to put your photographs online.

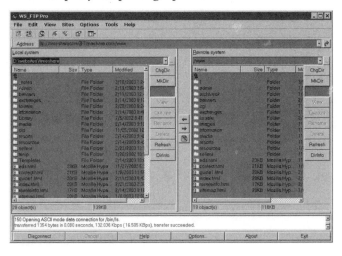

Figure 9.7   WS_FTP Pro screen.

Alternatives

Where else can you store your images? Well, there's no shortage of places.

eBay

You can store one image per auction free on eBay. This may be the best deal for most of your auctions. eBay charges extra for multiple images per auction, however, and if you need a lot of pictures for certain items, you might want to consider an alternative.

Storage Service

There are free places to store your images online. You can use one to save money. There are also inexpensive places to store your images. What you pick will probably depend on what services are offered and what price is charged. But storing images files is neither complex nor expensive, and you probably can't go wrong with a free service.

Presentation Service

Some storage services are more than storage. You get a presentation of multiple small photographs on a presentation panel. As bidders visit your auction ad, they can click on a photograph, and it gets bigger. This makes an attractive feature and is widely used for eBay auction ads (see Figure 9.8).

My experience has been that some of these presentation systems don't work for bidders about one time out of ten. That is, when a bidder clicks on a photograph, it doesn't get bigger. It stays the same size. You might be better off having a few photographs large enough for bidders to see something.

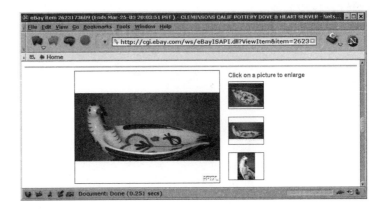

Figure 9.8   iPIX, a popular photo service for eBay sellers.

Auction Management Service

Auction management services typically provide a system for displaying your photographs. If you subscribe to such a service, use its image system. It is integrated into the overall system and should prove easy and efficient to use.

Host ISP

If you have a website separate from your dial-up or DSL ISP, you have a host ISP. You will have space to upload image files. If not, your host ISP should be able to provide you with some additional space for a modest monthly fee.

Choosing a Service

Many people like to play with their photographs. Photography is one of the most popular hobbies in the US. You can spend as much time as you want to taking photographs and doctoring the images. If that's your thing, there is plenty of software to keep you quite busy and plenty of image systems to make spiffy auction ad presentations.

But if photography is not your thing, keep it simple. This chapter outlines all you need to know and do to make attractive photographs that will help sell your merchandise.

10

Pricing

By far, the most important auctioning technique for both buyers and sellers is knowing the value. If you don't know the value of an item as a buyer, you are likely to underbid or overbid. If you underbid, you may lose out on a great bargain. If you overbid you will pay more than you need to for an item.

If you don't know the value of an item as a seller, you are likely to list the item with a minimum bid or reserve that does not maximize your sales price. If the minimum bid or reserve is too low and the bidders are few, you might end up selling a item below its maximum potential price. If you list the item with a minimum bid or reserve that's too high, you may not get any bidders.

There are even a few listing techniques you can use to encourage maximum bidding. But they all depend on knowing the value of the item. So, finding the market value of the item is your most important first step to selling success on eBay.

The question is, What market? More and more, the answer is eBay. That is, eBay is the market for an amazing number of goods. If you can find what an item has sold for in the past on eBay, you will have a good idea of what it will sell for today. If not, you can research values other places online and even offline to create data for making a value estimate (appraisal).

Prices

Prices are all over the place on eBay. For popular items, such as hot-selling name-brand merchandise, eBay prices might be a premium over the list price. For excess supplies being dumped on the market, eBay prices might be only 20 percent of list price. For a niche market in which there's one primary seller on eBay, the merchandise might go for 75 percent of list price. After a half-dozen more major sellers move into the niche, the merchandise might go for 60 percent of list price.

There are two things to remember about eBay. First, every item has its own market. It's difficult to make accurate generalizations about the markets for items, even similar items. Second, if you can make one generalization about eBay, it's that merchandise sells for less than in other markets. Why? Buyers seek lower prices as a reward for taking the risk to purchase an item from someone whom they don't know. But even this generalization doesn't apply to some eBay categories. So, you can see that value research is the first step in auctioning success.

eBay Research

You can access the eBay auction archives by clicking on Completed Items near the top of an auction listing page on the left. However, this link does not appear until after you've narrowed your search by using the search input. See Figure 10.1.

Suppose you have reached French Horn by clicking on a subcategory in the eBay category list (under Musical Instruments, Brass). You will not see the Completed Items link. However, if you narrow your search to double french horns by putting "double" into the search input at the top of the auction list page, the next auction list page will show the Completed Items link.

By clicking on the link, you will see a list of auctions that looks exactly the same as normal auctions except that the item prices are final. eBay archives about three weeks of auctions. By popular demand, eBay is considering the possibility of archiving more than three weeks. In any event, three weeks is enough for many items with regular sales and not enough for items with occasional sales.

Figure 10.1   Completed auction. ©1995-2003 eBay Inc.

This makes a pretty good research tool so long as the item you research has had regular sales. Unfortunately, even items with regular sales have up periods and down periods on eBay. One week you may find a half-dozen identical items up for auction, then the week after only one, and then none the week after that. Sales sort of ebb and flow, ebb and flow. Nevertheless, eBay archives can work well for you, particularly if you can take a couple of weeks to do your value research. But when the eBay archives fail for you, you have to turn to other sources.

Online Research

Thousands of manufacturers now publish their list prices on their websites. Although most such publications cover only current list prices for current merchandise, some websites also keep in publication the list prices for obsolete merchandise going back a few years.

List Prices

Magazines that review products often include the list prices in the reviews. Many magazines are now published online as well as in print. You can access past reviews online often going back as many as four or five years. This is a good source of list prices.

Another source of list prices is the product portal. Some enterprising individual (or company) compiles all there is to know about a product or a group of similar products. Such mini-portals often publish reviews or lists that include list prices.

If you know the list price, you can estimate the price for used merchandise. Indeed, many buyers use list prices as guidelines for purchasing. I know I do. Here are my general guidelines for purchasing on eBay:

New Items Must be priced at 40 to 55 percent of list price (i.e., a 45 to 60 percent discount).

Used Items (excellent condition) Must be priced at 35 percent of list price (i.e., 65 percent discount).

My guidelines work well for me, and I purchase quite a bit of new merchandise on eBay. But even though my guidelines work well for me, there are still plenty of exceptions where they don't work. Consequently, I occasionally make mistakes and miss bargains or pay more than I need to.

Advertised Prices

You can find advertised prices for merchandise at many stores and malls on the Web. This by itself doesn't tell you much. Some sellers (merchants) sell goods at a premium over list price. But one good place to get better information is a price comparison website. This is a website that automatically provides the latest prices for particular goods at a number of different stores or malls. For instance, at *http://CNET.com* you can get the latest prices for a specific model of a Canon digital camera at a dozen different online stores.

You will usually find quite a range of prices on popular new merchandise (from 50 percent under list price to 10 percent over list price) at price comparison websites. Most buyers using eBay aren't stupid. They do the research too. If you want to sell items that sell at certain online stores for as low as 50 percent of list price, you may have to meet the low prices or sell at even lower prices. That is, you will have to be competitive to be successful on eBay.

You can find merchandise sold online by using the search engines such as Google (see Figure 10.2). In fact, sometimes looking for merchandise via Google is almost like looking for it via eBay. Google works pretty well.

Figure 10.2   A Google search-result list for a consumer item. ©2003 Google

Prices for Used Goods

For used goods, there is not as much pricing information. You can frequent websites where used goods are sold, or the sales of used goods are reported. Some, like Amazon.com and Half.com, may provide pricing information in sufficient volume to be useful and dependable. Unfortunately, most such websites, even the largest, are limited to a fairly narrow range of categories of merchandise (e.g., Amazon.com and Half.com) and don't cover much ground. Pricing research online for most used goods requires ingenuity and persistence.

Offline Research

Unless you're very young, offline pricing research was your life until the Internet came along. You're probably an expert. You can use newspapers and magazines to find list prices, sales prices, and prices for used goods (e.g., brand advertising, merchant advertising, and classified advertising). Catalogs are a reasonable source of merchandise pricing for new goods. Special magazines devoted to a certain class of merchandise or collectibles may publish current market price lists. Even some trade organizations publish price analyses for both members and the general public.

And offline you can even go into a store and talk with an expert (sales clerk) to get pricing information. Or, there may be some other place where you can talk with an expert.

Appraisers

Appraisers are experts who estimate the market value of goods. Competent appraisals normally involve some work. Many involve a lot of work depending on the item to be appraised. Few appraisals require only nominal work. Consequently, most experts who do appraisals like to get paid for them.

Offline Appraisals

An offline appraisal costs more because you often deal with an expert on a face-to-face basis. That takes the expert's time and energy. In addition, an expert has to do a certain amount of time-consuming marketing just to get clients in the first place. The ongoing communication between appraiser and customer tends to be via telephone. If you can pay for it, an appraiser's services may be your best bet in determining the value of an individual item or type of item.

Online Appraisals

Many experts use a website to market their offline appraisal business. In such cases, the appraisal service usually doesn't have an online component. It's just the normal appraisal service delivered offline but advertised online.

Some experts provide online appraisals. These are appraisals perhaps researched online, prepared digitally, and delivered via email or in a document file attached to an email message. A website is often the sole marketing device used to get appraisal customers. Often the appraisals are assembly-line appraisals with one fee that fits all, even though some appraisals take more work than others. The ongoing communication between appraiser and customer tends to take place via email.

Such appraisals tend to be less expensive due to their efficient procedures and assembly-line production process.

Trial and Error

The worst valuing technique is trial and error. You have to experiment auctioning the same type of items with different minimum bids and reserves in a succession of auctions to find the sales price point. This is a lot of work and is the last resort to be reserved for those cases where research does not yield a clear value.

On the other hand, when you can't find the value through research, trial and error becomes the only technique to accurately set a value. And thank goodness that eBay provides a medium with which you can experiment and find a value—usually within a reasonably short time. Indeed, eBay offers an unprecedented and unique opportunity to accurately estimate a sales price.

The trial and error technique is particularly useful for scarce or rare goods. Moreover, it is so useful that many company marketing departments, as well as individual businesspeople, now use eBay as a testing ground to determine the prices of new merchandise. So, ironically, the worst technique for quick and easy pricing becomes a cost-effective and relatively efficient new technique for sampling the market and setting list prices for certain items.

Selling Strategy

Setting a price, minimum bid, and reserve price well is more a result of experience than instruction. Every market and every item is different. This section offers some ideas, but there are no immutable rules.

Setting a Price

The best strategy for selling is to know what the value of an item is and devise a strategy to sell it. For commodity items this is usually easy and quick to do. For instance, research the value in the eBay archives for the item. It takes only seconds, or minutes at the most. Then set a minimum bid and reserve price according to a predetermined strategy.

In other words, develop some predetermined strategies for various situations. As soon as you determine the value, use that value and a predetermined strategy to create your auction ad. It's quick, efficient, and effective. For example, a typical strategy would be to set the minimum bid to a low amount and set a reserve price a little below the market value of the item.

For unique items, estimating a price is more difficult. There may be no comparable sales in the eBay archives. You may have to do research both online and offline or even get an appraisal. Naturally, for low-priced items, it's often not worth the effort or cost.

You can use eBay to determine market value. If you don't want to give up one of the the items, auction the item with a high reserve and see how high the bids get. If you don't care about keeping the item, auction the item with a low minimum bid and see how high the bids get. (This process is not guaranteed to be definitive, though often it may be the best appraisal you can do anywhere.)

Setting Up an Auction

What's the best way to set up an auction? It depends on whom you talk to. Some say to set the minimum bid at $1 to attract bidders. But I don't think that necessarily attracts experienced bidders. Others say to set the minimum bid at a price significantly lower than market value. That shows that you're a reasonable seller and that the auction may be worthwhile for experienced bidders. While it may be more attractive to experienced bidders, it may not inspire novice bidders. Setting the minimum bid at market value is probably not a good strategy. Everyone looks for a bargain, and a minimum bid at market value doesn't look like a bargain even though it might be a great buy.

Buyer's Research

How do potential bidders know what the market value is? They research it just like you do as a seller. The higher the value of an item, the more likely that potential bidders will research the value carefully and thoroughly.

In any event, it's clear that an auction without a reserve price is more attractive to all potential bidders. Some bidders just won't bid in an auction with a reserve price. Buyers in a hurry to get something will typically avoid auctions with reserves. A reserve price often just takes the pizzazz out of an auction.

When should you set a reserve? When you're in doubt and can't afford to sell an item for too little. If you know the market—know the values—you can run auctions without reserve prices but with the confidence that you will sell profitably. It's when you don't know the values and can't sell confidently that you need to use a reserve price for protection against loss.

11

Special Auctions

If your products fall into certain categories, eBay may have a special auction for you. Some special auctions are separate auctions, and your items do not appear in the main eBay auction. Others are just sections carved out of the main eBay auction, and your items will appear in both the special auction and the main eBay auction.

These specialty auctions provide you an opportunity to reach your market more efficiently. That is, the specialty auctions draw more self-selected potential bidders. Keep alert, however, as some of these auctions have special rules and special fees.

An Experiment

The special auctions comprise an ongoing eBay experiment. They come and go from time to time. They even change names. The day this book went to press in February 2003 was just a snapshot of the eBay special auction situation at that time. By the time you read this book, the special auctions may be significantly different. Hey, they were different just a few months before I made the final edits for this book.

Special Section Auctions

These special auction sections are part of the main eBay auctions but get sepcial treatment.

Local

Local auctions for almost 100 US cities were an eBay feature while I wrote this book. Imagine my surprise when I found them missing from the eBay website during the final edit for the book. They just disappeared.

They were not separate auctions. Each was just a subset of normal eBay auction lists selected out of the main database and displayed as a stand-alone local auction. Apparently, they're now history. Whether eBay will bring them back in a reincarnation someday remains to be seen.

eBay has had problems making local auctions work well. They haven't quite figured out how to do it so far. Yet the potential for local auctions remains consderable. One must assume that someday when eBay is a much larger marketplace than today, there will be enough critical mass in many cities to make local auctions work well.

Real Estate

Real estate is enjoying a growing success on eBay. Because eBay isn't licensed (in most states), the real estate auctions aren't binding by eBay rules or by law. The real estate auctions are more of an advertising medium than a selling mechanism (see Figure 11.1).

Figure 11.1   Real estate on eBay. ©1995-2003 eBay Inc.

Classic Case

This is the classic case of advertising rather than selling on eBay. Real estate is a growing portion of eBay's business and gets special treatment that other categories don't get. It's almost a separate auction. Yet for most states, it's simply an advertising medium. It illustrates the advertising power of eBay.

Nonetheless, eBay has become licensed in real estate in several states and is experimenting with binding auctions. State laws require that a real estate auctioneer have a broker's license. If binding real estate auctions work well, look for eBay to get licensed in more states.

Everything Else

This is a catchall category. Unfortunately, there are a good number of significant categories that don't have a huge volume of auctions yet and therefore get lost in the shuffle. This new category includes all such auctions and gives them a little bit of a highlight on eBay. In other words, the miscellaneous category was somewhat overlooked before. Now it has a new name and some stature. This is a smart move. If you happen to have items that fall into the miscellaneous category, this new category will help your sales.

Separate Auctions

The history of separate auctions on eBay makes a colorful story. However, describing the current special auctions is about as much as this book can do without turning into a history book.

Live Auctions

Live, indeed. Yes, bidders bid in real time on auction items. The items are mostly art, art objects, fine arts, collectors' books and manuscripts, decorative arts, antiques, antique cars, high-end collectibles, wine, and the like. Bidders must register and be verified.

The sellers are auctioneers and auction houses. If you're an auctioneer, this is your cup of tea. If not, should you want to use this special eBay auction, you will have to find a licensed auctioneer to do your auctions for you or place your items with an auction house (see Figure 11.2).

Figure 11.2   Live auction webpage. ©1995-2003 eBay Inc.

Global

eBay is expanding across the globe. It now has auctions in over 20 foreign countries, and most are doing well (see Figure 11.3). Japan isn't one of them. eBay shut down its auction in Japan in 2002. It had an unbeatable competitor there. But it vows it will return someday. You can access the international auctions from eBay's home page. See Chapter 21 for a more thorough treatment of international business via eBay.

Figure 11.3   eBay Netherlands. ©1995-2003 eBay Inc.

eBay Motors

This is a very successful auction for used cars and trucks, antique cars, recreational vehicles, and almost anything with 2+ wheels. Many dealers have been successful in selling vehicles, and many even specialize in selling on eBay. One dealer in Dallas is reputed to have 176 vehicles in stock strictly for selling on eBay.

Because vehicles are a big-ticket item, this is one place where trust and customer service really count. eBay Motors really works, so don't take it lightly (see Figure 11.4).

Customer Service

The first rule of dealer sales is that you need to keep a vehicle available to eBay buyers until the end of the auction. Closing down an auction before the end because you sold the vehicle off your lot will not make you any friends on eBay and may damage your eBay reputation.

Figure 11.4   eBay Motors homepage. ©1995-2003 eBay Inc.

The second rule of dealer sales is to accommodate the buyer. In most cases, the buyer will travel from a distant city to pick up the car you sold him. He needs an out. That is, you need to guarantee satisfaction at delivery. If the buyer doesn't like the vehicle, don't hold him to the purchase. That's only fair. And buyers won't abuse such a guarantee. After all, they have to travel (at their own expense) to take delivery.

Accommodate a buyer in every way possible. Here are some means of doing so:

1. Provide information on your business.

2. Provide plenty of accurate photographs of the vehicle.

3. Describe the vehicle in your auction ad completely, including defects.

4. Agree to have the vehicle inspected.

5. Agree to close the transaction free.

6. Agree to close the transaction in escrow, if requested. (You can point out that an escrow closing is not necessary as dealers are licensed to properly close vehicle sales.)

7. Agree to mediation in the case of a dispute (e.g., Square Trade).

8. Pick up the buyer at the airport.

9. Agree to arrange for shipment should the buyer decide to take delivery at home.

Keep in mind that the buyer is in a very vulnerable position buying a vehicle unseen in a distant city. Do everything you can to build confidence in the purchase transaction.

Whatever you do, don't mislead or deceive. That's the kiss of death. Your death on eBay. Vehicle sales work well on eBay only because sellers play it straight and give good customer service.

Licensing

This section assumes you have a dealer's license. If not, get one in your state. You can't sell vehicles without one. If you're not a dealer because you're selling vehicles from a company fleet or otherwise selling legally without a license, act as if you are a dealer and follow the recommendations above.

Pricing

Vehicle market values are widely available on the Web from Edmunds, *http://edmunds.com*, Kelly Blue Book, *http://www.kbb.com*, and other sources. Many of your prospective buyers will check the value of the vehicle you have for sale, sooner or later. Most of the prospective buyers are bargain hunters. Why else would they even consider buying an unseen vehicle in a distant city? If you cannot offer a bargain price, you will probably not be successful selling a vehicle on eBay.

Consider putting a link in your auction ad to one of the pricing websites so that your prospective bidders can check the market vale of the vehicle you offer.

Use Your Imagination

You can afford some sales pizzazz for big-ticket items such as vehicles. Use your imagination. Remember, you're dealing with a weary traveler when the winning bidder comes to pick up the vehicle. How about a coupon for a free dinner at the leading restaurant in your town for every buyer? How about one free night at a motel? How about a full tank of gas and a free coupon for fifteen more gallons? How about a cooler full of ice and soft drinks?

eBay Stores

To have an eBay store, you must fill it with fixed-price (*Buy It Now*) items. There's an extra charge. It's essentially a mall sponsored by eBay. Chapter 17 covers it in more detail.

Half.com

Half.com is a place to sell new and used books and even textbooks (or anything with an ISBN number) at a discount. It is a huge book catalog similar to Amazon.com. It also sells music and movies (UPC code items). Not too long ago it expanded into video games, computers, software, consumer electronics, and a short list of miscellaneous categories including such things as sporting goods, jewelry, musical instruments, tools, and toys.

This is a fixed-price catalog website (see Figure 11.5) with its own rules and procedures. It even has a feedback system. It enables you to sell a limited range of items in a different selling format than eBay or eBay Stores.

Figure 11.5   Half.com catalog. ©1999-2003 Half.com Inc.

Gone with the Wind?

According to an article in the Los Angeles Times March 7, 2003, eBay has decided to close down Half.com. So, it may not be around by the time you read this. I find this hard to believe, because the book sales income Half.com gets from me each month must be enough to keep it going.

Auctions Houses

This special category is diminished from what it once was. Originally, it was set up to accommodate a number of old-line auctions houses and sophisticated dealers of art objects and the like (eBay Premier). In fact, eBay bought the old-line auction house of Butterfields in San Francisco and prominently ran auctions in eBay Premier. Then eBay made a deal with Sothebys (the old-line auction house in London and New York), and Premier disappeared. Now Sothebys has disappeared from eBay as a separate auction. The remnants of these operations (including Sothebys) can be found in Live Auctions.

eBayBusiness.com

This is eBay's business to business (B2B) auction. It has not caught on as fast as the retailing auctions and has a lot of competition from specialty B2B auctions across the Web. Nonetheless, it remains viable particularly for small businesses that are not plugged into specialty B2B auctions elsewhere. Indeed, it has a half-million auction listings and a billion dollars in sales (annualized on Q4 2002).

At the beginning of 2003, eBay moved this auction to a separate domain name *http://ebaybusiness.com* to give it independence from the primarily retail main auction site. This seems to be a marketing maneuver. At the time this book went to press, the new website and Business & Industrial category in the main auctions coexisted and appeared to be the same, although each had a different look. However, there was not a link on the home page to the new website. It's possible that by the time you read this, the new website will have completely succeeded the Business & Industrial category.

The main categories are:

- **Industrial Marketplaces** Includes agriculture, construction, industrial supplies, restaurant supplies, test equipment, etc.

- **Office Technology** Computers, telecom, office supplies, etc.

- **Wholesale Lots** Clothing, computers, sporting goods, etc.

- **Other** Commercial real estate, professional equipment, trucks, etc.

Take a look at the Wholesale Lots auctions if you're a wheeler-dealer and want to acquire some bulk inventory to sell at retail on eBay.

This is not the first time eBay has tried something different to make its B2B auctions stand out. Perhaps the B2B auctions for small businesses have not yet reached critical mass. But these categories increased 90 percent in 2001 and 2002 putting them on the road to an eventual success comparable to eBay retail.

If your business is one that sells primarily to other businesses, you will want to take a close look at this new eBay website. For instance, the owner of a metal fabrication business I talked with in Alabama told me that he bought machine shop tools (e.g., lathes) on eBay at prices significantly lower than he could otherwise. He was also building a 3,000 square feet metal building to expand his business and was buying construction supplies on eBay inexpensively. He told me he bought drywall for his new building several hundred miles away in Tennessee on eBay, and it was cheaper than buying it locally even after the cost of shipping.

Professional Services

Professional services have their own auction on eBay called Elance. Chapter 14 speculates (author's have their speculative vices) on how services might be sold on eBay. It also covers Elance in more detail.

The Reality

If you're looking to feel safe and secure betting your eBay business on an eBay special category or auction, get over it. eBay is experimenting and will continue to experiment with new ideas in auctioning; or, to put it more precisely, new ideas in selling. Today's special auction could be tomorrow's run-of-the-mill auction. That may not have much effect on your eBay business even if you fit in the special category of the special auction. But if it does, you need to consider the possibility that your special auction may evaporate leaving you to conjure up a new selling straetgy.

12

Fulfillment

Fulfillment is just a fancy name for filling the order. In the case of eBay, you've sold an item to the highest bidder, the bidder has paid you, and now it's time for you to deliver the goods. How you do that comprises your fulfillment operation.

Drop Shipping

Drop shipping is almost too good to be true for an eBay business. The manufacturer or distributor has the item packaged for a consumer in a warehouse ready to ship. Your job is simply to sell the item and notify the manufacturer or distributor to ship it to the buyer. You don't have to store any inventory or ship anything.

This is great work if you can get it. You just push papers (more accurately push digits), and make a profit. You never touch the product. You don't take any risk on holding inventory.

What's the catch? Well, not all manufacturers and distributors offer drop shipping. Those that do are likely to charge higher wholesale prices or a drop shipping charge. In other words, you pay for the drop shipping one way or another. The drop-shipping fulfillment may not be quick as today's online standards require. In fact, the fulfillment may be slow, and you may have no control over it. This will not make your buyers happy.

Drop Shipping Wholesalers

There is a certain ilk of wholesalers that will purport to make you successful in ecommerce (yesterday it was mail order) by selling merchandise to you wholesale and drop shipping for you. Many of these product offerings are weak, and you will waste your time trying to sell their lackluster merchandise. Indeed, the main feature of their offer is the drop shipping itself. Basing your eBay business on drop shipping rather than on saleable products will likely prove to be a disaster. Consider these offers very carefully before you commit to such a sales program.

Always Inquire

Always ask whether drop shipping is available. Any manufacturer or distributor that will drop ship for you will take part of the fulfillment burden off your back. If the wholesale price is right or the drop shipping fee reasonable, take advantage of the drop shipping. Drop shipping is on the rise. So, it will become available from more manufacturers and distributors in the future.

Should you use drop shipping, however, you will want to carefully monitor the reliability and timeliness of the fulfillment. You are, in effect, placing your eBay reputation in the hands of the manufacturer or distributor. A winning bidder waiting too long to receive the merchandise is not going to accept your excuse that it's the fault of another business.

Normal Operations

Fulfillment is the most tangible part of most eBay businesses. It requires an investment in inventory, equipment, and packing supplies, as well as space to operate. It also requires hard labor. Well, perhaps not hard labor (except for heavy products), but certainly tedious labor.

Inventory

eBay buyers expect delivery immediately. They are willing to wait through the shipping transit period but not beyond. That's why you need to have inventory in stock to be a successful seller on eBay. You need to ship immediately after the buyer pays. (This requires money to buy inventory unless you can get credit from your wholesalers.)

Warehouse

To hold inventory, you have to store it. You might do that in your closet, spare bedroom, garage, utility shed, your friend's garage, a mini-warehouse, or a commercial warehouse. You need to protect the inventory from heat, cold, moisture, and perhaps even rodents or insects. And don't forget theft. (Wherever you might do this outside your home, it's going to cost money.)

Shelving

In your garage or in a warehouse, you store inventory on shelves. You can buy inexpensive sheet steel shelving at a discount store. This is good for light merchandise. For heavy merchandise you need to upgrade to industrial shelving made from a heavier gauge of sheet steel. Industrial heavy-duty steel wire shelving is also appropriate. You need to look for a place to buy industrial shelving in your town. If you buy it on eBay or from a catalog, the shipping cost is likely to be high.

Assembly

Steel shelving comes disassembled in a box. It is easy to assemble. It takes only a screwdriver and perhaps a pair of pliers.

Steel shelving is a good investment. If you buy it for your spare bedroom (current warehouse), you can move it to the garage later when you expand. Eventually, you can move it to your warehouse when you get really big.

Look for retail stores or industrial businesses going out of business. Rush in and buy their warehouse shelving at a discount before someone else gets it.

Operational Space

Where you pack and label your merchandise for shipping is your operational space. It's not necessarily the same as your warehouse space, although convenience dictates that it usually is. This is where you use your fulfillment equipment, some of which may require electricity.

Most mini-storage units do not make very good operational spaces. They aren't set up to be used for operations, and in fact, they may have rules forbidding such activity. You are more likely to find operational space in an office-warehouse building or a warehouse.

Equipment

The equipment you might use for packing and shipping depends on the products you sell. At a minimum you will need a manual taping device to tape packages, a scale, and perhaps a postage meter. You might also need a pallet mover, a shrink-wrapping machine, a packing-material dispenser, or any one of a number of other machines. Plan your machines and your operation before you commit to your operational space.

If your operational space is separate from your administrative space, you will need separate communications devices, such as a telephone, a fax machine, and a computer (email).

Communication

A packing slip and a mailing label can act as a fulfillment order. Neither should contain any sensitive information such as a credit card number. Each can be attached to an email message as a text document and sent to your fulfillment site. Or, each can be delivered to your fulfillment site on paper.

Note this type of a system works well even when you do everything yourself in the same place (i.e., both administration and fulfillment).

Pay Online

If you use the Postal Service for shipping, you will save time and effort by using a postage meter to print and affix the postage on packages in your fulfillment operation. You can rent a postage meter for as little as $15 per month. You can also pay for the postage electronically from your home office. (Anything to keep you from waiting in line at the post office is a godsend.) In addition, some vendors enable you to print postage with your computer printer for as little as $4 per month.

With most systems, you can pay for your postage online with a credit card rather than take a trip to the post office to have your postage meter recharged (as in days gone by).

A postage scale with postage rates built in can save a lot of labor in your fulfillment operation. When the rates change, as they do periodically, you refresh the rate structure electronically to bring it up to date. Sometimes you can get a scale in a package deal together with a postage meter at an attractive price.

A combination of basic mailing equipment and services can cost little but do the following for you:

- Give a professional image
- Carry a custom message (printed with postage)
- Avoid overpayment (as with stamps)
- Eliminate post office visits

- Satisfy postal requirements for expedited shipping

- Make dropoff easier

Efficiency

The Postal Service doesn't permit mailing a parcel unless it's handled by a postal clerk. That means you have to wait in line at the post office to mail packages. The exception is a parcel with postage from a postage meter. That's a good reason to have a postage meter if you use the Postal Service for shipping. Dump those packages in the nearest post deposit box or leave them on the counter in the post office without waiting in line.

Using mailing equipment and services can really make a difference in bringing efficiency to your fulfillment operation. But you don't have to use the Postal Service for shipping. Competitors offer comparable services that may be more cost-effective.

Pitney Bowes

Pitney Bowes is the traditional provider for postage meters. It rents a complete line of postage meters and machines, scales, and other fulfillment equipment. It also provides free mailing tools (online software services). In addition, Pitney Bowes operates a special website to assist small businesses, PitneyWorks, one you need to visit (see Figure 12.1). There it offers additional free online software services. Moreover, you may be interested in using its new ClickStamp, a system that enables you to print postage with your computer printer (e.g., on shipping labels). ClickStamp also provides other online processing services that will catch your attention such as checking your ZIP codes for accuracy.

Pitney Bowes, *http://www.pb.com*

PitneyWorks, *http://www.pitneyworks.com*

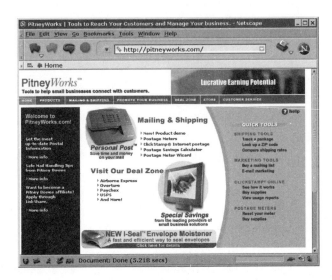

Figure 12.1   PitneyWorks small business website. ©2002 Pitney Bowes Inc.

Postal Service

The Postal Service has a new free service named Click-N-Ship. It provides shipping labels with or without postage all enabled right from your computer.

Stamps.com

Stamps.com is a service that enables you to print postage with your computer printer. This was the first such service. Additional services such as validating addresses and checking ZIP codes are also included. Plain paper shipping labels are a feature of this service (affixed to packages with packing tape) too. No messy and sticky labels to print. This is the type of service that can make your fulfillment much easier.

http://stamps.com

You might try their NetStamps. These are computer-printer printed postage stamps. (The day I visited the website almost 160 million postage stamps had already been printed by customers.)

Neopost

Neopost is another company similar to Pintney Bowes that provides equipment and supplies to mailrooms. Check out their website for competitive packages for your fulfillment operation.

http://www.neopostinc.com

Simply Postage

This is a hybrid service of Neopost. It appears on the website that Neopost is attempting to promote a service with better features over Simply Postage. It's the IJ25 postage meter package. It's a hybrid system with similar features for a slightly higher monthly fee. Like the other systems that enable you to use your computer to do postage, you need a computer to use Neopost's system, but you also need a minimized package of equipment from Neopost too.

http://www.simplypostage.com

Ascom Hasler

This company provides a range of mailing room equipment and services competitive with the others. Try PostLink, Hasler's product for basic mailing. It's a start.

http://www.haslerinc.com

Francotyp-Postalia

Yet another competitor in the postage meter business, this company's MyMail meter is a candidate for cost-effective use in a basic fulfillment operation.

http://www.francotyp-postalia.com

Pelouze

This is primarily a scale manufacturer that makes postage scales with updateable postage rates (see Figure 12.2). You need one of these, and you may be able to get one in an office supply store less expensively than from the postage meter companies. If you use a shipper other than the Postal Service, a Pelouze scale is a good choice too.

http://pelouze.com

Figure 12.2   Pelouze website. ©2002 Pelstar, LLC.

Packing Materials

Don't forget you need to store your packing materials as well as your inventory. Most likely you will use cardboard boxes for shipping, which don't take a lot of space (folded), or envelopes. However, packing filler can take up huge amounts of space. Typically, you store styrofoam peanuts in a huge plastic bag hung from the ceiling with a dispenser at the bottom so that you can feed them into packages with gravity. Bubble wrap comes in big rolls, which take plenty of space. Bubble envelopes take more space than plain envelopes. Newspapers take up the least space and cost the least. However, using newspapers as a packing filler requires more labor.

Buy your packing materials in bulk from a specialty supplier. In addition, as you might expect, there are some enterprising people like you who sell packing materials on eBay. So, check out eBay too. Below are some suppliers for you to consider:

Associated Bag Company All sorts of shipping supplies (*http://www.associatedbag.com*).

eBay Shipping Center A group of links to eBay auctions offering packaging and shipping supplies. Go Services, Shipping Center.

eSupplyStore Boxes and bags (*http://www.esupplystore.com*).

Mail Boxes, Etc. Local franchises providing packaging shipping supplies (*http://www.mbe.com*).

Paper Mart Boxes and tubes (*http://www.papermart.com*).

Speciality Bags Special bags including anti-static bags (*http://www.protectivepackaging.net*).

Uline Mostly shipping supplies (*http://www.uline.com*).

It's smart to protect items by placing them in plastic bags before shipping. Buy these in various sizes where you can buy in bulk at a discount.

Free Packaging

The Postal Service provides free packages for Priority Mail. If you ship via the Postal Service, you will want to find out what's currently available. Get a list of free packages. In addition, other shippers also offer free packaging, which can save you money. Inquire and get a list of what's currently available. Most of this packaging doesn't offer much protection for your auction items, but a little bubble wrapping can solve that problem easily.

Resources

You undoubtedly have local stores where you can buy fulfillment equipment and supplies inexpensively. For instance, you can get a commercial-quality taping device for under $10 at a discount store. The tape is inexpensive too when purchased in a six-pack. So, visit your discount stores and discount office supply stores to price what you need to buy for your fulfillment operation. Compare such prices to other sources and to national catalogs.

You will find that you can buy what you need in such stores inexpensively so long as you don't need to buy in bulk. For bulk buying (e.g., 500 cardboard boxes), you will get better prices from a specialty vendor.

Global Industrial Equipment A catalog with a huge amount of industrial equipment, some of it for shipping rooms and warehouses (*http://www.globalindustrial.com*). See Global's website in Figure 12.3 .

Figure 12.3   Try Global equipment for many things you need in a warehouse. ©2003 Global Industrial.

Shipping

Most people ship via UPS (United Parcel Service) or the Postal Service. Federal Express Ground (Home Delivery) is a competitive new entry into this market that you will want to consider. Note that UPS provides $100 insurance included in the normal shipping charge. The Postal Service charges extra, and it's not cheap. For overnight use FedEx, UPS, or Express Mail. There are also other overnight shippers such as Airborne Express and DHL.

Many of your customers will want to track their packages. If you use a shipper that makes tracking available, send the requisite tracking number via email to your customers automatically. The capability for your customers to track packages will save you a lot of tedious communication.

To learn more about shipping, visit the requisite websites:

Airborne Express, *http://airborne.com*

DHL, *http://www.dhl.com*

Federal Express, *http://fedex.com*

Postal Service, *http://usps.com*

UPS, *http://ups.com*

All of these shippers enable you to work via the Internet to manage your shipping. They also provide robust proprietary software with various levels of digital complexity to enable you to set up your own shipping system. Plan on spending some time at each website to determine what they offer, and then choose a shipping management package that suits your situation.

This is a very competitive industry, and the various programs evolve constantly and change regularly, even at the Postal Service. The trend is in your favor. The services are getting more robust, and they're available to small businesses that are digitally savvy.

Shipping Education Center

You can learn some basics about shipping with eBay's free tutorial. Go Site Map, Selling Tools, Shipping Education Center.

Shipping Rates

Shippers rates are somewhat straightforward when you ship one package. When you ship multiple packages every day, however, the rate structure gets less expensive but more complicated. You can take advantage of quantity shipping and get reduced rates and reduced pickup fees among other benefits. It pays to study the rate structures to determine which shipper will be the most cost-effective for you.

Shipping Services

Automatic shipping arrangements and charges are offered via shippers' websites. Anyone can use such free services. The auction management services tap into the shippers' websites to arrange shipping automatically. Such software calculates the shipping charges and adds them to the buyer's checkout. They also print the shipping labels. Of course, you can do all this manually, but it's a lot of work. It's easier to use an auction management service.

Plain Paper Labels

Shipping labels can be printed on plain paper and taped to packages. You don't necessarily have to use pre-printed labels with sticky backing that require special handling in regard to your computer printer.

In addition, you can get a variety of services that may give your fulfillment operation a boost, even actual fulfillment services.

FedEx Home Delivery

This is part of FedEx Ground but specializes in delivery to residential homes. If you're selling to consumers, you will want to investigate this service carefully to determine what advantages, if any, it offers.

Fulfillment Services

There are fulfillment services almost everywhere that would love to do your fulfillment for you. Until you grow to a large volume, they are most likely not cost-effective. Nonetheless, it doesn't hurt to inquire.

iShip

This is a retail shipping management service that you may find handy when you grow large (*http://iship.com*).

Mail Boxes, Etc.

MBE is a local franchise with a physical presence that supports small businesses with a wide variety of goods and services. You can buy packaging and shipping supplies there. Such supplies are sold at retail prices, although you might be able to negotiate quantity pricing. You might even contract with MBE to do your fulfillment. They have the equipment, supplies, and shipping arrangements to do a competent job. The only question is whether they will do it at a cost that you can live with.

Shippertools.com

This is a delivery confirmation service for Postal Service Priority Mail. Want to know if your item got delivered? Use ShipperTools, *http://shippertools.com*. You pay a reasonable membership fee.

UPS

UPS offers UPS Supply Chain logistics. You might investigate this when your business grows to a substantial volume. In most cases you will have to have a sizable fulfillment operation to make such services cost-effective.

More importantly, UPS also offers a service called MY UPS.COM. You will want to investigate this to see if it fits your fulfillment operation.

Insurance

Protection against risk of loss in transit is the business of the insurers in the shipping industry. The question is, When do you need insurance?

Low-Value Items

Insurance for shipping is too expensive, quite frankly, to justify for low-value items. Most sellers leave it up to buyers as to whether they want insurance and then make them pay for it. This is total insanity!

What happens when the buyer doesn't get the item you shipped (no insurance)? No matter what you tell him, he's going to be mad and will likely give you negative feedback unless you ship a duplicate. You really have no choice but to ship another item to the buyer. I recommend you do this on a self-insured basis. In other words, just bite the bullet and send a duplicate. Don't pay for insurance or ask the buyer to pay for it.

For unique items (one of a kind), you have a problem. You will have to replace it with a comparable item or refund the buyer's money. But this is basic customer service. It doesn't get much more basic.

Proof of Delivery

Of course where you have proof of delivery through Shipper-Tools or through return receipts, you don't necessarily need to send a duplicate should a customer claim they didn't receive the package. Send them the proof of delivery.

UPS and FedEx Ground

UPS and FedEx Ground automatically insure parcels up to $100. You might want to consider this when you pick your shipper.

High-Value Items

For high-value items, you probably cannot afford to be self-insured. You need to purchase shipping insurance. The question is, Who's going to pay for it?

Insurance can be expensive. This is something you will want to investigate carefully when you choose a shipper. Many buyers will elect to not purchase insurance. What happens when the buyer doesn't get the item you shipped (no insurance)? The answer is the same as it is for low-value items. The buyer is going to be mad and hold you responsible. Therefore, it seems prudent to include the cost of insurance in your shipping and handling fee. Don't give the buyer a choice.

You will want to investigate Universal Parcel Insurance Coverage (U-PIC). This is independent of any shipper, works for all, and can save you money. If you deal with a number of shippers, getting all your insurance through U-PIC may save you hassle as well as money. Check out their website:

http://www.u-pic.com

Pickup

Assuming you have sufficient volume, have your shipper pick up your packages. You have to have a certain volume to justify the expense. Some shippers are pretty good about coming by about the same time everyday to pick up your packages.

You will go nuts trying to deliver the packages to your shipper. Ever wait in line at the post office or UPS? One way around a lengthy wait is to have all packages labeled and paid. Then the delivery to your shipper is just a quick drop off.

Ship by Truck

Read carefully. This subsection is a hot tip! The big three shippers have limitations (weight and size) on parcels they will accept for shipment. About 70 pounds is the maximum weight. Everything else must be shipped by truck (or bus, see below). This creates a huge problem.

How much is the trucking going to cost? The shipping cost could be a huge percentage of the value of the item or even exceed the value. For example, how much does it cost to ship a desk worth $150 from Portland, Oregon, to Miami, Florida?

For shipping via the big three, you just look at a fee schedule, and you know exactly what the shipping will cost. For shipping by truck, what do you do? Therein lies the problem. The uncertainty stifles eBay business for large or heavy items. In fact, the uncertainty practically eliminates such business.

If you can accurately determine easily and instantly what shipping charges will be for large heavy items (via truck), you can start selling items that no one has sold yet on eBay. You can take the uncertainty out of the shipping cost. You can perhaps find a profitable niche more quickly and easily.

And you can do this with a relatively new service: freight-quote.com (see Figure 12.4). This is simply an online service that enables you to calculate the shipping cost by truck for an item quickly, easily, and at no expense. Try it at:

http://freightquote.com

Freightquote.com, of course, would like to have your trucking business for its affiliates, but there's no obligation to use the cost calculator.

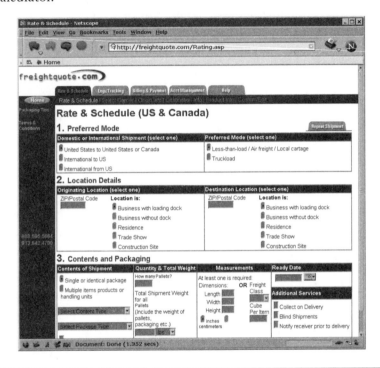

Figure 12.4   Freightquote freight rate calculator.

Example Business

Suppose you know an artisan in your town who manufactures beautiful cherrywood tables the size of office desks, which people love to use as desks in nice offices. The tables are also appropriate for dining. The tables are 36 x 72 inches and weigh 150 pounds, much too large and heavy to ship except by truck. The artisan tells you he can make as many as you can sell on eBay, and he will sell them to you at a wholesale price. You can make a reasonable profit selling them for $1,200 each on eBay.

The table is comparable to tables in a nice furniture store selling for about $2,200. It looks like a good opportunity, but the shipping cost makes it uncertain. For buyers, the shipping cost has to be low enough to keep the overall cost of acquisition well below $2,200, or why not just buy a comparable table at a furniture store?

You discover freightquote.com and decide to sell the tables. In your auction ad, you publish a list of sample trucking costs at several distances from your town. Now buyers will have more information to make a purchasing decision.

Quick Check

A quick check on freightquote.com indicates that the trucking for the table will cost about $400 coast to coast, less for a shorter distance.

Convenient to Whom?

For whom is this service a convenience? In the example, you could have called a local trucking company and asked for shipping costs to cities 500, 1,000, 1,500, 2,000, and 3,000 miles away and published such costs in your auction ad. That might take more time, however, than you want to spend.

Freightquote.com provides a convenience to you, because you can calculate shipping costs on freightquote.com more efficiently than calling a trucking company. Actually, estimating freight costs is not as simple as you might think. You will have to learn a few things before you can do it accurately. But you will be able to list sample trucking rates in your auction ad and then give a winning bidder an immediate quote for the specific trucking costs.

Again, let me point out. It is new services like this that spawn new businesses.

By Bus

How do you ship by bus? You take the package to the bus station in your town and pay for the shipping. Your customer picks up the package at the bus station in her town. You can ship packages larger than the common shippers will accept, although you cannot ship larger packages than will fit in the luggage compartments under the bus. Try Greyhound (see Figure 12.5). It has an interesting variety of shipping services:

http://www.shipgreyhound.com

Figure 12.5   Greyhound webpage for shipping by bus. ©2003 Greyhound PackageXpress.

House Spouse Fulfillment

You need to do your own fulfillment for a while just to learn that part of the business. When you find yourself pressed for time, you may come to the same conclusion that many eBay businesses do, that you want to hire someone else to do the fulfillment part of your business operation. You can hire an employee. However, as advised in Chapter 3, you are probably better off hiring an independent contractor (see Figure 12.6).

The house spouse down the street with a garage might be a good choice. Most stay-at-home parents, whether men or women, are looking for a business they can run at home. A fulfillment service isn't a bad choice, even if the service has only one customer: you.

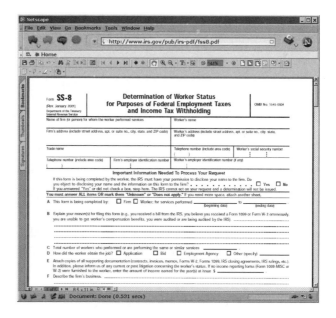

Figure 12.6   IRS guidelines regarding independent contractors.

Don't hire such a person. Suggest that they become an independent contractor. Give the house spouse information, perhaps a book, but don't organize their business for them. Keep in mind that you cannot control an independent contractor. You can set standards, specifications, and deadlines, but in the end an independent contractor controls the management and operation of the fulfillment effort.

Once an independent contractor is organized to do business, then direct them to information on the fulfillment business so that they can learn how to provide services to you. Then recommend suppliers and give them your standards, specifications, and deadlines in writing and in detail. Finally, make sure you have a signed contract with them, one that clearly spells out that they are in fact an independent contractor.

There are two things that you will provide to them. First is a packing slip. It specifies all the merchandise to be shipped but contains no prices, credit card numbers, or other sensitive information. Second is a shipping label. In return, they should provide you with an accounting of the items shipped.

If convenient, deliver the paperwork to them via email. Naturally, you have to deliver the inventory to them yourself or have it delivered to them. They are responsible for safeguarding it.

Same Considerations

Although this outline of an independent contractor relationship is focused on a fulfillment operation, the same applies to any part of your operation that you might hire out.

Administration

The rest is paperwork. You need to administer the fulfillment operation even when you farm out part of it. That will entail delivering the packing slips and labels. If you use an auction management service, the service should provide a system for managing fulfillment and cranking out the paperwork.

Understand that the term "labels" above can mean shippers' labels as well as plain labels. The labels that you deliver to your fulfillment independent contractor can be shipper's labels, even ones with prepaid postage. Whether it's you or your fulfillment contractor, it doesn't make sense to stand in line to process packages. One way to avoid it is to have all your paperwork (labels) and payment work done before the packages are dropped off (or picked up).

To drop off properly labeled packages with shipping prepaid requires that you have to learn something about shipping before you can pick an auction management service. You want to have a system that handles all the paperwork and payment work of the shipping with the least effort possible. Digital technology makes this feasible, but you're the one who has to implement it. Choosing the best auction management service for your situation can make sure you integrate your shipping processes into your overall system so that everything works more smoothly and more easily.

The alternative is to cobble together your own computer system made up of various programs obtained here and there. That's possible if you're especially computer savvy. You might even get a system that's less expensive to buy and operate (although there's no guarantee). But why bother? An auction management service can do it all for you. That seems the least painful way to go.

Finally, part of your job is to estimate a fulfillment cost per item. To do that, you need to know the cost of one box, one bag, X amount of packing filler, X amount of packing tape, etc. Each item is different. This process will enable you to estimate your handling cost for each item, which potentially can be billed to your customers.

Inventory Control

If you don't systematically account for your inventory, the business will get away from you before you know it. You can do it on a spreadsheet or with a database program. But the best way to do it is with an auction management service that includes an inventory control system. Such services will integrate this function with your other auction management functions and thereby coordinate your entire management and accounting effort.

What about doing it manually? You're not going to save money doing it manually; it will take more time; and your records will be less useful ultimately.

Inventory control includes taking a physical inventory periodically. Many traditional businesses take inventory once a year. It's a huge job. Yet for an eBay business, particularly one in the start-up phase, your inventory will be smaller with more turnover. You may need to take inventory more often to keep your records accurate. When you sell things that you thought you had in inventory but don't, you invite serious customer service problems. Remember the feedback system?

The Digital Goal

What's the goal of fulfillment? Just-in-time inventory control. Many manufacturers and even distributors keep the minimum possible amount of inventory in stock. Instead, they have the inventory delivered just before they need it.

Just In Time

What does this require? First, it requires manufacturers and distributors that ship orders very promptly. Second, it takes predictable shipping times. For instance, if your distributor processes all orders and ships via UPS within twenty-four hours and USP takes two days to deliver, you can count on having new inventory in three days. Third, it requires you to be very organized with very tight inventory control. You need to order regularly. Each time you order, you need to know the up-to-the-minute status of your inventory.

Why is this a desirable goal? The less inventory you have on hand, the less operating capital you need, and the less space you need.

Customer Service

What's another goal of fulfillment? Customer service. It's great to plan a just-in-time inventory system and operate it. But don't lose sight of the customers, your eBay buyers. You must keep enough inventory on hand to make sure you can ship immediately to each customer. If any buyer has to wait for you to order from the distributor, it's not good customer service, even with only a three-day wait.

Only with Software

Quite frankly, I don't know how you can manage your inventory precisely and efficiently without software. Don't try a just-in-time system manually. Software on your computer—or better yet an auction management service via the Web—not only helps you account for money and inventory but also enables you to do things not possible without digital assistance (e.g., a just-in-time inventory system).

Automakers

According to numerous articles written about auto manufacturing, the automakers keep an inventory of parts measured in hours at their assembly plants. This is a just-in-time system. They do it with software and trucks. If there's a bad snowstorm slowing the trucks, the assembly line comes grinding to a halt.

Quantity Buying

How does just-in-time inventory work with quantity buying? Usually, when you buy in larger quantities, you get a lower wholesale price. This will increase your short-term capital requirements but presumably increase your profits too. However, it doesn't necessarily have to interfere with your just-in-time system. Have the merchandise shipped in staggered shipments of smaller quantities rather than all at once.

Another technique is to have everything shipped to cheap storage. Then move small quantities just in time to the more expensive real estate where your fulfillment operation is located.

The Super Business Model

Just-in-time inventory enables you to activate a super business model. Take advantage of it!

Most retailers would be very happy to turn over their entire inventory every six months, but most don't. Not only that, but they have to store their inventory in high-rent retail shops instead of low-rent storage space. Operating capital for inventory alone is a huge requirement.

You can turn over your inventory quickly. Auctions are only 3, 5, 7, or 10 days. If you use a just-in-time inventory operation, you will need only a small amount of inventory. Your can keep your operating capital requirement low and use a comparatively minimal amount of low-cost storage space. It doesn't get any better than this. Well, maybe it does; see the section in this chapter on drop shipping.

13

Receiving Payment

Receiving payment is important to you as a seller, but believe it or not, making payment is even more important to a buyer. If you're serious about running a business on eBay, effective customer service dictates that you offer your customers as many different ways to pay as you can.

Each customer's situation is different, and often there is only one way a customer can pay. If you don't accept that particular means of payment, you lose that customer.

257

Merchant Credit Card Account

To accept credit cards, you will need a merchant credit card account. You get such an account at a bank or through an organization that has an affiliation with a bank.

Although I'm not trying to sell Costco (a membership warehouse discount store operating in many states), the Costco example below is relevant because it's a group deal, like group insurance. Consequently the fees are a little lower. Costco, because it's a place where many small retailers buy merchandise at or near wholesale prices, offers a wide range of small business services. One such service is a merchant credit card account. This represents the low side of the range of fees you will discover when you research merchant accounts.

Costco's Merchant Account Program

As of late 2002 in a brochure, Costco offered the following terms to its members who elected to arrange merchant credit card processing through Costco for mail-order and phone-order retailing:

- 2.03 percent of charge plus $0.28 per transaction.

- $18.99 per month equipment lease (or $549 equipment purchase).

- American Express, Discover, and Diners Club an additional $0.10 per transaction.

- $10 charge-back fee.

This seems like a reasonable deal, although you will do well to shop around to get the best fees. Costco and the bank have made arrangements with Nova Information Systems to offer this traditional service that requires you to clear all transactions via the phone. This arrangement is subject to Bank approval, and those with poor credit may not get approval.

Why Do You Need Good Credit?

The bank is worried that as a merchant you will put through modest fraudulent charges to increase your operating capital or large fraudulent charges to built up your cash reserves just before you disappear.

How does this work? This example of the sale of a baseball cap on eBay shows:

$9.32 (sales price of cap) $\times$ 2.03% = $0.19

$0.19 + $0.28 = $0.47 fee

This is a sizable fee for an item that sells for a low price. Indeed, it's 5 percent of the sales price. Let's look at another transaction, the sale of a digital camera on eBay:

$151.65 (sales price of digital camera) $\times$ 2.03% = $3.07

$3.07 + $0.28 = $3.35 fee

This is not such a large fee. It's only 2.2 percent of the sales price. As you can see, with a fixed fee you pay a premium on low-dollar sales but get a better deal on high-dollar sales.

But, you know what? We didn't take into account the cost of the equipment rental. Suppose you have 119 sales per month. That's an additional fee, in effect, of $0.16 per transaction ($18.99/119 = $0.16).

Keep in mind that this doesn't include the additional charge you will pay for online (Internet) processing, which takes place in a website shopping-cart-checkout process. Online processing fees will be in addition to normal merchant account fees.

For online sales, you don't need the equipment ($18.99 per month) that Costco offers for clearing charges, since your transactions will all be online and cleared as part of the online check-out process. (Of course, if you do take telephone orders, you will need the equipment.) Nevertheless, you may be required to rent the equipment whether you need it or not.

Your Bank

You may end up getting your merchant account from your bank. Many retailers do. Your bank may not offer the lowest fees, but your credit card processing is likely to be part of a larger group of services the bank provides to you.

Online Processing Charges

Electronic processing of credit card charges for online sales will cost you additional money. In fact, the charges tend to look like the merchant credit card charges, albeit somewhat lower. But when your buyer goes to the checkout, you need the online processing.

eCommerce Software

In order to handle sales online from your own website, you need ecommerce software. That might cost anywhere from $200 to $10,000.

Miva Merchant is a leading example and is inexpensive for the functionality it provides. It costs around $500. You don't have to be a programmer to set it up for your website, but it's not easy to do.

Perhaps a better approach is to find a Web host provider that includes ecommerce software as part of a package of services. Web hosting is a competitive business, and almost every host provider offers some kind of ecommerce software for no additional fee, or in some cases, a modest additional fee. Whether such software will meet your needs adequately is one thing you will want to determine up front. There are even host providers that offer Miva Merchant free or for a modest additional fee (good deal!).

This is a wild software market. Look over every offering in detail to make sure it does what you need it to do and doesn't have any hidden costs. Don't agree to pay on a per-transaction basis for the software, and don't agree to pay a high fee either. You don't have to. Beware of software deals that tie you into an online mall for which an extra fee is charged. The mall is very unlikely to boost your sales.

Note that the software must be compatible with the online processing service to which you subscribe. They must dovetail. For instance, Miva Merchant has plug-ins for a variety of online processing services. These plug-in are mini-programs (add-on programs) that provide Merchant with extra processing (extra functionality).

If You Can't Get a Merchant Account

If your credit isn't well enough established to get a merchant account from your bank or via another low-cost source such as Costco, you can still get one, albeit at a higher cost. You can get one through an intermediary that provides merchant credit card accounts for ecommerce websites.

A recent review of the fees charged by such an intermediary were as follows:

- 2.25 percent transaction fee
- $0.29 per transaction fee

- $25 per month minimum
- $29.95 monthly fee
- $95 annual fee
- $99 one-time fee

This is probably going to cost you more than a merchant account from your bank. Unfortunately, there are so many different fees involved in using a merchant account online, you will do well to analyze each offering carefully and totally. Banks and other financial services providers can be unscrupulous in dealing with novice business customers. Add up each fee including the merchant account fees, the online processing fees, and the cost of ecommerce software to determine what your total cost is. You may find that in some cases using an intermediary is less expensive than using your bank.

Money Orders and Cashier's Checks

Money orders can be a risky form of payment to accept. They can be easily counterfeited. It's possible the day might come when we see an increase in money-order and cashier's-check fraud on eBay.

My Bank

My bank is a huge bank with branches in many states. Yet its money orders and cashiers checks, generated by a computer on a laser printer with almost plain paper, look like they are counterfeited---poorly counterfeited---even though they are perfectly legitimate. I always wonder whether the eBay seller many miles away will accept my money order.

Are these money orders and cashier's checks easy to counterfeit? You bet they are. Just duplicate them. But a counterfeiter wouldn't even bother to duplicate them. A counterfeiter might just make up his own form for a money order and put the name of any bank at the top. Who would know the difference? Do you know what a Bank of Iowa cashier's check looks like?

Many sellers accept only money orders. They do so to protect themselves. A buyer can't get her money back if she's dissatisfied with the merchandise as she can with a credit card chargeback. So, the seller gets a sense of finality in the transaction. But I'm sorry to be the one to inform you: This practice is not good customer service.

Compared to Credit Cards

Payment by credit card or through a payment service online is as easy as providing a credit card number and other information. It takes but a few seconds. On the other hand, to pay by money order or cashier's check, a customer has to go someplace (e.g., a bank), wait in line, deal with a clerk (e.g., teller), make payment for the money order, put the money order in an envelope, mail the envelope, and wait an extra few days before the goods are even shipped. Why would anyone do this? I certainly wouldn't. (I have done this several times in the past but would not do it again.)

Still some people are used to using money orders routinely in their financial dealings and feel perfectly comfortable paying this way.

If you're interested in good customer service, you need to accept money orders and cashier's checks. But learn something about detecting counterfeits. And, if you're interested in good customer service, you will not limit your payment methods to only money orders and cashier's checks. Many people just won't buy from you (me included), and those who do may be unhappy about the payment method.

Should You Wait

Should you wait for a money order or cashiers check to clear? Theoretically, the issuer (e.g., bank) stands behind them, and you don't have to worry about insufficient funds. But what if the money order is a counterfeit? If it's from a familiar source such as the post office, you can probably tell whether it's real. If it's from my bank, you better hold the merchandise until the money order clears.

Another Point of View

Having thoroughly alarmed you, let me soften my point of view a little. The leading money orders are easily recognizable, and you will see them often enough to know when to suspect a counterfeit. In addition, a counterfeiter online leaves a trail (his Internet access account). He also leaves a trail offline, the delivery point. This normally makes it easier for law enforcement authorities to catch him. So, counterfeits aren't as likely as they might seem. So, don't refuse money orders and cashiers checks based just on what I've said above. But do be careful.

Here are some of the leading providers:

Postal Service The Post Office is the classic issuer of money orders. They are comparatively cheap if you're talking money. They're expensive if you're talking time (waiting in line). One can also send money orders from the Postal Service website.

BidPay.com This is Western Union's answer to online service. Remember the telegraph? This is one of the latest reincarnations. Western Union has certainly been in the money payment business for a long time. Today you can buy a money order on line with a credit card, and BidPay.com will send a money order in the mail anywhere in the country and to foreign countries. (The only foreign currency you can deliver, as of early 2003, is British pounds.) The cost is enough to make you want to buy an antique telegraph on eBay and go into competition with BidPay.com.

7-Eleven This convenience store and others sell money orders. They also have ATM machines. They are one-stop financial centers. A customer can get money from the ATM and buy a money order. The 7-Eleven money orders are comparatively cheap. The ATM charge for withdrawing money? Who knows? Let's hope it's not more than the item being purchased.

SendMoneyOrder.com This new service is designed for online auction payments. You can send a money order anywhere in the world. (As of early 2003, you can deliver funds in 40 foreign currencies.) It's not cheap for buyers, but you can put a link on your website that enables your buyers to go to SendMoneyOrder.com immediately and send you a money order. They buy the money order with their credit cards. This is another mechanism designed to create the most transaction fees possible in an auction sale (similar to BidPay.com).

Banks I get free money orders and cashier's checks at my bank because I have a deluxe account. For those without a special account, the cost is outrageous. And you still have to wait in line.

As you can understand, insisting that your customers pay via money orders may reduce your market, perhaps significantly.

Late Check

A late check to get the latest rates before the book went to press revealed that SendMoneyOrder.com was not online for several days. What that means I do not know. What I do know is that it's tough to write a book when many important eBay-related services are starting or going out of business monthly.

Cost

Unfortunately, money orders and cashier's checks tend to cost a lot. It's a harsh policy to force your customers to use them.

Table 13.1   Cost of Money Orders to Buyers

Company	$25 Money Order	$150 Money Order
Postal Service	$0.90	$0.90
BidPay.com	$2.95	$5.00
7-Eleven	$0.99	$0.99
Bank	Varies from free to $5.00+	Varies from free to $5.00+

I don't know about you, but the thought of paying 12 percent for a money order is my idea of extortion. Even the idea of a 4-percent cost seems out of line. It's not something I would want to force on my customers. Nonetheless, some people live on cash and buy money orders when they need to pay by check; and they use money orders like checks.

Checks

Checks probably cause more problems than other forms of payment. First, counterfeits (or forgeries) can be a problem, although a normal check would certainly be more difficult to counterfeit than my bank's money orders or cashier's checks. Second, there is always the risk of insufficient funds. Even though a check written on insufficient funds constitutes a criminal offense, such an offense is seldom handled as a real crime in most locales. Consequently, checks written on insufficient funds are quite common.

Most sellers on eBay know enough to wait for a check to clear before sending the merchandise. Indeed, this is a good practice. Every eBay seller who has done high volume sales has a story to tell about the merchandise they sent before the check cleared and how they got burned. Don't let it happen to you. Wait for the check to clear.

Do accept checks, however. Most of the world still operates on checks (about 60 percent), and it's good customer service to accept them.

You can also accept checks by email or by phone (possible since 1996). Here's how that works:

1. The buyer provides you with all the relevant information from one of her checks on the phone or in an email.

2. The buyer authorizes you to write a check for the purchase (a specific amount).

3. You input the buyer's check information into a program such as TurboCheck (*http://www.turbocheck.com*). The program prints a check on a check form run through a computer printer. You sign the check on behalf of the buyer and deposit it.

4. You wait for the check to clear and then send the merchandise.

The biggest problem you have with this technique is convincing the buyer that it's OK. But it's really no more risky for her than giving someone a check, which she does everyday. No extra information is revealed.

You need to protect yourself against a potential claim of fraud by the buyer. Keep a record of the email authorization. The authorization should include a statement that the buyer authorizes you to write a check for a certain amount. If you take the check by telephone, you should make a recording and archive it.

This is also good customer service. If a customer feels comfortable paying with a check this way, the customer will get the goods sooner. The period that the check would otherwise be in the mail is eliminated, and shipment is made a few days sooner. (See Chapter 20 for more information on Miva Merchant, which offers check writing as a means of payment.)

Online Payment Services

Payment services are go-betweens between a seller and a customer. For example, a credit card is a payment service. With the consent of the buyer, the credit card service takes an order from the seller to credit funds in the seller's account for a purchase and then simultaneously debits the buyer's account.

Online payment services normally work a little differently. They constitute another level of service overlaying traditional payment services. PayPal provides a good example and is the leading payment service on the Web.

PayPal

PayPal is the largest Internet payment service and was purchased by eBay in late 2002. PayPal verifies that the credit card the buyer is using belongs to the buyer by going through verification procedures that most retailers don't use. It also enables a buyer to have her bank account debited (like writing a check). Once a buyer has set up a PayPal account, she can use it just like a credit card with any seller that will accept it. The payment notification is actually emailed from PayPal to you (seller).

You can place a PayPal link in your auction ad to take a winning bidder directly to a PayPal payment page to make payment. It's essentially a checkout device. The PayPal payments you receive as the seller are held by PayPal in your PayPak account. You can have the money electronically deposited directly into your checking account, or PayPal will send you a check. You can also keep money in your PayPal account for making payment on things you buy online.

A buyer can make a chargeback, which comes back to you. If so, you will pay a fee just as you do for a merchant credit card account chargeback.

Being a seller for PayPal is not free. In fact, those who receive the money via PayPal are the ones who pay the fees.

Table 13.2   PayPal Fees for Receiving Payment

Rate Plan	Fee	Preferred
Standard Rate	2.9% + $0.30	
Merchant Rate	2.2% + $0.30	0.7% + $0.30

You get different rates by meeting PayPal's different seller qualifications. PayPal has a Seller Protection Policy to protect you against chargebacks and fraud. You can review the details at the PayPal website (*http://paypal.com*). PayPal requires that you ship only to confirmed addresses.

Be aware that PayPal has its own style feedback system. It keeps track and publishes how many PayPal transactions you've done.

This system works very well and has been very popular. It even integrates with QuickBooks (accounting software). The fees include transaction services fees making this service very competitive with a merchant credit card account.

PayPal is available to buyers in 38 (and growing) countries; and outside the US PayPal pays in 5 (and growing) foreign currencies.

I speculate that eBay intends to make PayPal the first international online currency. It already works well within the US. It has the potential for making international trade for small businesses safer and easier. If eBay can pull it off, PayPal will dramatically increase eBay's international business.

With the above in mind, it will be worthwhile for you to study PayPal and use PayPal. Feeling comfortable with PayPal will, I predict, pay many dividends in the future.

Billpoint

An alliance of eBay and Wells Fargo Bank, Billpoint was the official eBay means of payment until eBay purchased PayPal. eBay has phased out Billpoint completely. PayPal is now the official eBay method of payment.

Cash on Delivery (COD)

This is an old favorite from the days before electronic credit services. It's now out of vogue and more trouble than it's worth, not to mention expensive. A few people may still want to use it, but this is one payment method you need to avoid unless you have a specific reason for accepting it.

Don't Sell on Credit

If you sell on credit, it is certain that you will get burned regularly by people who will not pay you what they owe. Selling on credit can be a good business practice if you understand what the statistical risks are and set yourself up to be a bill collector. If you want to avoid all that, however, don't sell on credit.

It is particularly important that you don't sell in bulk on credit. This is the kind of sale where the demand for credit will be the most intense. Someone wants to buy something from you at a wholesale price in bulk to resell at retail. Since four out of five businesses fail in the first five years of their existence, you are likely to get burned, sooner rather than later, selling in bulk to other retailers on credit. The loss for a bulk sale on credit is likely to be substantial compared to credit losses on individual items.

In fact, as I pointed out elsewhere in this book, when you finance someone's inventory, you are in essence financing their business. If there is any financing of inventory to be done, make sure it is a wholesaler financing your inventory, not you financing another retailer's inventory.

Having said that, I understand it is difficult to sell at wholesale in some industries without providing credit. If you are forced to provide credit, make sure the credit periods are short (e.g., monthly). Then keep on top of your collectables. In fact, be brutal about collecting on time. If anyone is late in paying, cut them off. Of course, before you do business with someone, let them know what to expect in regard to your collection methods. And be sure to check their credit.

Fortunately on eBay, most people don't have to worry about collections. Buyers expect to pay immediately and do not expect to receive credit. Consequently, most of your credit demands will be from retailers buying in bulk from you, people who you deal with outside the eBay marketplace.

What Should I Do?

Getting set up to receive payments is sobering. Each means of payment has its advantages and disadvantages. And you need to offer multiple means to buyers just for the sake of good customer service.

The big question is, Can you get by with an online payment service and forgo getting a merchant credit card account? The answer is probably yes. PayPal may be all you need if your sales are strictly on eBay. PayPal gives you the flexibility of collecting payment off eBay as well as on eBay; and PayPal is so popular that it may be even better than having a merchant credit card account. Merchant accounts are less expensive when you reach high volume. However, just starting out, you may want to use PayPal exclusively for a while. Keep in mind that anyone with a credit card or a bank account can get a PayPal account.

Whatever you do, consider everything very carefully. The financial arrangements for many means of payment are somewhat complex and require substantial analysis. There are so many schemes available that it would be fruitless to analyze more than a few samples. The providers will not help you sort things out either. In fact, they are more likely to confuse you hoping to sneak by those little fees, those insidious little fees that add up to big dollars.

Take a look at a variety of payment schemes. Pencil out each using a range of products with different prices. Try to determine which is the least expensive before choosing one.

You will be shocked at how expensive credit cards and payment services are for low cost items. It's tough to make a profit on products with a narrow margin. For big ticket items, the costs are a lower percentage of sales price, but they're still significant.

Auction Management Services

Some auction management services have checkout devices and online processing that you can use for both your website and your eBay auctions. If one of these services will work for you, there's no reason to duplicate it with some other service.

14

Selling Services on eBay

This chapter is about services, that is, experts providing informational services or physical services for a fee. A lawyer is a good example. A lawyer gives advice, drafts documents, and occasionally goes to court. Another example is a landscaping service. A person or team with landscaping skills visits your property and takes care of the foliage. This chapter is not about branded services such as a vehicle oil change, lube, and checkup. Such services are essentially products and can be marketed as products on eBay.

This chapter is also speculative. Today you will find few services being sold on eBay (but see Elance at the end of the chapter). This is likely due to four factors. First, some professional organizations have prohibitions on self-promotion. Rules covering marketing and advertising are strict. In regard to nonprofessionals, few people are aggressively trying to sell services via eBay. They haven't persistently pushed the envelope, so to speak. Second, service providers who have tried have not been visibly successful. They haven't figured out productive techniques. Third, due to a paltry offering, people don't look on eBay for services. They aren't conditioned to do so yet. Fourth, selling services is primarily a local endeavor. Until eBay figures out how to do local auctions effectively, perhaps services will not come into their own on eBay. Consequently, this is an opportunity waiting for the further evolution of eBay.

Because the idea of selling services on eBay is speculative, this chapter is a collection of speculative ideas, not proven techniques. It just seemed to me that selling services should not go unaddressed in a book about eBay business.

eBay does have a special auction Elance devoted to certain types of professional services (covered below). However, it has not been a smashing success, although it is growing. So, no one seems to have found the magic formula yet.

Advertising

Selling services on eBay is essentially a marketing campaign, not a money-maker. It's a opportunity for a provider (to use a generic term) to meet potential customers.

The nature of the typical service project is that it's open ended. Until the customer's problem is pinned down, it is difficult for a provider to even propose a course of action or set a price. Indeed, in some cases, the problems are so complex that it's impossible to even predict the duration of the services or the outcome.

The bottom line is that few services are packaged and priced. In other words, what does a provider have to sell on eBay? The answer is, not much. To create a package of services, a product, might be a good approach.

Some Service Packages Do Exist

Certainly some services are packaged and priced. A residential real estate appraisal, for instance, is normally a uniform product with a uniform price performed by a knowledgeable real estate professional. But as soon as a particular residence falls outside the normal parameters of residences, it becomes a special case. The appraiser has to do extra work and will charge a custom fee.

Where services are packaged, you can attempt to sell them on eBay like any other product. Such an effort might turn into a money-maker with some experimentation and marketing savvy. Still, it's more likely to be a loss-leader and justified as advertising.

eBay essentially delivers an opportunity for providers to advertise. The advertising will be ineffective unless it falls into a general marketing scheme. But a unique opportunity exists to reach a market of exactly the potential customers you need to reach at a bargain marketing cost. Unfortunately, you have to sell something in order to use eBay for advertising. If you're a provider, what do you sell?

What to Sell?

To sell services on eBay, you might try turning a certain set of services into a package. That is, you need to create a product. This is not a new concept for providers. Every profession or trade has their bread-and-butter money-makers.

Many lawyers, for instance, offer annual checkups for small corporations. The lawyer prepares the minutes for the annual meeting, holds the meeting, and reviews any matters of importance for the year. This is a perfunctory service of minimal importance for most small businesses for which lawyers often charge a set fee. It's not an unnecessary service because the corporate owners are required by law to do certain things every year. But it is normally a routine and uneventful, almost a ceremonial, occasion. You can bet when the annual meeting is anything but routine (e.g., two stockholders fighting) and grows into an extensive effort for the lawyer, the lawyer will start charging an hourly fee, not a set price.

Service providers often create packages where the work is quantifiable and predictable. Often a set fee goes with the package. Providers spend little work for some customers who purchase the package and a lot of work for other customers who purchase the package. The idea is that it will all average out into a product that is profitable.

This chapter focuses on creating service packages for marketing purposes only. As such, the packages don't have to be profitable. In fact, they can be loss-leaders. The goal is not to make money on the packages but rather to get new customers who are willing to pay for your services repeatedly.

But If You Can

If you can put together a service package that's profitable to sell, and you sell it regularly on eBay, it might be a money-maker. But in effect, you will be selling a product just like anyone else who sells a product. If so, you should focus your attention on other chapters in this book more relevant to selling profitably. This chapter is essentially about advertising.

Packages

How do you design a package of services for marketing or advertising purposes on eBay?

Saleable The product has to be something that people will buy. To have your auctions go without bids again and again is an embarrassment and probably doesn't do your business image much good.

Low Cost High cost products attract fewer bidders. You will probably want to offer packages at entry-level pricing.

No Obligation There should be no financial obligation over and above the price of the package for the customer purchasing the package.

Geographical Limitations You should be realistic about geographical limitations. A lawyer in Baltimore is not likely to give a potential client in Albuquerque adequate advice on real estate legal matters in New Mexico. A landscaping service in Baltimore cannot provide a potential customer in Albuquerque with the work needed. It's physically impossible to do cost effectively unless it's a big contract.

Painless Using the package should be as painless as possible for the customer.

Recurring Offering The package needs to be offered on a regular basis to have adequate advertising impact.

Specific Service The package should offer a specific service or a specific group of services, not a broad range of services.

eBay Home The package needs to appear in the proper place (in the proper category) on eBay. If there is no obviously logical category, it's a waste of time to make the offering. Choose another package that has a home on eBay.

Information Products

Books, booklets, pamphlets, reports, white papers, references, lists, directories, audio tapes, video tapes, CDs, DVDs, and software are all saleable information products. Service providers have traditionally used these to promote their businesses. Why not sell them on eBay?

Again, it is important to distinguish between creating information products to make money and creating them to drum up business. If they are legitimate products with commercial potential, create them and market them to sell well. In other words, get into the publishing business. Use ISBN numbers and UPC numbers and spend some money to give your products an attractive and commercial appearance.

If you offer the products just to promote business, and not to make money, design them differently. They will cost less, and you will have more flexibility in selling them on eBay.

For example, a security consultant might write a book, *How to Make Your Office Secure,* to sell for $25. It might cover physical security, computer security, and personnel security—in 230 pages. Now that's a book a lot of people might buy. Print it commercially, have a three-color book jacket designed, copyright it, and get an ISBN number for it (you have to register as a publisher). Sell it on eBay and Half.com to make money.

The same security consultant might write a report, "How to Choose an Electronic Security System for Your Office" (35 pages), to sell for $5. Print it with a laser printer, bind it with a standard office binding, and sell it on eBay. Don't bother to register a copyright. You have a copyright automatically just by creating it, albeit with fewer rights. In fact, you might want to include a license with each copy for the purchaser to make copies of it for friends, relatives, and colleagues so long as no one sells it. Remember, you're trying to get business, not make money.

1-2-3 Review

Ideas for service packages are limited only by your imagination, but here's one that might work well. Suppose you are an advisor who charges $100 per hour for your time. Offer a review package. The first hour costs $25, the second $50, and the third $75. After that your normal rate applies. The buyer gets charged only for the time she uses. The goal of the package might be to identify the customer's problems and recommend a course of action to solve the problems. If the customer has a simple problem, another part of the goal might be to start to solve the problem. In fact, some problems are simple enough to be solved in three hours or less.

Here's what this package does for you:

- Introduces you to a potential paying customer at a reasonable marketing cost.

- Gives you an opportunity to solve a customer's simple problem and turn the customer into a salesperson for you and your services.

- Gives you the opportunity to make a longer-term proposal to solve a customer's problems using your consulting assistance.

- Gives you an opportunity to ask for referrals.

Here's what the package does for the customer:

- Limits the customer's financial obligation.

- Enables the customer to understand her problems better.

- Reveals a workable course of action to take to solve the problems.

- Gives an opportunity to solve a simple problem at a low cost.

- Enables the customer to decide whether she wants to work with the advisor further.

There is one other feature this package should offer: timeliness. Make this an impulse purchase. Promise a quick appointment for consultation (e.g., within the next twenty-four hours). But this is virtually impossible for a busy advisor, right? Not necessarily. What if you limit the consultation to the phone and only one half-hour at a time? Offer to give the consultation outside of normal office hours. Under such circumstances, even a busy advisor can probably give the first half-hour of consultation sometime within the next twenty-four hours. Many customers will be less threatened by a telephone review than an actual face-to-face meeting even though they may eventually want to meet you in person.

Outside Office Hours

The social value of this type of after-hours offering cannot be underestimated for certain situations. People don't always need a advisor during business hours. Sometimes the distress impulse comes outside the 8-to-5 workday. An abused spouse seeking legal assistance is a good example.

The example given assumes a fixed price (*Buy It Now*). What about payment? Payment should be made the normal way for the full amount. In the example the payment is $150 ($25 + $50 +

$75). It could be charged on a credit card or paid through PayPal. The consultant is obligated to refund the cost of the unused portion, if any, of the consulting package.

If you have to make a refund, you will be unable to recover your eBay fees. But that's OK. This is a marketing idea, not a money-making idea. And the fee isn't much.

Without a Fixed Price

If this is not to be a fixed price auction, the bidder should be bidding on the entire three hours with the idea the first hour is to be charged at 16 percent of the final value, the second hour is charged at 33 percent of the final value, and the third hour is charged at 51 percent of the final value.

There are dozens of variations on this idea. Certainly many advisors (e.g., lawyers) offer an initial free consultation, and you can even work a free hour or two into the formula.

Be Creative

You can turn a traditional free consultation into a paid consultation on eBay. Set the minimum bid for a one-hour consultation at $1. Offer this deal often enough so that the bidding never goes to more than a few dollars. This is essentially a free consultation that you sell on eBay.

Task Packages

Where does that leave the landscaper who provides mostly physical labor rather than information? Package some landscaping tasks. Put 10,000 square feet of lawn mowing together with five bush trimmings and three dozen flower plantings into a Welcome Spring landscaping package to be sold on eBay.

Again the likelihood of a customer needing such a service might be remote. Who has 10,000 square feet of lawn, five bushes, and wants a dozen flowers? Most people need custom landscaping services. But the object is to advertise on eBay. And the Welcome Spring package has possibilities. The following press release illustrates how eBay might be used to sell merchandise that is difficult to sell on eBay: soft drinks. It's an analogous situation to selling services on eBay.

> PLANO, TEXAS, Feb. 6, 2003 - Dr Pepper/Seven Up, Inc. today announced that it has entered into a strategic alliance with eBay, the World's Online Marketplace^{TM}, to develop a comprehensive marketing platform for brands such as Dr Pepper, 7 UP, Sunkist, A&W Root Beer and Canada Dry. In an effort to forge stronger relationships with consumers, Dr Pepper/Seven Up will work with eBay to develop an extended loyalty program, advertise brand news within the eBay community and drive trial sampling of new products.

Will Dr Pepper/Seven Up be successful on eBay? Who knows? But you can't fault them for not trying something new.

Strategy

There is no magic formula for selling services on eBay. It will take a lot of experimentation to find something that works. It's an advertising campaign and should fit into an overall marketing plan. Your customer service needs to be superb; the offering is just the bait to get a customer. Timeliness is often essential to success. Follow-up is important. This cannot be a disorganized fishing expedition. This is serious business.

Location

If your service business is tied to a state or locale where you are licensed or need to meet people face-to-face, state that in your auction ad. If instead, you can provide informational services via telephone and email that aren't tied to a state or locale, develop your marketing strategy to create a national clientele. Then move to Maui, Park City, or Sanibel Island where you can run your business and have fun too.

Online

As covered elsewhere in the book, you can sell on eBay without any other online presence. In fact, that may be the most productive approach for selling most products. Still, I think services are an exception to that notion.

Build a website, not to sell your services but to provide customer services. As mentioned earlier, even a brochure website has value to potential customers. Start out doing something simple things for customers and then build on it. Remember, the Internet is an informational medium, and many services are informational in nature. The two make a nice fit. Take advantage of that. Even services that are not informational in nature often require more explanation to customers than a typical product.

Do you expect a person selling refurbished Canon digital cameras to have an independent website? Probably not, so long as he can get all his inventory into his eBay store.

Do you expect a lawyer to have an independent website? Sure. The website is a psychological substitute for an office. The website better look good and provide good customer service, even if the customer service is something simple.

Do you expect a landscape service to have an independent website? Yes. It sure would help to know something about a landscaper's capabilities. There are so many different kinds of landscaping tasks.

Information

Don't spare the information. The Internet is an informational medium. Your auction ads need to be brimming over with information. Your offering needs to be simple and understandable. However, if it interests potential customers, many will want to know a lot more details, not only about the offering but about you too. Don't disappoint them by being cryptic. Give them a lot to read.

Don't get me wrong. I am not advocating boring your potential customers to death. You can arrange your information in such a way as to show the priority of its importance. This gives people the option to keep reading and learn more or to quit reading and go on to something else. Here's a potential format for use in your auction ad:

- **Offering** Simple, all text, about 50 words.

- **Detailed Explanation of Service** Text and possibly other media, 200 to 1,000 words depending on complexity.

- **Resume** Text and photographs, as much as 2,000 words and a half-dozen photographs. Covers people or business, or both.

- **Referral** Referral to website, all text, about 50 words including URL (but not hyperlink).

- **Transaction Details** How to pay and that sort of thing, all text, about 100 words.

Hey! This isn" a classified ad. This is the Internet. This is eBay! Provide plenty of information. In the format outlined, the progression of information goes from the simple to the more complex. For those who need more information to make a decision, give them something to chew on.

Elance

Elance is eBay's special auction for professional services. It works a little differently than eBay and is somewhat narrow in scope. But if it fits your profession, it's worth a try (see Figure 14.1).

Figure 14.1   Elance website. ©1995-2003 eBay Inc.

Auction Procedure

Customers who need professional services post their projects on Elance. You bid on doing the projects for them. In other words, it's a reverse auction. The low bid wins the project theoretically. However, the customer is not obligated to accept the low bid and can pick a provider with a higher bid.

This auction has nine main categories:

- Web Design and Development
- Software & Technology
- Business Strategy
- Legal
- Accounting & Finance
- Graphic Design & Multimedia
- Writing & Translation
- Training & Development
- Administrative Support
- Engineering and Design

Thus, if you offer a service providing meeting and event planning for businesses, you would list yourself (or your company) under Administrative Support. You would be one of about 311 listed providers for that particular service (at the end of February 2003).

A customer looks at the Administrative Support list of providers. She can take one of two approaches. She can go through the list looking at the details of each provider and choose one (or more) to submit her project for bidding, or she can put her project up for bid to the entire list. Listed professionals can choose to bid or not to bid on any project available for bidding. eBay claims that the total new projects each week number about 1,000. It also claims that it has over $75 million in posted projects and 300,000 freelancers ready to work. (Figures for the end of February 2003)

When you complete a project, you are rated on a scale of 1-5 by the customer, and the average of your ratings goes in your listing. The dollar amount of business you've done (on Elance) also goes in your listing (see Figure 14.2).

Figure 14.2   Elance Writing & Translation Service Providers (948 total). ©1995-2003 eBay Inc.

One good thing about Elance is that it's not necessarily a free-for-all. Your have to qualify. You don't have to compete against people who allege they are qualified but are not.

Fees

The fee to be listed varies with the category and the duration of the period to be listed. It's $75-$250 per month or $360-$1,200 per year. In addition, there is a transaction fee of 8.75 percent of the project amount for any project originating on Elance. There is an additional bid fee for the number of projects bid over a certain free monthly amount.

The average amount paid on projects appears to be somewhat low, which raises the question as to whether this auction makes economic sense for providers. It seems to me that this auction makes more sense as a service to introduce you to potential customers with whom you can do repeat business rather than as an opportunity to obtain significant and profitable projects. It is not self-evident that this auction will be profitable for you, and it appears that the only way to find out is to learn how it works, try it, and work it intelligently.

Profitable?

The fact that I've devoted most of this chapter to speculating about how professional services might be sold on eBay and less on how Elance works reveals my skeptical point of view about Elance. (Authors often get carried away.) But don't let that deter you from trying Elance from time to time to determine whether it can work for you. Clearly eBay has got something going here, and it's certainly worthwhile to give it careful consideration.

Advertising

If you look at Elance as an advertising opportunity and you do some loss-leader bidding, you will be following the ideas discussed earlier in this chapter but on Elance instead of eBay. Might work!

Buy!

Take yourself out of the selling mode and put yourself into the buying mode, and Elance looks great! It provides you with a great opportunity to get professional services you may need at a reasonable cost. It introduces you to professionals who may not be available in your community. In short, Elance looks to me like a buyer's market. When you need special professional services to get your eBay business off the ground, keep Elance in mind.

IV

Unpleasantries

15

Dealing with Buyer Fraud

Buyers watch out for sellers who do not deliver the goods, probably the greatest fear of all on eBay. No one wants to pay for an item and then never have it arrive. But fraud is not limited to sellers. There are plenty of fraudulent buyers too. How do you, as a seller, protect yourself against them?

Fraud

This is a section about some crimes and illicit practices all arbitrarily labeled *fraud* here. You need to be aware and be cautious about all of these.

Non-Payment

A number of eBay members think eBay is a game and don't understand, or don't care, that eBay is a legal marketplace. Undoubtedly, most of these are neo-postadolescents, but even some adults aren't above acting with this kind of distain for the system too. This is a real problem for sellers, perhaps the number one problem. If the winning bidder doesn't pay up, a simple auction turns into an unpleasant task of bill collecting.

Set up a system to notify winning bidders about shipping and handling charges and requesting payment. If they do not pay after successive requests, notify eBay and relist the auction. eBay will relist free in this case. Always give negative feedback to the non-payers, but don't get emotional. Just state the facts.

Payment Fraud

If you don't ship until payment has cleared, you are doing as much as you can, as a practical matter, to protect yourself. Although counterfeit checks, cashiers checks, and money orders are easy to make, it's unlikely that someone would use them for Internet purchases. The culprit could likely be traced both through the Internet access account and the delivery address. Nonetheless, it pays to be cautious, particularly on big orders.

Realistically, you will probably ship before cashiers checks and money orders clear. But you are taking a chance in doing so. Don't ever ship before a personal check clears. Too many eBay sellers have been burned by "insufficient funds." This is certainly the common wisdom of eBay.

Nevertheless, another version of wisdom you might want to consider is customer service wisdom. Ship as soon as you receive payment. Sure, you will get bounced checks on which you can't collect. You just factor that into the income and expense calculation. That's what physical stores have to do everyday. You will build your customer service reputation by shipping immediately.

When to Ship

Deciding when to ship is not easy, considering that waiting for payment to clear is not good customer service. If you sell five dozen $25 items each week and experience only one or two bounced checks, you might opt to ship as soon as the checks are received. Your loss is small. You need a lot of customers. And it's good customer service to ship immediately. Still, if you sell three $1,700 items a week, you might want to wait for payment to clear before you ship.

If you do get a bounced check, run it through again if it doesn't cost anything at your bank to do so. In the end, when you have lost your patience and have not been paid, report it to eBay and give negative feedback. If the loss is large enough, pursue a remedy.

Credit Card Fraud

Credit card fraud is widespread. Stolen credit card numbers abound. The most quickly growing crime is identity theft. The object of the identity thief is usually to get cash and merchandise using someone else's credit, specifically their credit card.

It's not a good idea to ship to a different address than the one for the credit card used to purchase the item.

The future for the safe use of credit cards looks brighter. Some cards have a CVV2 number (printed in the back of the card). Some require a PIN (personal identification number). The use of enhanced safety features will be much more widespread in the future. If you can use these safety features, do so. Until then, be careful.

SET

The credit card companies created a system a few years ago that is substantially more secure than the haphazard system we live with. It's called SET (Secure Electronic Transactions). As credit card fraud continues, you may see it become more popular.

In general Americans have been slow to adapt more secure personal payment systems. For instance, the Smart Card, which contains a small microprocessor, has been popular in Europe for a long time. Only recently has it started to gain a foothold in the US. The microprocessor in the card gives it additional functionality including additional security.

Credit Card Chargebacks

Many eBay sellers won't accept credit cards. They've been burned by unjustified chargebacks. That happens when a buyer contacts his credit card issuer and claims that the seller did him wrong. The issuer charges the purchase amount back to the seller and credits the buyer's credit card account.

The issuer is invariably a financial institution such as a bank. Some banks do chargebacks automatically or perform only a cursory investigation. Others investigate as they should. When the bank does investigate, the bank will naturally have a tendency to favor its customer, the buyer. Nonetheless, some banks favor the seller, oddly enough. It's a crap shoot. But don't let someone get away with an unjustified chargeback too easily. Contest it.

Customer Service

Thus, credit cards are not risk free. Walking out your door in the morning isn't risk free either. There are some risks you need to assume in order to do business. Accepting credit cards is one of them. Accepting credit cards is good customer service and is well worth the risk of chargebacks.

Fraud with a Valid Credit Card

Here's an example of how credit card fraud can cause a loss. The names have been changed to protect the used-to-be innocent. The buyer, Mr. Slick in New York, sees Mr. Sellwell's new computer in an eBay auction ad. He contacts Mr. Sellwell in Los Angeles by email to put in an order to buy 12 new computers to be shipped to an address in Pakistan. He gives a credit card number. Mr. Sellwell, being no dummy, gets a phone number and calls Mr. Slick to verify the order. Mr. Slick verifies the order on phone. Mr. Sellwell ships the computers. A month later the bank notifies Mr. Sellwell that Mr. Slick has charged back the purchase claiming he never ordered any computers.

Mr. Sellwell calls Mr. Slick to find out what's going on. Mr. Slick denies ever making the order. (Yes, it's the same person on the phone.) Mr. Slick's email address is now defunct. Mr. Sellwell reports this to the bank, which refuses to do anything about it. Mr. Sellwell then reports it to the Attorney General in New York State and is told the case can't be won in criminal court. It's just Mr.

Sellwell's word against Mr. Slick's word. So, the Attorney General won't even investigate the case. Mr. Sellwell has no recourse through eBay, because the transaction took place outside eBay. Mr. Sellwell has just taken a loss equal to the cost of 12 computers.

This true story illustrates two things. First, sellers can be the victims of eBay fraud. Second, don't ship to an address different from that given for the credit card.

International Fraud

International fraud is so prevalent, that few sellers will sell to those outside the US, at least in regard to the use of credit cards for payment. Although you might have some workable remedy inside the US, as a practical matter, you have none outside. If you do not get payment before you ship, you are taking a substantial risk of loss. In particular, countries you should avoid include:

Afghanistan

Austria

Belarus

Romania

Cuba

Colombia

Egypt

Hungary

Indonesia

Iran

Iraq

Libya

Latvia

Lithuania

Malaysia

Macedonia

Mexico

Nigeria

North Korea

Pakistan

Philippines

Russia

Rwanda

Serbia

Slovak Republic

Sudan

Thailand

Ukraine

Yugoslavia

To be fair, my list was procured second hand. You need to research your own list when you plan your foreign sales program. Note also that PayPal is an exception, because PayPal verifies its credit card holders and also allows members to use bank accounts.

Chapter 21 outlines strategies for safely doing export business internationally.

Resources for Fraud Information

You can get additional information on fraud in order to protect yourself against loss at the following websites:

- Antifraud.com, *http://antifraud.com*

- CyberSource, *http://www.cybersource.com*

- eBay, Services, go Buying & Selling, Fraud Protection

- Internet Fraud Complaint Center, *http://www1.ifccfbi.gov*

- Fraud.org, *http://www.fraud.org*

- ScamBusters.org, *http://www.scambusters.org*

A checklist for handling credit cards safely will help protect you against fraud:

1. Require that complete information be submitted with each order (e.g., name, address, telephone, email address, etc).

2. Don't accept orders originating from free websites or email addresses. Accept only ISP or domain-based addresses.

3. Verify submitted information routinely.

4. When in doubt, call the telephone number given for the order.

5. Use HTTP_USER_AGENT and REMOTE_ADDR code in your forms that gather crucial information on buyers.

For electronic checks, call the bank to verify the account name and number.

Remedies?

Remedies are probably not worth pursuing once you have determined a buyer has put one over on you. About the only two things you can easily do are filing negative feedback and reporting to eBay.

Feedback

You can always file negative feedback on a buyer who has won your auction. This is not a remedy. You won't get reimbursed. But you will warn other eBay sellers about the buyer, as you should.

Administrative Remedies

You can report fraudulent buyers to eBay. If it's just a dispute, eBay isn't interested. You will be left to work it out with the buyer. However, if there was fraud committed, eBay will take your complaint and maybe even do something about it. eBay will at least penalize the buyer or cancel the buyer's account.

eBay is quite serious about getting rid of criminal activity in the auctions, and it devotes substantial resources to chasing petty criminals.

There's not a great likelihood that you will get reimbursed, but you might be successful getting the buyer in significant trouble with eBay. In fact, eBay might even forward the case to a district attorney.

Legal Remedies

You can always sue the buyer. If the buyer lives in your own state, you can sue him in small claims court or even in the court of general jurisdiction (which will require a lawyer). If he lives in another state, the loss will have to be huge to justify the expense of litigation in a far away place. Just write it off, and put it behind you.

In any event, the court will award you damages, assuming you prove your case. Court is one place where you can really find a remedy. Unfortunately, getting a judgment against someone doesn't guarantee payment. It just gives you the right to chase after the buyer trying to collect by using certain legal devices, such as filing liens against the buyer's real estate, if any, or taking possession of the buyer's personal property (e.g., vehicle).

Remedies in civil court are impractical in many instances. First, if the buyer is a petty criminal, you're probably going to have trouble finding him. If you can't find him, you can't sue him. Second, the cost of litigation is too high to justify unless the loss is in the tens of thousands of dollars, or unless you handle your own case in small claims court.

Criminal Complaints

A criminal complaint that results in a criminal conviction doesn't reimburse your loss, but it punishes the buyer. It may also warn other sellers against the buyer in some cases. It's your duty as a citizen to at least file a complaint in regard to criminal activity. The question is, Where?

Online

FBI, *http://www.fbi.gov*

Postal Inspector, *http://www.usps.com/postalinspectors*

FTC (Federal Trade Commission), *http:// http://www.ftc.gov*

I have filed several complaints at these websites (not involving eBay) and was actually called by a governmental official on my cell phone while attending a dinner party in regard to one of the complaints I filed.

Offline

FBI Office (where you reside)

Post Office (where you reside)

FCC (Washington, DC)

Police (where buyer resides)

District Attorney (where buyer resides)

State Attorney (where buyer resides)

For more details on handling feedback and pursuing remedies, read my book *eBay the Smart Way.*

Some Afterthoughts

Nothing is ever simple. The eBay market is dependably honest. But every once and a while some petty misdemeanant will get you. Nonetheless, you can't run your business as if every buyer is a potential petty criminal. You have to bend a little. Wait until someone does get you to be become unmerciful.

A Different Address

For example, can you really refuse to ship to an address that's different from the address that goes with the credit card? What about Christmas presents? Many people will want to buy online in November and December and ship to relatives. What do you do? What about customer service?

Feedback

Some sellers are afraid to give negative feedback to a buyer for fear that they will get retaliatory feedback. If you present your negative feedback in a straightforward, factual, nonemotional manner, most people will see through the retaliatory feedback, if it materializes. If you warn people in your auction ad that you will give negative feedback to bad actors, you will scare away many of these troublesome little hawbucks. But don't overdo the scare tactics, or you will scare away your honest customers too.

V

Making It Work

16

Software Features

Software to manage auctions, business processes, and accounting for an eBay auction business is a prime ingredient for success. Don't think about trying to do without it. First think about what you need, and then find software or a software service (auction management service) that satisfies your needs.

I have listened with total astonishment to hear eBay businesspeople complain about the cost of auction management software services. They must lack experience running a business with employees. Indeed, the software services are very inexpensive for what they do: eliminate employees.

Database Solution

You will find a revised outline of a three-use database system for doing business on eBay in Appendix 4 . This was first published in eBay the Smart Way. At that time the auction management software packages were somewhat unsophisticated, and setting up a database application to cover inventory control, bulk auction submission, and catalog data for ecommerce made sense.

It doesn't any longer. The database system outline in Appendix 4 is included just for an optional review of the concepts behind using a software application to manage your business processes for your eBay business. I advise you to forgo creating your own database system (unless you're a programmer with extra time on your hands) for eBay and use one of the very competent auction management services now available.

On the other hand, if you are using pre-existing software systems that you want to keep, you can use the information in Appendix 4 to devise a system that integrates your eBay operations into your present system.

Auction Management Software

In recent years, auction management software has migrated from CDs to websites. This presents you with some new facts of life:

1. You don't buy the software, you rent it.

2. You don't have to worry about annual or semiannual upgrades. The upgrades are added as soon as they become

available. Since you use the software through your browser, the upgrades are transparent and require no action on your part.

3. The software services are easier to use with a broadband connection. They're a little slow with a dial-up connection, maybe too slow.

4. Most services offer a comprehensive but integrated package of features for running your entire eBay business.

As they say, the problem today is not running an eBay business—the auction management services do that—the problem is finding a niche in which to sell something.

Auction = eBay

Most auction management services handle auctions besides eBay auctions. I do not consider this an important feature, although it may be for some people. I consider the word "auction" in "auction management service" to be a substitute for "eBay," and it's used to keep from confusing it with eBay's own auction management software.

Desired Features

This chapter will consider some of the features you need in a software package to run your eBay business. The next chapter will review one sample auction management service to see how it measures up.

Inventory Control

For most people selling on eBay as a business entails selling lots of items. You need an inventory control system not so much to save money but to retain your sanity. Inventory control is not optional, and if you do it with paper, it's a lot of trouble. It's an essential part of an auction management service.

Presentation

You can't make individual webpages for each auction on a custom basis. You just won't have the time. You can use templates to save time, but that's still inefficient. Best is to use a system that incorporates webpage templates. (If you can customize the templates, so much the better.) This is a typical feature of an auction management service and a welcome one.

Auction Management

Auctions are just like inventory, numerous. You need to keep track of them. In addition, you need to have them uploaded to eBay automatically at times that you schedule. Software to do this takes much of the busy work out of your eBay business. This is an essential function of an auction management service.

Customer Communication

Potential bidders, bidders, and customers will contact you about one thing or another. It's convenient to keep track of these communications separate from other matters in your business or personal life.

Auction Follow-Up

Rather than contact each winning bidder personally with the requisite information to close the purchase transaction after an auction, the software should contact the winning bidder automatically via email.

Transaction Checkout

A transaction checkout device, just like one at an ecommerce website, makes paying easy for a winning bidder. The checkout should be able to handle a variety of payment choices. This is a highly desirable feature of an auction management service.

Shipping

Having the checkout handle shipping with the same automation as payment is important too. As you may recall from Chapter 12 on fulfillment, the shippers provide the requisite information on their websites that auction management software can tap into for the correct up-to-date shipping charges. In addition, a process for tracking shipping can reduce unnecessary communications with customers. Again, the shippers provide tracking service requiring only a tracking number. An auction management service should print the package label with the tracking number and otherwise provide the tracking number where needed (i.e., to the customer via email).

Documentation

Documentation should include an email receipt for customers, an email notice that their account has been charged, a packing slip for the package (and to instruct warehouse personnel), a mailing label for the package (printed to the specifications of the shipper), email instructions regarding tracking shipment, and the like. All documentation should be automated. Auction management services cover many of these requirements.

Write Once

A person (employee) should never have to enter any data into the auction management service more than once. Data entry should be quick, easy, and convenient.

Prime Feature

This is a prime feature of any software system and an absolute requirement. Don't overlook your basic need for a "write once" feature.

Accounting

A record of each transaction and each customer must be stored in an archive (database) for future reference. The archive system should dovetail with your accounting software to enable you to seamlessly transfer your records into your accounting system.

Database Applications

Most applications that contain lists, directories, catalogs, transaction records, inventory items, and other groups of data are database applications. At their core is a built-in database. Auction management programs are database applications too. They process data, use data for processing, accept the input of data, archive data, and export data to other applications (e.g., accounting systems).

eCommerce Software

eCommerce software for small businesses is generally thought to be a catalog, shipping cart, and a checkout device. Invariably, this is a database application. In function, it has some overlap with auction management services, but it is not exactly the same. If you are going to operate a website where you sell inventory, it would be especially useful to be able to integrate your ecommerce system with your auction management system instead of running separate systems.

In fact, you may be able to use an auction management system in place of an ecommerce system. If an auction management service provides a catalog, a shopping cart, and a checkout device, you can probably use it on your website. That would be a feature to look for when reviewing auction management services. Two for the price of one. Or, take a look at it the other way round. Find an ecommerce program that offers auction management features. These combinations are covered in the next chapter.

17

Software Assistance

Running an eBay business requires a lot of paperwork. To make it easy you need to do two things. First, you need to use a system to manage the paperwork. Second, you have to turn much of the paperwork into digital work.

eBay provides some programs for you to use in managing your eBay business. They're competent and mostly free, and you may be able to get by just fine using them. Some third-parties, however, provide comprehensive auction management services that make managing an eBay business almost automatic.

Keep in mind when considering software that delivery via the Web may be preferable to using software residing on your own computer. Here are some attractive features:

- No maintenance required

- No updates to install

- Continually updated by vendor

- Low monthly cost

- Files saved in a system that's backed up each day

- Can store redundant files on your computer too

- No strain on your operating system (fewer crashes)

- Use all Web software in Web browser

- Can use anywhere and on any computer connected to the Internet

As one who wonders why Microsoft's own programs don't run on Microsoft's operating systems as well as Adobe programs do, who has to reinstall Microsoft Office every three months to keep it working, and who is many years weary of pampering his bizarre operating system, I can tell you that I am a believer. Software services via the Web are a godsend. I'm looking forward to the day when all I need is an operating system and a Web browser.

However, you do need a broadband connection to make software services work well. They sputter along on a dial-up connection.

eBay's Programming Aids

You don't have to go any further than eBay to find help with your selling tasks, and many sellers don't. The starting place to decide on what software services to use is on eBay. Then review what eBay offers and compare it to what third parties have to offer.

My eBay

This is a free system that keeps track of your auctions. It has been around for a long time, and some sellers find it perfectly adequate. It offers lots of features. Give it a look before you decide you need something more. You can find it on the eBay menu bar under Services.

Picture Service

eBay offers its own picture service. You get one photograph free per auction. You pay for a variety of additional services. One additional service is inclusion in eBay's Gallery where bidders shop by picture, an appropriate place for some merchandise but not all.

Management Software

At the time this book went to press, eBay's management software seemed to be in transition. One gets the feeling that in addition to the new services in existence there will be more new services to come soon, and old services will disappear.

eBay Selling Manager

This is a new service available only online for a monthly charge of $5. It enables you to schedule listings, monitor bidders, send customized mail to customers, relist items, and print invoices and shipping labels. It also keeps sales records. *It does not create new listings.* It's comparable to Seller's Assistant but has more features.

eBay Seller's Assistant Standard

This is an offline program (use it on your computer) similar to Selling Manager but without as many features. It's the same price at $5 monthly.

eBay Seller's Assistant Pro

This is a beefed up version of Seller's Assistant Standard for $16 per month. It offers the additional features of feedback management, inventory management, reports, and the capability to automate certain processes. You use it offline on your computer.

Turbo Lister

This is a free listing program you can use offline for both individual listings and bulk listings. Used together with one of the other eBay management programs, you will have a great deal of auction management capability. Entering your listings offline can be faster than online. Once you've entered the listings into Turbo Lister, the program then uploads them to eBay.

Turbo Lister is more than just a submission vehicle. Once you have entered your listings, you can look at your auction ads and further tune them before submittal (see Figure 17.1).

The Turbo Lister can also import and export standard comma delimited data files (also known as .csv files). This is a breakthrough. For years eBay didn't accept standard data files. One had to submit bulk listings in HTML pages, a rather awkward format for data submission. Indeed, in past eBay books I presented an elaborate and cumbersome database-mail-merge scheme to automate the bulk listing process as much as possible.

The significance of this new capability is that you can now use your own database application and export the data in comma delimited format to Turbo Lister. Then you can make a bulk submission to eBay. The database application might be one that you created yourself or an off-the-shelf inventory management program that you've used for many years. Most business-processing software uses a core built-in database. Now through Turbo Lister, you may be able to use such software to export the data necessary to create eBay listings (auction ads).

This is particularly relevant to businesses that have a physical presence and use traditional retail software. If this is you, check with your accountant to determine what new possibilities now exist for integrating your existing business software with eBay processes via Turbo Lister.

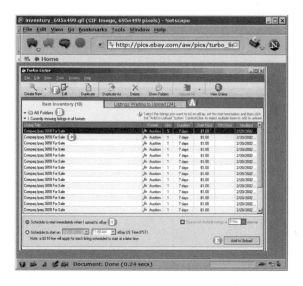

Figure 17.1 Turbo Lister's table list of items. ©1995-2003 eBay Inc.

For those who have built or want to build their own database applications to manage their eBay activities, Turbo Lister now enables you to submit bulk listings easily and almost directly with data exported from your database.

eBay Checkout

The eBay checkout system isn't bad but seems to be overlooked by most sellers. Now that eBay has purchased PayPal and phased out BillPoint, perhaps the eBay checkout will catch on with sellers. You can find a checkout tutorial for sellers in the eBay Seller's Guide. Give it a try, particularly if you do not use an auction management service.

Andale

Andale is one of the auction management service leaders. Reviewing software is better done by current magazines than books, and this should not be considered a critical or even a complete review of Andale. Rather Andale is presented here as a good example of an auction management service. By taking a look at some of Andale's leading features, you can better understand auction management services and can better choose one that's right for you.

This section does not even attempt to cover all of Andale's features, which are truly extensive. You are encouraged to visit the Andale website to more fully appreciate the extent of Andale's potential support for your eBay business. But keep in mind also that Andale has some energetic and capable competitors, and you need to carefully review what they have to offer too.

Andale's a la Carte

Andale (*http://andale.com*)offers its features as individual components priced individually, although it also offers certain packages of components for various levels of volume. Taken altogether, the Andale components provide you with a comprehensive eBay management service.

Research

The research function is free but is an amazing service. You enter the item, and Andale automatically researches the sales in the eBay archives. It returns the following:

- The average selling price
- A list of all the auctions
- The success rate of the auctions
- The average number of bids per auction
- The listing categories used

In addition, it provides further analysis of the auction statistics. It's a valuable tool for determining value and for developing tactics to sell a particular item. See Chapter 10 to understand how important this is.

Rare Information

eBay started out providing current statistics regarding eBay auctions on its home page. Over the years such information has gradually disappeared. Today we are stuck with the statistical information that eBay releases at its annual conference in June. No one else has accurate statistics on eBay.

eBay Magazine published useful eBay business statistics but is now defunct. Today, where can one turn to find useful eBay business statistics? The Andale research function is a rare place where you can actually get accurate and useful statistical information that will help you with you eBay auctions. And it's free!

DeepAnalysis

HammerTap (*http://hammertap.com*) sells DeepAnalysis, a program which amazingly extracts statistics from an eBay category or keyword grouping. It's quick, comprehensive, and handy for analyzing sellers as well as products. It's a rare source of eBay statistics.

Images

Andale offers an image service comparable to many others. It stores images on the Web for you, and you can use them in your auction ads or anywhere (see Figure 17.2). The primary advantage to Andale's service is that it's integrated with Andale's other services. This makes it quite convenient to use if you use other Andale services. Andale charges a minimum of $3 per month, and that includes up to 3 MB, which is approximately 50 average-size images.

Listings

The heart of an auction management service is the listing service. The listings are the auction ads. Andale's minimum charge per month is $2 which includes 10 listings.

Andale claims that you can create an auction ad in 30 seconds in contrast to 3 minutes on eBay. The service even provides a spell checker. You have 100 themes (templates) from which to choose to make your auction ad look professional. You can also schedule the ads to appear on eBay at any time for many months in advance, and the service includes a bulk listing feature. An inventory manager is part of this useful service too. But that's not all. I could write a chapter on all the features included. This particular service is a good one to compare to the listing services offered by Andale's competitors.

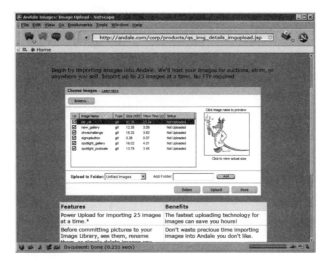

Figure 17.2   Andale image listings. ©1999-2003 Andale Inc.

Counters

Andale provides free counters for your auction ads. In fact, you can use these counters in any webpages anywhere. You can also access traffic reports based on the counters.

Gallery

The Gallery is an add-on feature. That is, it is automatically added into eBay auction ads, emails, and other presentations. It includes four visible items (from four other auctions) with one thumbnail photograph each (see Figure 17.3). Note that if all the items in the Gallery are not eBay auctions, its use may be outlawed by eBay rules.

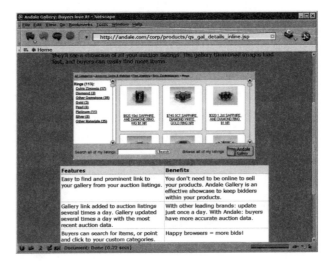

Figure 17.3   Andale Gallery. ©1999-2003 Andale Inc.

It costs $6 per month. The point of using it is to cross sell and increase overall sales; that is, with the Gallery, you are referring people to your other auctions. Neat feature. Read more about the Andale Gallery in Chapter 19.

Checkout

Providing winning bidders with a checkout device can save you a substantial amount of time that you would otherwise spend exchanging email. The Andale checkout costs a minimum of $2 per month for ten checkouts and is a full-fledged payment-shipping service. It can handle twelve payment methods and can automatically calculate shipping charges. It generates invoices, packing slips, labels, and reports. See Figure 17.4.

And you can use it anywhere you want to, not just for your auctions on eBay.

What a Deal!

Want to avoid running separate ecommerce software at your website? Andale's checkout might be what you need. Check out Andale's total offerings, including the Andale store, to determine what you can use for ecommerce at your website.

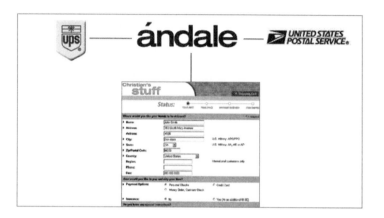

Figure 17.4   Andale checkout. ©1999-2003 Andale Inc.

Feedback

Providing feedback to others is a sensitive endeavor. You had better handle your routine feedback carefully or it will turn back to feed on you. The benefit is that when you provide positive feedback for winning bidders in a timely manner, they in turn are likely to take the trouble to do the same for you. Andale provides a free feedback management service, which works automatically. It also alerts you immediately when someone files negative feedback on you, a very useful feature.

Reports

The Andale reports provide dozens of analyses of your operations. These are mostly financial analyses. It's like having a CPA working for you. This is the kind of information that can keep you from making dumb mistakes and can show you the way to greater profitability. The cost is $20 per month.

Read Them

Many people who subscribe to analytic reports on their business operations have a tendency to put them on the shelf for later reference, even though most analytic reports are not cheap. Don't make this mistake. Set aside an hour or two each month to review the latest reports on your operations. It's tough to do when you're busy, but it's smart. Think of it as keeping score in a game, and keeping your eye on the score. The sooner you respond to your business statistics, the more money you will make.

Andale Store

The store is similar to the listing service featuring catalog pages for auction items. It's a substitute for the eBay Store. It looks better and operates with more features. In addition, you can use your Andale store anywhere, not just on eBay. Indeed, you can use it as a catalog in a separate website! It includes a shopping cart and a checkout device. It also offers both inventory and sales management. It costs a minimum of $6 per month for 20 items.

Another Chance to Save Time and Money

Using your Andale store as a catalog on your website can potentially save you the effort and cost of separate ecommerce software. Focus on the effort potentially saved. Who wants to run two programs that do the same thing, one for your eBay auctions and one for your website? Use Andale store in both places.

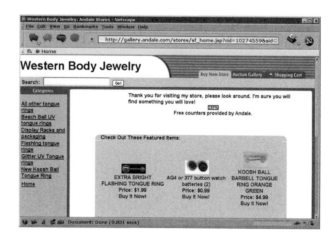

Figure 17.5   Andale store, a popular feature. ©1999-2003 Andale Inc.

Email Offer

Have you always wanted to SPAM? Andale gives you your opportunity. Actually the email goes only to your customers, past and present, so it's not really SPAM. But it does give you the means to easily communicate with everyone in your Andale database. Promote new products or wish everyone a Merry Christmas. For $6 per month, this is an easy way to keep in touch with your customers. Does this violate eBay policy? I don't think so. These are your customers, not potential customers.

Lister Pro

Andale does it all for you. But there's one thing that Andale or any other software cannot do for you: data entry. You or an employee must enter the information about products, prices, and the like. In a well-designed auction management system, you need to enter the requisite information only once. But you do have to enter it at least once. See Lister Pro in Figure 17.6.

Data entry online via a dial-up connection can be slow. With a broadband connection it goes faster. It goes the fastest, though, on your own computer in the rows and columns of a database table.

Lister Pro is a free Andale program you use on your own computer to enter and then upload data to your Andale services. It looks like a database table or a spreadsheet. It makes data entry easy and efficient! Without this program, the work you have to do to make Andale services work would be more tedious. Learn how to use it.

In a Table

Don't underestimate the efficiency of data entry or changing data in a table format rather in a form format. You or your data entry employee (independent contractor?) can do much more in much less time.

Packaged Services

Andale has packaged services for different levels of selling according to average anticipated needs. The following schedule indicates about how much it will cost you per month to use Andale depending on your monthly volume.

40 auctions	$11
110 auctions	$35

275 auctions $100

1,100 auctions $230

Not all of these packages offer the same services. Since Andale offers its services a la carte, your monthly costs will be different unless you specifically buy one of these packages.

Cost Dilemma

You can see that the cost ranges between 21 cents and 28 cents per auction. This poses a dilemma. The higher the volume, the more you need this service; but normally the higher the volume, the lower the price per item. This cost is a significant expense for a low-price item and an insignificant cost for a high-price item. This is the same dilemma faced with many of the other fees necessary to do business on eBay.

Figure 17.6   Andale Lister Pro. ©1999-2003 Andale Inc.

Broadband

With programs (used on your own computer) being replaced today by services (which you use through a browser), you need a broadband connection to the Internet. A DSL phone connection, cable Internet service, or even satellite Internet service is up to 30 times faster than the fastest dial-up modem. In addition, broadband connections are full-time connections. You are always connected. There's no waiting for a connection to be made as there is with a dial-up modem. You don't necessarily need a powerful computer for your eBay business, as I've stated elsewhere in this book. But a broadband connection is a real convenience.

Go Broadband and Save

As mentioned in Chapter 4, if you use a voice-over-IP phone service, you may be able to save enough in long distance telephone charges to pay for the a DSL line or cable Internet access.

Merchant-Veeo

Miva Merchant (*http://www.miva.com*) is a robust ecommerce program, which accepts third-party add-ons (plug-ins) to augment its features. Chapter 20 covers Merchant in greater detail. That chapter briefly covers the Veeo eBay plug-in for Merchant, which you can use to extend the capabilities of Merchant to do eBay auction management.

Veeo Action Plus (*http://veeo.com*) enables eBay auction setups and auction monitoring via Merchant. It provides full eBay controls but processes auction transactions through the Merchant checkout. There is a Pro version, which handles email to winning bidders. Because Merchant itself includes an inventory management system, the addition of Veeo Action Plus works out to a be a sensible overall system.

Nevertheless, this approach to operating your eBay business is recommended only if you operate a website from which you sell merchandise. Otherwise it makes more sense to use a service such as Andale.

Auction Management Services and Software

Below is a list of auction management services:

Andale, *http://andale.com*

AuctionHawk, *http://www.auctionhawk.com*

AuctionHelper, *http://auctionhelper.com*

AuctionWatch, *http://auctionwatch.com*

Auctiva, *http://auctiva.com*

ChannelAdvisor, *http://channeladvisor.com*

CollectorOnline, *http://www.collectoronline.com*

HammerTap Manager, *http://www.hammertap.com*

ManageAuctions, *http://manageauctions.com*

Zoovy, *http://zoovy.com* (see Figure 17.7)

Figure 17.7   Zoovy.com website. ©2003 Zoovy.

Some of these services include software that you use on your own computer. If you would rather use software exclusively on your own computer, check out the following software offerings:

AuctionTamer, *http://www.auctiontamer.com*

Auction Wizard 2000, *http://auctionwizard2000.com*

Easy Auction, *http://auctiontools.net*

MyAuctionMate, *http://www.myauctionmate.com*

ShootingStar, *http://www.foodogsoftware.com*

Timber Creek Sold!, *http://www.timbercreeksoftware.com*

Various programs, *http://www.hammertap.com* (see website in Figure 17.8)

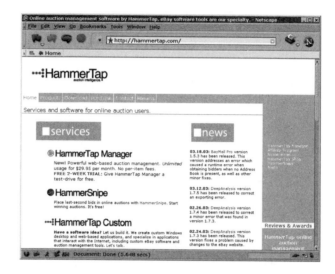

Figure 17.8   Hammer Tap website. ©2000-2003 Hammer Tap.

As you might expect, there is free software available from some of the vendors above that might prove useful. However, I recommend that you do not look at price when it comes to auction management. Auction management software can save you so much time and effort that you need to choose a service or software package that feels comfortable to you. This software niche is competitive, and the prices are reasonable. Choose the service or software that you want to use, not the least expensive.

Re-Advisory

As reported in Chapter 1, my bias is for auction management services. For most people making a livable business on eBay, an auction management service is a godsend. So is eBay's array of software.

Chapter 1 gives a call to action. It advises a trial period of eBay selling using your own system of keeping track of your merchandise, auctions, and sales. Once the trial is over, however, don't continue on with a patchwork system. Even before your volume picks up, get started with an auction management service. You won't regret it.

Custom Programming

If you find yourself paying for custom programming, you should have a specific reason for using such programming. Generally speaking, off-the-shelf programming, such as Miva Merchant and a service such as Andale, is competent to handle everything you need to do in your eBay business. There is no reason to pay to reinvent the wheel.

Custom programming can be very expensive when you use it to recreate functions already available in off-the-shelf programs. Still, it can often be surprisingly inexpensive when you use it to create a minor function that's otherwise not available. Consult with a freelance programmer if you need a special function. It can't hurt to ask.

Accounting Software

As long as we're considering software, take a look at Intuit, *http://intuit.com*. You can do your accounting now with Quicken (personal accounting), move up to Quicken Premier Home & Business, and finally to QuickBooks (business accounting). Many of the auction management services and software dovetail with QuickBooks (as does Miva Merchant) making it seamless for you to integrate your operations with your accounting. This type of overall system 15 years ago would have cost you a few hundred thousand dollars and would have required three full-time employees to operate it. Today it costs peanuts, and you can operate it by yourself. It even dovetails with PayPal. And you can use various QuickBooks services such as Payroll to save yourself the trouble (see Figure 17.9).

Figure 17.9   Intuit (QuickBooks) Payroll Services. ©2003 Intuit Inc.

There are other appropriate accounting programs, too, some of which also dovetail with certain auction management services and software.

If You Have Employees

If you need to have employees, you will need competent services or software to do your payroll. Intuit offers payroll service as do other sources. This makes having employees bearable. Don't try to do your payroll manually.

18

Customer Service

Why is customer service so important? Because there isn't anything else. If you can't keep your customers happy, you don't have any future selling on eBay.

Customer service is getting more robust on the Web. Another way to put this is that the trend is to more and better customer service. Commerce on the Web is very competitive, and much of that competition takes place in the customer service realm.

If you think you can just sell something on eBay and that's the end of it, you are in for a surprise. When you sell something on eBay, that's only the beginning of it.

I suppose as an individual selling occasionally on eBay, you might be able to avoid being concerned with customer service. But even that notion is dubious. And when you make a business of selling on eBay, customer service must hold your continual attention.

Is this something new, invented online? No, not at all. The offline businesses that give the best customer service are among the most successful. Business online or on eBay is no different than offline. The name of the game is customer service. The customer is always right. Always!

Feedback

Your indoctrination to customer service on eBay is the feedback system. This can be a harsh introduction if you're not careful. The customers (buyers, bidders) get to speak out if not treated well. And they will. The feedback record is permanent and public. Your mistakes can stay with you for a long time. It's better to think things through from the beginning and develop a customer-oriented approach to your business. That will help keep your feedback record clean.

But that may not be enough. You really have to buy into the customer service philosophy. You have to believe that providing good customer service is the right thing to do in the retail business. You have to be a believer. With such an attitude, you won't have to worry about getting negative feedback.

Make no mistake. The feedback system works. Potential bidders not only check the feedback of sellers but they avoid sellers with significant negative feedback. Having a clean feedback record is essential to your success.

Read, *Trust Among Strangers in Internet Transactions: Empirical Analysis of eBay's Reputation System*, 02/05/01 draft, *http://www.si.umich.edu/~presnick/papers/ebayNBER/RZNBERBodegaBay.pdf*, and visit an author's (Paul Resnick) webpage at *http://www.si.umich.edu/~presnick/* if you like an academic flavor to your eBay information. The conclusion of the paper is that sellers with better reputations are more likely to sell but not likely to get a higher price. Also read Daniel Reeves' paper, cited in the beginning of Chapter 24, which concludes that an increase in a seller's positive feedback yields an increase in auction prices.

Credit Card Chargebacks

Anyone who pays with a credit card and is dissatisfied with a purchase can ask for a chargeback (a refund to their credit card account). Banks issue credit cards. Some banks routinely honor a chargeback request without any investigation. Some investigate. Of the banks that investigate, some will seem to favor the buyer and some will seem to favor the seller.

This is not a game you want to play. Your customer service should prevent chargebacks. If a customer makes a chargeback, your customer service has failed. Design your customer service from beginning to end so that customer dissatisfaction never goes as far as a chargeback.

Guarantees

The most analogous industry to ecommerce is the mail order business. How do mail order firms talk people into buying merchandise, often sight unseen, from faraway places? They give guarantees. That's what you need to do too.

Look at it this way. Whether you want to or not you will have to exchange merchandise with or make refunds to unhappy customers. Otherwise you won't survive on eBay. Why not turn that fact of life into a positive instead of a negative? Guarantee what you sell. Mail order firms do it. Leading offline merchants do it. Why not you?

Now, there are situations where manufacturers handle the guarantees or warranties (e.g., consumer electronics), and you don't have to do it. There are situations where guarantees aren't appropriate and aren't expected (e.g., used goods sold "as is" with fully disclosed defects). But if you sell something after saying that it is in good condition or that it works, it better be in good condition or it better work when it gets to the buyer. The feedback system is too powerful for you to carry a lot of unhappy customers on your back.

As Is

What does "as is" mean? You see this used a lot on eBay. Is it used by a seller who sells something that works well, who wants the maximum price, but who doesn't want to take any responsibility?

Or, is it used by a seller who is not sure whether the item works well, and who expects a lower price? Who knows?

This is an expression you want to avoid using in your auction ads. If you're the first seller (above) who doesn't want to take responsibility, you're going to have a tough time on eBay, and you're going to get a lower price for the item in any event. If you're the second seller (above) who doesn't know about the item and is willing to take a lower price, you might be mistaken for the first seller. You can't win.

Give it up. My advice is that if something doesn't work well or is not in good condition, don't sell it. Why ask for trouble?

If you want to insist on selling something "as is," make sure that you provide complete information on why you are doing so. Selling something "as is" can be legitimate in some cases, but it requires full disclosure. It should never be a routine abdication of responsibility.

Types of Product Guarantees

Different guarantees go with different industries. Here are some possibilities for product guarantees:

Not DOA (dead on arrival) This is a guarantee popular with some retailers (e.g., computer hardware retailers). It means that the hardware is guaranteed not to be DOA. So long as it works when it gets to the buyer, the guarantee is valid. If it breaks a day later (or an hour later), there is no guarantee. This seems reasonable for used computer hardware so long as it is well explained.

Short-term This is a guarantee with a specific short time limit (e.g., 90 days).

Long-term This is a guarantee with a specific time period of longer duration.

Limited This limits the reasons justifying the return of the merchandise (e.g., only if defective).

You want happy customers, but there's a limit to what you can do. The least you can do is a short-term, limited guarantee; and that may be enough. The fact that you guarantee your goods at all will put your potential customers at ease. Take a look at what your competitors are doing both online and offline. Go them one better if you can.

Satisfaction Guarantee

The ultimate guarantee is a *satisfaction* guarantee. This is not a product guarantee. This is a purchase guarantee. If your customer isn't satisfied with the purchase for any reason, she can return it for a refund. This is essentially what the leading merchandisers guarantee offline (e.g., Target, Costco). This is a very powerful guarantee to give on eBay. It's the ultimate in customer service. It's not appropriate for all merchandise, but you need to seriously consider giving this type of guarantee. Many leading eBay sellers do.

Payment

Different means of payment are not conveniences for you, they're for your customers. You need to be ready to accept payment as many ways as possible. At the very least you need to accept the following:

PayPal It's the leading payment method on the Web. If you accept credit cards, you can probably get away without accepting PayPal until you grow large.

Credit Cards Visa and Mastercard are a must, but it's nice to accept American Express and Discover too. If you use PayPal, you can probably get away without accepting credit cards until your volume grows.

Electronic Checks Accepting electronic checks is easy to do. Do it.

Checks Most of the world still runs on checks.

Money Orders and Cashier's Checks Some people deal strictly in cash, and this is as close to cash as they can get short of sending currency.

People (customers) are creatures of habit. Others are fussy. Whatever the reason, some people will not purchase unless you offer their chosen method of payment. Don't be foolish. Don't throw away a significant portion of the market. Be flexible in regard to accepting payment.

Escrow.com

This is the eBay recommended escrow service for completing eBay auction transactions in escrow. Should you agree to closing a transaction in escrow?

No seller wants to use escrow. Sellers perceive that as long as they don't have to deliver before they get paid, why bother with escrow? Sellers know they're honest. They don't need an escrow closing. Unfortunately, that attitude completely ignores the point of view of the buyers.

Every buyer has a line that he or she will not cross. It might be $50, $500, or $5,000, but at some price a buyer will simply not pay a seller without some assurance that the item will be delivered. Just for reference, my threshold is about $1,000. I can buy something more expensive than that, but I wouldn't unless the seller agreed to an escrow closing. If you don't agree to an escrow for your $1,400 item, you will eliminate me as a potential bidder. And dozens of other potential bidders! (You'll never know the people you've eliminated.) Consequently, I recommend that you agree to an escrow closing upon request.

Who pays? Escrow closings aren't cheap. For the $1,400 transaction at Escrow.com, the fee is a whopping six percent for a credit card transaction or three percent for a check transaction! That's $84 or $42. I recommend that the buyer and seller split the cost. That's fair and what is commonly done in real estate transactions.

What's in it for you? First, it increases your credibility. If you offer it, the buyer may decide not to use it. If you refuse it, the buyer may insist upon it (or just not bid). Second, it gives you protection against a chargeback on a credit card transaction. It will be difficult for the buyer to argue that the merchandise is unsatisfactory after a successful escrow closing. After all, the seller isn't paid until the buyer accepts the merchandise.

So, go to Escrow.com (*http://www.escrow.com*) and learn about escrow closings. You don't necessarily have to offer it for high cost items, but agree to it, if asked; and agree to split the cost. This is basic customer service.

eBay also recommends escrow services for foreign transactions, which makes sales abroad more feasible. Of course, there are other online escrow companies, and you might want to search for one and use it. I'm sticking with eBay's recommendation, because this is a sensitive matter for which eBay's recommendation carries some weight.

Licensed Dealer

If you are a licensed dealer (e.g., vehicles), you can argue that the state regulates dealers and their transactions. Therefore, the buyer has protection and doesn't need an escrow closing. Licensed dealers normally are obligated to go through a state-sanctioned procedure to close transactions. And a buyer can check up on licensed dealers ahead of time through the licensing state.

Square Trade

If you get in a dispute with a buyer, Square Trade is a lifesaver to settle the dispute fairly. Mediating the dispute is done online and by other means of communication. Hopefully, nobody goes home mad, and everyone keeps their reputations intact. This is essentially a service you offer to buyers with a notice (seal) in your auction ad. Go to the Square Trade website for details.

http://www.squaretrade.com

This is not a major expense and is one you will do well to offer.

Authentication Services

If you sell collectibles, art objects, and various other items that buyers expect to be authenticated, you need to provide authentication. The authentication simply states that the item is what it purports to be. Various items are authenticated in different ways, but the idea is that experts do the authentications. When you're dealing in items that require authentication, line up the proper experts to do the authentication for you.

Returns

Set up a policy and system for returns and inform your buyers. This will give you some control. You don't want returns coming in that you can't identify or about which you have no information. Publish your policy in your auction ads.

You need to coordinate your return policy with your guarantees. Both should be explained to your customers. For instance, if you allow the return of defective merchandise only, you need to require your buyers to state the defects when they return something.

Timeliness

Handle all communications with customers immediately. Face and resolve all problems immediately. If a customer isn't happy, it's a burden—to the customer. Get that burden off their back as soon as possible. Make it right. This is how you build a business.

Full information

Always provide full information on the items you sell. It's a convenience to bidders; it will result in more bidders; and it will save you time (i.e., less email from potential bidders). If you don't take care to do so, it makes you look like you're in a hurry or don't care. Either interpretation signals that you will probably be difficult to deal with if something goes wrong, a signal not well received by buyers.

Full information is especially crucial for used or defective merchandise. People want to get the full story. They won't appreciate surprises.

Software

Use software wherever you can to streamline and automate communications and customer service. A good example is to follow up an auction immediately with an email to the winning bidder. However, know when to handle communications on a personal basis. It's difficult for software to handle the unique problems that arise from time to time.

Seek new ideas in customer service software. You need to review the customer service software market at least once a year to discover what's new. Go to trade shows that focus on customer service. Note that much customer service software is expensive and designed for large businesses. Seek inexpensive customer service software designed for small businesses. It's not necessarily inferior. It's just designed for a smaller-scale retail operation.

Auction management services contain customer service software. Keep up to date on this software and stay aware of new features being offered.

Offline Customer Service

Just because you have an online business doesn't mean you need pay attention only to online customer service. Always keep in mind traditional (offline) customer service and combine it with what you do online. The goal is to keep your customers happy. For instance, sometimes you need to use the telephone to resolve a problem. Email just doesn't get the job done. Sometimes even a letter (on real paper) is appropriate.

Experiment

Online customer service is being invented now. Review what your competitors and retailers in other industries are doing. Imitate some procedures. Reject others. Experiment with your own ideas. eBay and other successful ecommerce operations are not well seasoned processes that have reached maturity. They are early experiments that are working. Invent something to make your customers' experience more satisfying.

Amazon.com

Amazon.com continues to be the model of effective retailing online. It is 100 percent customer service. Review what's going on at Amazon periodically. You will get some ideas you might be able to incorporate into your own retail business.

Off the Ground

The founder of Amazon.com, Jeff Bezos, could have been up and running in two months in 1996 with quite powerful existing ecommerce software. Instead he chose to create his own system. He spent a year in a garage with several programmers inventing Amazon.com before the website went online. The rest is history. Amazon.com has invented at least half of the leading ecommerce customer service techniques and continues to be innovative.

Take Advantage

eBay offers a lot of digital devices that provide customer service. Aggressively experiment with all of them. Use the ones that work for you and your customers.

If you have a website, your host ISP will have a bag of digital tricks you can use free. There are CGI scripts and perhaps JavaScripts to be incorporated into your webpages. Some of them will be appropriate for customer service. An example is a guest book where customers sign in. Their name goes on a mailing list for a newsletter or future promotional emailings.

Not Just This or That

Customer service is the sum total of what you do for your customers to make things easy, convenient, and satisfying for them. It's your accounting, your procedures, your communication, your eBay advertising, your policies, and many other things. Think through everything you do with your customers in mind.

VI

Operate Smart

19

eBay Storefront

So you want to have a storefront where you can sell more items than you auction! eBay provides a good place to start. If you want more than eBay offers, Chapter 20 gives you some ideas. Here, however, we'll stick to a brief discussion of the eBay seller auction listings and eBay Stores.

What Is a Storefront?

Before we consider the eBay offerings, it's useful to discuss what a basic storefront is, and then see how the eBay offerings measure up. A storefront is a website that sells products. In other words, it's an ecommerce website.

eCommerce websites or storefronts can be plain or have a lot of character. For instance, Costco.com sells discount merchandise (just as it does in its physical stores). That's pretty straightforward. Many ecommerce websites, however, include some type of attraction or perhaps even entertainment. For example, Amazon.com has book reviews on its website. This is not only relevant to selling books but very useful to buyers. The Fly Shop website (*http://www.theflyshop.com*) has a catalog of fly fishing equipment and supplies, its primary business. It also offers fly fishing trips abroad, local guide service, fishing in local private waters, a fly fishing school, and a kids camp. The kids camp portion of the website features a memories section for the camp going back four years and includes photographs for each year. The overall website furnishes plenty of information about the area where the physical shop is located, which is a national destination area for fly fishing (Redding, California). The customer service spans from the physical location right onto the website.

Regardless of what else an ecommerce website might offer, the ecommerce portion of the website inevitably offers a catalog, a shopping cart, a checkout, and occasionally other functionality.

Catalog

A catalog is essential to ecommerce. It's simply a list of products available for purchase. It might appear as one product per webpage with some scheme of hierarchical navigation, a list of products to be browsed, a list of products resulting from a search, or even a combination of these. A well-done catalog contains a photograph of each product, a description of each product, and the price of each product. It might also contain choices for the product. For instance, an article of clothing might contain a choice of four colors and eight sizes.

Some catalogs are elegant with artwork that will knock your socks off. Others are rather plain. The most desirable feature of a catalog, however, is usability. It must be easy to navigate and easy to use. Because 90 percent of ecommerce websites miss the mark, that's worth repeating:

The most desirable feature of a catalog is usability.

Shopping Cart

A shopping cart is a digital device that accumulates purchases as the buyer browses through the catalog much as one throws products in a shopping cart as one goes through a department store. One can check the cart to determine what's in it and can even take products out (delete them).

Checkout

When the buyer finishes shopping, he goes to the checkout where he gives his name, address, and credit card information (or other payment information). The digital checkout device usually calculates sales tax, if any, and adds shipping costs. Then it collects the total payment.

Other Functions

An ecommerce website may have other functions, too, such as enabling a buyer to rate the product (review it). Other buyers can view the rating (or review) to assist them in making purchasing decisions.

Informal eBay Storefront

The eBay seller auction list is like a catalog. The catalog list contains all the current auctions for a seller. eBay generates such a list automatically for each seller.

A link to the seller's list of auctions appears near the top of the auction page near her eBay ID. Most bidders are aware of this link.

At the top of the auction list, three tabs enable a buyer to use the list conveniently. One tab presents all auction items. Another presents all *Buy It Now* items. And one presents the combination of the two. When a buyer clicks on an item on the list, the auction ad for the item appears exactly the same as in the normal eBay auction scheme.

This is not a fancy catalog (see Figure 19.1). Indeed, it's exactly like the remainder of eBay. There are no visible shopping carts and no special functions. The checkout device is the normal eBay checkout device (see Chapter 17).

It's not much, but it's free and may be adequate for your eBay business. It's functional and easy to use for buyers and may be all you need.

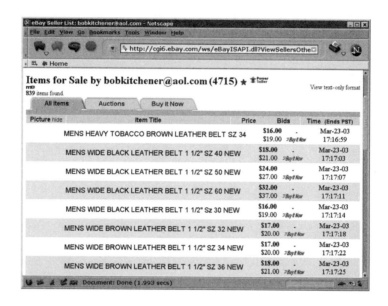

Figure 19.1 eBay seller auction list. ©1995-2003 eBay Unc.

Fee

There is no additional fee for the list of all your current auctions. The eBay system automatically generates the list.

About Me

One thing your eBay auction list lacks is information about you and your business. You can take care of that, however, by making a brochure website on your *About Me* page on eBay. This is discussed in Chapters 8 and 20 at more length. With a little HTML (see the tutorials in Appendixes 5 and 6), you can make your *About Me* entry on eBay a long webpage providing information on both you and your eBay business. The link to your *About Me* webpage appears beside your eBay ID (login name) on an auction webpage. It's great for your business whether you promote the eBay auction list or not. And it's free.

eBay Stores

eBay Stores are strictly for fixed price (*Buy It Now*) items that are not current auctions. These items appear only in your eBay Store. Your eBay Store items are not listed in the eBay auctions.

eBay Stores have a little more pizzazz than a seller auction listings but not much. You get a heading above the list of items that you can customize. The possibilities are not great, but you can add some text and a digital graphic or photograph. The list of items itself is virtually identical to eBay auctions.

Although an eBay store is a lack luster storefront, it does put you where the traffic is and doesn't cost much. That's a good combination. It's as easy as eBay to use. And it's likely to be more cost-effective than operating your own website. A link beside your eBay user ID in your auction listings goes directly to your eBay store. Look for the traffic for eBay Stores to increase as buyers catch on to the stores. The eBay Stores make up the eBay mall, in effect, and have the potential to become another major focus of buyers' attention someday soon.

What Else?

OK, so the eBay seller auction list or the eBay Store aren't exactly spectacular as ecommerce websites. But they're easy to use and easy to navigate. Every one of your auction webpages links to them. You can even use your eBay Store URL to link to your Store from elsewhere on the Web. (You can do the same with the URL for an auction list and an auction ad.) Not a bad deal! After you read Chapter 20, it may look like a better deal than it does now.

Andale Store

The Andale Store is simply the Bay store dressed up (see Figure 19.2). It has a pleasant appearance with thumbnail photographs and is easy to use. A click on an item (thumbnail) takes you directly to the requisite eBay auction.

Andale projects part of the Store to the bottom of every eBay auction ad (only four thumbnails show) as the Gallery. This is a cross-selling device. It enables a bidder to easily click and enter a sellers gallery. So long as all the items in the Andale Store are eBay auctions, eBay should have no objection to the link.

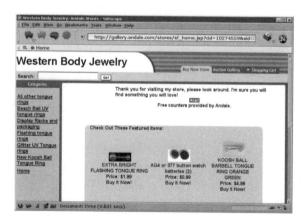

Figure 19.2   Andale Store. ©1999-2003 Andale Inc.

Dangerous Threads

Bob and Debbie have been in the retail business for 13 years selling clothing and leather goods (Dangerous Threads). In 2001, they closed their store in Nashville and focused on building up their eBay retail business, primarily in leather goods.

Previously, they manufactured the leather goods sold in their store (see Figure 19.3). Today they have the leather goods manufactured to their designs and specifications. They also distribute the leather goods and components to a few hundred retailers and wholesalers nationally. And they sell the leather goods on eBay to consumers. Bob says that they are now (early 2003) to the point where just the eBay retail sales are enough to support them without taking into account the manufacturing and distribution businesses.

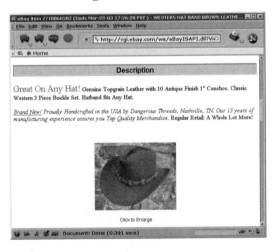

Figure 19.3   eBay auction ad featuring a Dangerous Threads leather hatband with conchos. ©1995-2003 eBay Inc.

Bob and Debbie do everything themselves in regard to the eBay sales. That's incredible considering they run 1,500 auctions a week. About 30 percent result in sales. That's 450 items a week to be accounted for and shipped. They use a combination of a manual system and eBay's auction management services to keep track of everything. They also use Andale's Gallery. They are interested in using more of Andale's services, but do not have the time to fully investigate and learn to use new software. They do take the time to carefully write copy for their auction ads and to carefully photograph their auction items with a digital camera.

About half their business is sales via *Buy It Now* on eBay. About 5 percent of their winning bidders don't complete the purchase transaction. They give a satisfaction guarantee, in effect, even though they don't necessarily advertise it. They haven't experienced any buyer fraud or credit card charge-backs and do most of their transactions through PayPal. They operate a separate website but make only a small percentage of their sales from that website. Their seller's list of auctions on eBay is a huge catalog by itself. Bob and Debbie do not have an eBay store. They have chosen to use the Andale Gallery instead.

They have reached the point where they need employees to break through to the next level of eBay retailing. As Bob told me, "Today, we don't have any employees. But call me back in a month, and we might have ten employees." If my other conversations with Bob are a predictor, were I to call back in a month, he would still not have any employees. He might, however, have several independent contractors helping him with his eBay business. He runs his manufacturing and distribution businesses using independent contractors exclusively.

Marketing

Remember that when you use an eBay storefront, you have little marketing burden. Your marketing is essentially internal (in eBay) and just a matter of links. It's all done for you. You are taking advantage of eBay's tremendous marketing power. In addition, you can enhance your marketing by writing good copy for your auction ads and *Buy It Now* ads. That is, you can include almost anything you want in the auction ads. This is one of the great benefits of an eBay Store—no huge marketing effort. The Andale Store is just a pretty version of an eBay seller auction list and fits right in with the concept of letting eBay do the marketing.

20

Other Storefronts

Carrying on your online retailing business beyond eBay is not advisable in many cases, for reasons that this chapter covers. The primarily reason is a marketing consideration. Although eBay reduces your need to market considerably, the minute you step out of the eBay system, marketing will consume 50 percent of your time, money, and effort. This is probably a situation you can wisely avoid without shortchanging your online retailing business.

Marketing

Read Chapter 1, which briefly mentions the role of marketing in any successful business. eBay is the only way to beat the 50 percent rule. The 50 percent rule states that 50 percent of your time, effort, and resources in any business will be devoted to marketing and selling. So, if you want to sell outside of eBay, you need to be ready to devote the necessary resources to your marketing and selling efforts.

Suppose you create a nice website for your business with all the appropriate ecommerce software. How are you going to get people to come to your website? Here are some things you can do:

Search Engines Get found by the search engines; that is, get near the top of the list on the first page of the search results. There is only one way to do this successfully. Hire a consultant who knows how to make it happen. You will find that just identifying such a consultant who's competent is tough.) It will cost you between $5,000 and $10,000, and in addition, it will require a huge amount of your time. There are no short-cuts here. This is online marketing at it's most effective, per-haps, but it isn't cheap.

Don't Believe

Don't believe anyone who tells you that they can get you to the top of the search engine lists for a $100 registration fee or by subscribing to a monthly newsletter. Never happen. The process is tedious and expensive.

Banner Advertising The word is out that banner advertising is not effective. That's not true. Advertising on other websites can be effective if part of an intelligently and professionally run advertising campaign. Unfortunately, it costs a lot.

Trading Links This will work. You can do it yourself. But you need a lot of links, and each takes time to arrange. It's doubtful that this alone is enough to sustain an online retailer. Joining a link-exchange group will help, but oddly enough that will hurt you in the search engine sweepstakes.

Affiliates Get affiliate websites to sell your merchandise. To do this effectively, you need affiliate software. modStop (*http:// modstop.com*) makes inexpensive affiliate software that plugs into Miva Merchant (see below), so cost is not a barrier here. Nonetheless, you will spend a lot of time arranging affiliate relationships.

Offline Advertising Can't beat this. But it sure is expensive. And you had better be ready to take the telephone orders that this approach will generate. They are likely to be greater than online orders.

Email You can build mailing lists (takes a long time) or buy a spamming campaign (requires huge numbers and can cost a lot). This can be effective. But various governmental agencies are moving toward controlling spam, making the future for this marketing method doubtful.

Discussion Groups Participation in discussion groups is another effective marketing technique for some merchandise. But participation often takes a huge amount time.

Community

Participating in the eBay community is not a prerequisite to success on eBay. Neither is participating in a community relevant to what your sell. But at least the latter has the potential of generating some sales. Only you can decide the best use of your limited time.

If you do participate in a community (forum, discussion group, listserv, mailing list, etc.), go lightly. Don't flood the group with thinly veiled sales information. Most groups frown upon crass commercialism. The groups use email in one form or another to communicate. Use email carefully. Email tends to be direct and abrupt, and it often seems rude. You can offend other participants quite easily.

These are not the only marketing techniques you can use to promote a website business. The sampling here illustrates that marketing requires large resources of time, effort, and money. It's likely your website will not get the traffic required to sell a reasonable amount of merchandise without effective marketing.

Selling from a website is a much different business than selling on eBay.

Website

To be effective for ecommerce, a website must meet certain criteria. It should be attractive and have a professional look. It requires ecommerce software, including a catalog, shopping cart, and checkout device. It also requires coordination of the business arrangements with the use of the software. And the website must be useable.

Your Own Website

Unless you can do most of the construction yourself, you're going to pay a few thousand dollars, at least, to build a commercial-quality website. Even if you can afford the money to construct it, you will have to pay additional money to operate it effectively. This is not a lightweight undertaking. You had better make sure you really need it before jumping into such a major project.

Can You Do It Yourself?

You can create your website yourself if you want to take the time to learn and experiment. Using HTML (Hypertext Markup Language) is not programming. Anyone can learn it, and webpage authoring programs minimize the amount you'll have to learn about HTML. See Appendices 5 and 6 for tutorials.

A Mall

There are a lot of malls on the Web. The idea is that they attract business just because they have a lot of stores. They usually provide webpage templates to use for storefronts and the usual ecommerce software.

The problem is that they don't really attract many customers but often charge fees as if they did. As a marketing method they perform poorly. The few malls that do have effective markets, such as Yahoo and Amazon, charge a lot of money; and you have to decide whether they are cost-effective.

On the other hand, if you don't use your website for selling, creating a relatively inexpensive brochure website in an obscure mall may prove cost-effective for customer service.

A Brochure

If you listen to Web gurus, you will learn that a website that's nothing but an online business brochure is worthless. That's crazy. It depends on what you want to do with it. If the idea is to attract customers, the gurus are right. It won't work. However, if the idea is to provide customer service, a brochure website can work just fine.

A printed business brochure explains the business, features the key personnel, provides some color pictures, includes the address and telephone numbers, and perhaps even provides references. A brochure website does the same. For a physical location it might even include a map to your store. It's easy and inexpensive to construct this type of website, and it works.

Customers want to know something about your business. It helps them decide whether they want to do business with you. They want to know how to contact you. And local customers want to know where to find you if you have a physical location. This makes things easier for your potential customers. Voila! This is a low-level customer service. And you can provide it even without ecommerce software.

You refer your customers there just to learn more about you and your business, and if you have a good story to tell about yourself, so much the better.

A Lot of Leeway

About Me serves this purpose on eBay and for an eBay Store. *About Me* isn't infinite, but just one webpage gives you a lot of leeway in creating an online business brochure.

I like brochure websites and *About Me*, but they do not by themselves generate any new prospective buyers.

Domain Name

When you create a website, you need a domain name. One way to look at the domain name situation today is that the pickings are slim. All the straightforward one-word names are gone, owned by someone else. They have value because they're easy to remember, and people actually use them to find things. For instance, if you sold clocks and put up a website at clocks.com, your customers would be able to remember your website address easily. A certain number of people looking for clocks will just type in "clocks.com" to see if they can find some, and they would find your website.

Another way to look at the domain name situation is that millions of two-word combinations are still available. Many might be suitable for your website and your business. For instance, "elegant-clocks.com" might be available and might fit your clock business. Or, how about "jonesclocks.com" if your name is Jones.

Your Domain Name

If you are starting from scratch, make your business name and your website address the same. It will be easier to build your brand, and it will be more convenient for your customers to find you:

> Elegant Clocks (*elegantclocks.com*)
>
> ElegantClocks (*elegantclocks.com*)
>
> Jones Clocks (*jonesclocks.com*)
>
> JonesClocks (*jonesclocks.com*)

Avoid extensions such as .net, .org, .biz, and the like. The good one-word names are taken for those extensions too, and the offbeat extensions will make it confusing for your customers to use your Web address. Stick with .com.

Go to the Whois search at *http://www.netsol.com* to find out if a name you have chosen is available. If not, choose another. You can register a domain name for as little as $9 per year at a domain name registrar. As soon as you make your choice, register the name immediately. Someone else could make the same choice at any time and register before you.

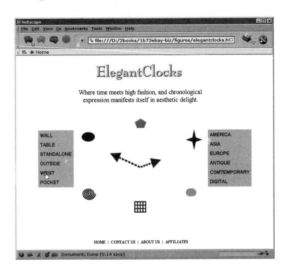

Figure 20.1   Mock website for Elegant Clocks.

Keep in mind that your email address will be the same as your website.

suzanne@elegantclocks.com

suzanne@jonesclocks.com

or

admin@jonesclocks.com

sales@jonesclocks.com

staff@jonesclocks.com

Domain names are not case sensitive; that is the characters can be uppercase or lowercase or any combination. Thus, you can publish the Web addresses mentioned as:

ElegantClocks.com

JonesClocks.com

Suzanne@ElegantClocks.com

Sales@JonesClocks.com

Names are important. Take some time to read about domain names in an Internet book and familiarize yourself with how they work.

eBay ID

Make your eBay ID the same as your domain name to help build your brand. The easier you can make things for your customers, the better. This will require you coordinating an eBay ID that's available with a domain name that's available.

If you're dead set on getting a one-word name that suits your business, that name may be available for sale. Look up the owner in Whois, and try to negotiate a purchase. The value of domain names seems to go up and down with NASDAQ (the virtual stock market). When NASDAQ is low, you may be able to purchase the domain name you want inexpensively.

Prefixes

You can add a prefix to a domain name, and it's like getting a completely new domain name. For instance, if you have the domain name clocks.com, you can use

alarm.clocks.com

grandfather.clocks.com

sundial.clocks.com

and the like. (Only the owner of the root domain name can arrange this.) You simply put a period in front of the domain name and add whatever you want to. The prefixed domain name acts just like any other domain name. It will cost you an extra monthly fee for each additional name that you create this way with most host ISP's, but it might be worth it if you have a use for it. Unfortunately, you will have to educate your customers to put in that extra period.

eCommerce Software

If you sell from your website you will need to use ecommerce software. Such software is available at virtually every host ISP. However, there are dozens of different ecommerce software programs, and you will want to find one you can stick with. If you use whatever is available today and then change to another host ISP tomorrow, you may have to start over again. That would be very painful. It's better to find ecommerce software you like and then find a host ISP that operates that particular ecommerce program. If you grow to dislike the ISP, you can switch to another ISP that supports your ecommerce software.

Features

The typical features included in an ecommerce software package are a catalog, shopping cart, and checkout device. That seems simple enough. However, the software features for creating a catalog vary greatly. A shopping cart is reasonably straightforward. But a checkout device can run dozens of different processes, which may or may not be included. Therefore, it pays to compare ecommerce software packages carefully to know exactly what you're getting.

Miva Merchant

Miva Merchant (*http://www.miva.com*) has evolved to be one of the leading ecommerce software packages for small businesses. It features the requisite catalog, shopping cart, and checkout device. Its features, as is, are very robust. In addition, Miva has designed Merchant to accept plug-ins so that third-party software developers can write add-on programming for it. As a result, you can buy plug-ins (add-ons) to make Miva do almost anything except dance the polka at a German restaurant. One of the plug-ins I like best is one that creates an affiliate marketing system for you.

What's the significance to you? With Miva, for an inexpensive price you can create an ecommerce system that equals the features of a corporate system costing hundreds of thousands of dollars. This is a terrific advantage for you once you build up some business volume.

Merchant on eBay

eBay with all its catalog programming expertise chose Miva Merchant to operate the eBay Store for a few years. This is where eBay sold T-shirts and other eBay souvenirs. Today it has been renamed the eBay-o-rama and operates on a different system.

Miva Merchant costs about $500, with yearly upgrades costing about $200. It quite possible for a nonprogrammer to install it, but it isn't the easiest thing you'll ever do. Once set up, it's very stable. It accepts uploads from a database to populate (fill) the catalog (see Appendix 4 for a description of a website system). This is the best way for a small business to operate a website catalog.

modStop

This software developer has created dozens of plug-ins for Merchant. Check it out (*http://www.modstop.com*). Just trying to understand what each of their plug-ins does is the equivalent of taking a business course in ecommerce.

Figure 20.2   modStop website. ©2002-2003 modStop.com.

Veeo

This software developer (*http://veeo.com*) has created a Merchant plug-in for eBay auction management. This gives you the choice of using an infinitely flexible program designed for ecommerce and of having an auction management program as well. It's worth comparing to the other auction management services available.

Miva Host ISP

To use Merchant your ISP has to have a Miva server. Over 200 ISPs run Miva servers, so you have choices. You can also find a

Miva host ISP that will provide Miva Merchant to you so that you don't have to buy it. In other words, the host ISP sets up and operates Merchant for you leaving you only to populate the catalog with merchandise from a database. This can save you a lot of work and perhaps some money too.

Miva Website

I'm not trying to sell you Miva Merchant, but it's worth reporting to you just because it's such a robust program, particularly as extended by all the plug-in written for it. A visit to the Miva website (*http://miva.com*) can be very educational because everything you need for ecommerce is there. If Miva doesn't provide it, Miva provides a link to it.

Database

A catalog for products is the heart of every ecommerce program. Invariably an ecommerce catalog is a database. You enter data about your products, and the software turns the data into (populates) a catalog.

Using an ecommerce catalog database can be slow and tedious for a small business using a host ISP. If you have a lot of items in your catalog (i.e., over 100), you will probably find it easier to maintain your catalog database offline in a database manager like Microsoft Access. You simply enter data and make changes on your own computer and then export the data in a data file (in an ASCII delimited file). You upload the data file into Merchant. That updates your website catalog.

Uses a Database

Andale Lister Pro (see Chapter 17) is essentially a database that works just as described above. You use its table easily and quickly offline and then upload the data to create your auction ads or eBay Store ads.

A large business works in a database on a dedicated server system that also powers its website online. This is not cost-effective for a small business. Instead, working in a database on your own computer is fast and efficient. Then uploading the updated data to an ecommerce application is quick and easy (once you catch on to the routine).

What's the difference between a database for a large business and one for a small business in regard to use online? It's not necessarily the number of records (rows) and fields (columns). There is one small business I know of that uses Merchant for 9,000 different products. Rather, the difference is the number of *concurrent* users (the number of website visitors downloading catalog webpages at exactly the same time). Database systems for large businesses are built to handle many more concurrent users.

Concurrent Users

In general, you can think of databases handling concurrent users as follows:

Access	4
Microsoft SQL Server	100
Oracle	10,000

Remember, the concurrent users are just a small percentage of the people visiting your website at any time. Visitors are using your website only while they're downloading a webpage, not while they're reading it.

Merchant has its own built-in database. There is no relationship between how Merchant performs online and what database you happen to use on your own computer to maintain your data.

Auction Management Service

If you use an auction management service to manage your eBay business, you may be able to use its ecommerce devices on your website. Such services often provide both database listings (catalogs) and checkout devices. By using the same system for both your eBay auctions and your ecommerce website, you will save a lot of confusion and eliminate a few learning curves.

How Many Domains?

Can you have your website at more than one domain? Yes, you can. For instance, suppose your domain is clocks.com hosted by Online King ISP. You like Online King because it provides you with almost all the Web services you need. But it doesn't provide Miva Merchant. You don't want to change to an ISP that does provide Miva Merchant. In fact, you don't have to. You can stay at Online King and get your Merchant services somewhere else.

Example

Supposed the host ISP Commerce Master (commerce-master.com) does provide Merchant. You can keep your ecommerce services (Merchant services) with Commerce Master. Your root Web address will be commerce-master.com/clocks/, and the various URLs for your Merchant service will follow from that.

The links to your Merchant service from your website (clocks.com) will take website visitors away to the other domain (commerce-master.com/clocks/). Since you control all the webpages (and links) at commerce-master.com/clocks/, however, it doesn't matter. You can bring your website visitors back (via links) as easily as you sent them there. In other words, you can seamlessly integrate the two domains into one website. You can even integrate additional domains into the website. This is what you have to do when no host ISP provides all the services you need.

Will Website Visitors Notice?

Will your website visitors notice if you take them from one domain to another via your website links. Not likely. It will all seem like one website to them.

A Grander Website

As you will have gathered from reading this chapter, individual websites (or services offered at individual websites) can be (building blocks) for a grander website. So, consider this idea. You build a brochure website with your own domain name, a good idea in any event. You use Andale (or comparable auction management service) to manage your eBay effort, a good idea in any event. You integrate your Andale catalog and checkout device into your brochure website. And voila! You have an full-fledged ecommerce website. This is an easy and intelligent way to go that will work for many eBay businesses.

When you're in business on the Web, choosing a host ISP can become one of your most important decisions. Let's take a look at four different situations:

1. Your dial-up ISP provides you with a website as well as a connection to the Internet, and you only need a brochure on

the Web. Use the website provided by the ISP for your brochure. It won't cost you any extra. Suppose your dial-up ISP is Local Digicenter. Your Web address might be localdigicenter.com/clocks/.

2. Your dial-up ISP provides you with a website as well as a connection to the Internet, and you only need a brochure on the Web. But you want to use your own domain name. Ask the ISP to provide your website with your domain name. This will cost extra, but you can use your own domain name for your Web address.

3. Your dial-up ISP doesn't provide websites. You only need a brochure on the Web. Get a free website at a place like Geocities at Yahoo (*http://geocities.yahoo.com*) and use it for your online brochure. Or, go to a host ISP for a website and pay a fee.

4. You want to operate a full-fledged business website including ecommerce software. First, you need to plan your website and determine what services you will need. You need to carefully compare the offerings of a number of host ISPs. Pick one that offers you the most useful selection of services. If you need additional services not offered, use another host ISP just for those special services (i.e., two domains for one website).

Bonding to eBay

If you can bond your ecommerce website to your eBay auctions, your website might produce significant sales. Notice that I didn't say "link." eBay no longer permits a link from your auction ad to your website. Consequently, to bond your auction ads to your website to generate traffic, you have to figure out some clever way to do so that doesn't break the eBay rules.

One way is to put your URL in your auction ads as part of your address:

ElegantClocks
541 Grainline Street
Topeka, Kansas 61301
www.elegantclocks.com
(492) 606-8749

A URL by itself without the HTML anchor (link) markup is just a published URL, not a link. This is a simple way to let potential buyers know where to find your website so long as eBay continues to permit it. eBay could outlaw it as eBay has outlawed the link. Indeed, eBay has strict rules about it that you need to review.

Before you construct your own website with the idea of bonding it to your eBay retailing, you need to ask yourself, What am I trying to accomplish that I can't accomplish with an eBay store? If you simply want to sell more of the same items, beefing up your eBay store is probably a better strategy.

You need a special situation for the bonding idea to work well. Suppose your core business is selling items in bulk, say a dozen at a time or a gross at a time. If you sell just individual items on eBay, it can act as a lead-in to selling the same items in bulk on your website. For example, suppose you sell doorknob-locksets to residential construction customers (e.g., do-it-yourselfers or small residential contractors). You offer one model in an eBay auction each week and make it apparent in your auction ad that you have plenty more available. A potential bulk customer using the eBay search engine will find your auction ad and presumably find out about your website by reading the ad.

The customer will then go to your website and buy two dozen sets for a construction or rehab project. In other words, the auction ad is a lead-in for larger sales. If you can make this work, you may be able to justify the cost of constructing and operating a website without doing the immense amount of marketing it takes to promote a website. Again, you need to review the eBay rules to make sure you're not breaking them with any scheme you implement. This is one area in which the eBay rules have been evolving and getting stricter.

About Me

You can still put a link to your website in your About Me page. And you can put a link to your About Me page in your auction ad. Do it.

eBay's Hidden Market

The eBay market is $14 billion per year as eBay claims (2002), right? Not exactly! The eBay market is larger, although how much larger is difficult to say. Here's a real life example.

We were buying network equipment (new) to build a network for our new charter high school campus. We needed fiber optic cable. We found three reels on eBay from one source, enough to wire our entire campus. The eBay transaction was $1,200 for three spools. Incidentally, this was a savings of about $9,000. We drove to San Jose (from the northeast San Francisco Bay Area) to pick up the cable and were very happy to save so much money for the school.

The seller was a digital company that was getting out of the wiring business. The seller had a huge surplus inventory of new network parts. While picking up the reels of cable, we vowed to return with a wish list and purchase equipment and odds and ends.

As construction projects go, ours changed. A trench was rerouted to save $5,000 in construction costs. Unfortunately, it required our Tech Committee to install fiber optic cable runs for an extra 500 feet. In addition, cabling experts advised us that we needed a little more cable for our original runs. The bottom line was that we needed a lot more fiber optic cable. The cost was to be about $20,000 (to save $5,000, right?). Fortunately, the original seller had plenty of additional fiber optic cable. Our cost to purchase it was only $2,300. This transaction resulted from a few phone calls and happened off eBay. (The seller had not diligently pursued selling the additional cable on eBay.)

When we drove down to pick up the next few reels of cable, we took our wish list of network parts. We spend almost three hours going through the seller's inventory. As a result our total purchase for the day was about $3,800 (including the cable). On the $2,500 (list) of new network parts we bought, we saved about $1,000. Again, this happened off eBay.

Out of Compliance?

Was our $3,800 second purchase in compliance with eBay rules? Yes. The additional cable was not currently offered on eBay. The new network parts, such as cable organizers and RJ-45 jacks, were not currently offered on eBay. Indeed, we didn't know whether these items had ever been offered for auction on eBay. The eBay rules did not govern our second transaction, even though it was three times as large (in dollars) as our first transaction.

Implications

What are the implications for off-eBay sales? First, you must consider them as an important part of the eBay market. Second the implication for eBay is a loss of potential revenue. Third, any seller can pursue aggressively off-eBay sales (resulting from eBay) to maximize profits. However, if you get too blatant about it, you may be violating an eBay rule.

The Hidden Market Exists

The hidden market exists. It's an important market. It results from bringing a buyer and seller together for one transaction, who later do another transaction not necessarily via eBay. Although impossible to estimate accurately, the hidden eBay market may be almost as large as the visible eBay market.

eBay's Loss of Potential Revenue

There are two aspects to eBay's loss of potential revenue in regard to the hidden market. The first is the loss on transactions that break the eBay rules. This happens when a buyer contacts the seller about an item being auctioned and then buys it outside the eBay auction process denying eBay its fee (see Rules below).

The second is the loss on transactions between a buyer and a seller introduced to each other by an eBay transaction, who proceed to do additional business with each other regarding items not auctioned on eBay. eBay will never be able to do much about this hidden market. The only way it could attempt to control this market is through the honor system, and that would never hold up for transactions involving items that were never even offered on eBay.

Nonetheless, you have to sympathize with eBay. It misses collecting revenue for a huge number of transactions between buyers and sellers that it introduced to each other through its online auction process. Because eBay has created a huge new market that offers wonderful new opportunities to us, it's in our best interest to take into account the eBay hidden market when considering eBay fees. We need to make sure that eBay continues to do a great job of regulating and expanding this huge new market, and to do so eBay needs adequate revenue. Keep this in mind the next time you complain about eBay fees and regulations.

Pursuing Off-eBay Sales

One of the themes of this book is to communicate the importance of customer service. It motivates buyers to do business with you again in future auctions. In a real sense, you continually build your brand on eBay. A better brand (a better reputation, better feedback) sells more online just as it sells more in a bricks and mortar business environment.

Additionally, the hidden market (off-eBay) is an omnipresent opportunity for you. For instance, let's say you purchased a carton of baseball caps and are selling them one at a time in individual auctions on eBay. A buyer buys a cap at one of your auctions and likes it so much that he contacts you about buying ten more of them for his baseball-fan buddies. This is the type of purchasing that you want to encourage.

Let's say that when the buyer requests to buy ten more baseball caps, you are currently running four auctions selling individual baseball caps on eBay. Do you have an obligation to eBay to refer the buyer to your auctions? Perhaps not. The buyer may not even know about these auctions. The buyer may only know about the one completed auction in which he bought the first baseball cap. He's not trying to get around eBay. He's just trying to buy more caps. And he's probably going to ask for a quantity discount. Even if you referred him to the current four auctions, he would still be six caps short.

Your obligation to eBay is to not make a sale outside of eBay in regard to a specific auction that has introduced (or reintroduced) the buyer to you. In this case, you have no knowledge that any of your current four auctions has introduced (or reintroduced) this buyer to you. As mentioned above, the buyer may not even know about these auctions. The buyer was introduced to you via a prior completed auction wherein eBay received its requisite fee. This buyer is simply approaching you to buy something (a bulk purchase) not offered on eBay. Therefore, this is a potential transaction that is not out of compliance with eBay rules.

Reintroduction

The hypothetical buyer seeking to purchase ten baseball caps is different from the buyer who previously bought a T-shirt from you and now seeks to buy a baseball cap. She sees one of your baseball cap auctions. Instead of bidding, she contacts you directly and requests to purchase a baseball cap. The baseball cap auction has, in effect, introduced her to you, and you are obligated to sell to her through the auction. This is, in actuality, a reintroduction, but it would violate the spirit of the eBay rules to treat it as anything but an introduction.

Difference of Opinion

Keep in mind that eBay—or someone else—may have a different interpretation of the eBay rules than the author of this book.

You can see from this legalistic discussion of off-eBay transactions that you always have an obligation to eBay to determine whether you are in compliance with eBay rules. Certainly there are huge numbers of situations where you can make sales resulting from contact with eBay buyers that do not violate eBay rules. These sales can be a profitable and routine part of your eBay operations. Selling additional items (particularly bulk items and expendable items) is a strategy you need to back up with promotions and advertising. It's all part of building your brand.

Rules

When a buyer contacts the seller about an item being auctioned and then buys it outside the eBay auction process, it denies eBay its fee. This is a breach of a member's agreement with eBay and is unconscionable. Biting the hand that feeds you (denying revenue to the organization that has created this wonderful new market) is not a sound business strategy. Nor is it a morally defensible business strategy! Everyone should follow the rules, and pay eBay the fees it deserves.

One can sell a series of items on eBay that lead into more sales off eBay for which one doesn't have to pay an eBay fee. And one can do it without breaking eBay rules. Why would anyone break the rules to stiff eBay for its fee on one of the auctions they ran on eBay? Not nice. eBay is a wonderful marketplace. Everyone should do their share to support it. Follow the rules and pay eBay its fees.

Advertising

In your advertising, you can expand your business by appealing to the hidden market. For instance, when you sell one item on eBay and have many more in stock, you can offer to sell multiple items in your eBay auction ad. Sample:

> Buy this high-quality Yankees baseball cap and wear it for years. It's made from a cotton-polyester blend that keeps you cool and yet is highly durable. The triple-sewn visor

has a waterproof stiffener that will not melt in the first rain. Contact us at sales@tagf-inc.com for team availability and quantity pricing.

In *eBay the Smart Way* I suggest that one can use an eBay auction as a form of advertising. In the early days of eBay, you could even put a hyperlink to your ecommerce website right in your auction ad. Today eBay outlaws the link for most auction ads (real estate is one of the exceptions) but doesn't outlaw advertising words that express a web or email address.

Links Outlawed?

Does eBay absolutely outlaw seller website links in auction ads? Sort of. You can't put a real link (HTML) into an auction ad, but you can advertise a link. That is, you can publish a non-functioning link expressed as a Web or email address (without the HTML markups). And many sellers do so.

When you have only one item to sell, you can still advertise your ecommerce website and your email address in your auction ad. You want people to visit your ecommerce website and potentially buy additional merchandise. You want people to be able to get a hold of you easily; it's part of good costumer service. And when you have additional inventory of the item in the auction ad, you will want to advertise that more items are available upon request. When you do this, the advertising can be effective. One item always being auctioned with an effective auction ad can be a terrific ongoing advertisement and help you sell many more items off eBay than on eBay. But be sure to include your website and email addresses.

In Practice

In order to generate a reasonable number of off-eBay bulk purchases or even individual purchases, you will need a considerable number of eBay auctions.

Buyers

Put yourself in the place of a buyer. You find a set of steak knives you need in an eBay auction ad. But you need more than one set because you're buying for your bridge club of 225 members. Unfortunately, eBay tends to cater to individuals rather than bulk buyers. In addition, many sellers shoot themselves in the foot by putting a bare minimum of information in their auction ads. So, you get ads like this:

> Set of six deluxe stainless steel steak knives with brown wooden handles.

A much better ad, at a bare minimum, to generate both individual purchases and bulk purchases might include the following:

> Set of six high-quality stainless steel steak knives with 5" blades and extra-large oak handles lacquered to a lustrous golden brown. These knives will look good on any table and will never rust. Just the right size for gracious dining. Money-back guarantee. Contact us at sales@tagf-inc.com for quantity pricing.

eBay Stores

You can take advantage of the hidden market using an eBay store instead of a separate website. In this case, eBay gets its fees. I think for many eBay businesses an eBay store is a better investment than a separate website. You can put a link in your auction ads to your eBay store. And eBay puts a link to your eBay store beside your name at the top of the auction listing.

About Me Webpage

When all is said and done, you may want to forego doing your own ecommerce website. Everyone is different. Every eBay business is different. And every situation is different. This chapter gives you some alternatives for creating a full-fledged ecommerce website. This chapter also sends you the message that you may not need an ecommerce website. It just may not be worth the time and effort because of the marketing effort you will have to expend to make it work.

One thing is clear. It is worthwhile to do a good presentation on your *About Me* page as mentioned in Chapters 8 and 19. This is your opportunity to have a one-page business brochure website right on eBay, free. You will have to know a little HTML (see the HTML tutorial in Appendix 6) to do reasonable job of publishing your information, but it's well worth the effort. And unlike the auction ads, you can include a hyperlink to your website in your *About Me*.

One great thing about *About Me* is that eBay links to it from your auction ads and from your eBay Store ads. Regardless of what other website you create, be sure to put up a generous *About Me* page. Then link to it from everywhere, even outside eBay. It may be all you need.

21

Selling Internationally

Believe it or not, many American goods are in high demand outside the US where people cannot buy them or cannot buy them as inexpensively as they can in the US.

For instance, in Europe computer books are normally about three times as expensive as in the US. Consequently, Europeans like to buy computer books in the US, and what better place to buy them than eBay or Half.com.

Well, what about language? That's certainly a barrier to commerce. Keep in mind, however, that English has become the international business language. And it's growing. According to the Foreign Language Department of the Curso Experimental Bilingue, Sao Paulo, Brazil, (*http://the_english_dept.tripod.com/ esc.html*), about 750 million people speak English as a second language. Another 375 million speak it as a native language (about 275 million in the US). If you're wondering whether those abroad can use eBay (in English), there's hundreds of millions of people who can, if they have a computer.

English in Hyderabad?

What's one of the official languages of India, a country with a billion people? English. India has so many languages that even many schools are conducted in English, the common denominator.

There is a huge market around the world for American goods, a market that can speak English, just waiting to be tapped via eBay. This is an exciting opportunity for eBay businesses that want to expand their markets.

Selling

When I started selling some of my eBay books on eBay, about one-third of the buyers were from abroad. They sent cash in envelopes to make purchases. Don't ask me why. I suppose it was the easiest means of payment for them, and they didn't want to be refused the merchandise.

This is not a practice you want to encourage. If the envelope gets lost or comes without the money (not unlikely), the buyer will become frustrated and perhaps angry. You may be in danger of getting negative feedback. Give buyers abroad a specific means (or several means) to make payment.

What's the Difference?

What's the difference between selling here or abroad? Communication, shipping, payment, and fraud.

Communication

Sometimes the communication can become a little difficult because most people abroad don't speak English as well as you do. But you can usually work through that. Most people who learn a language academically can often write better than speak. So, be persistent with email.

The telephone is still not cost-effective for calls abroad, perhaps, but occasionally it makes sense to use it anyway.

Vonage

Vonage, the voice-over-IP telephone service mentioned in Chapter 4, provides low-cost telephone rates to many countries abroad. My wife recently spent two weeks in Singapore. I talked with her every night for 6 cents a minute via Vonage. Sounded like she was a block away.

Don't overlook digital online translators to communicate in another language. They are alleged to work haphazardly. Nonetheless, I found Babel Fish Translation at AltaVista (*http://babelfish.altavista.com*) to be reasonably accurate, and free.

Shipping

Although shipping is not as complicated as you might expect, it's a little more difficult to manage than domestic shipping. Here are some possibilities:

Airborne Express, *http://airborne.com*

DHL, *http://www.dhl.com*

Federal Express, *http://fedex.com*

Postal Service, *http://usps.com*

UPS, *http://ups.com*

You can get help with a variety of shipping and export issues on some of the websites above. These shippers ship to most countries.

Modern international shipping is more convenient, faster, and more dependable than in yesteryear. The expansion of modern shipping around the globe has really revolutionized shipping and opened great new opportunities for international trade. eBay is firmly planted in the middle of this revolution. Unfortunately, international shipping via many of the companies above is relatively expensive.

Payment

Receiving safe payment is the most difficult problem to resolve for international sales. Many eBay sellers just forgo the opportunities rather than deal with the complications and the rampant international credit card fraud. Fortunately, some reliable and safe payment methods are falling into place.

Read eBay's tutorial on international trading under services for buying and selling. It's the best introduction available free.

Western Union

Western Union enables people in other countries to send you payment via wire for an auction item purchased on eBay in the US. Whether the price is right is the question. But it's possible and secure.

PayPal

eBay had a good progressive partner in Wells Fargo Bank with which it put together the BillPoint payment system to compete with PayPal. Nonetheless, PayPal was the market leader and remained so. In fact, PayPal was so successful, it was taking over the world, literally. That's what motivated eBay to buy PayPal and give up its relationship with one of the most innovative banks in the country. I believe eBay sees an opportunity with PayPal to establish the leading international online currency for consumers. And, of course, that's good for the international auction business.

PayPal is now available in the following countries:

Anguilla

Argentina

Australia

Austria

Belgium

Brazil

Canada

Chile

China

Costa Rica

Denmark

Dominican Republic

Finland

France

Germany

Greece

Hong Kong

Iceland

India

Ireland

Israel

Italy

Jamaica

Japan

Luxembourg

Mexico

Netherlands

New Zealand

Norway

Portugal

Singapore

South Korea

Spain

Sweden

Switzerland

Taiwan

United Kingdom

As of late February 2003

Keep in mind that PayPal is relatively safe. The PayPal credit card holders are verified, and many PayPal members use their bank accounts instead of credit cards anyway. In regard to the countries above, PayPal has a variety of arrangements. The arrangements are changing—improving—and PayPal will bring more countries into the fold soon. Expect PayPal to expand rapidly and offer expanded transaction services worldwide.

Figure 21.1   PayPal multiple currencies webpage. ©1999-2003 PayPal.

Could it be that PayPal will end up being the tail that wagged the dog? Remember, PayPal is not limited to use on eBay. eBay with all its success is still only one marketplace. But PayPal can potentially go everywhere online. This is particularly important in international markets.

Make Your Peace

A number of sellers have had trouble dealing with PayPal. That doesn't surprise me. The explosive growth that PayPal has had to handle has resulted in significant lapses in customer service, I'm sure. But you can't afford to be at odds with PayPal. If you are, make your peace, and move on—with PayPal. If you try to go it alone without PayPal, you will not only hurt yourself in the US but will be at a significant disadvantage internationally.

This book cannot present an accurate picture of PayPal internationally. Things are moving too fast. Take some time and research PayPal's international services; and make it a point to refresh your understanding periodically. It's your license to international sales.

Even with PayPal

Even with PayPal you are going to have to learn about international financial transactions and currencies. If you're going to export, learning is the price of admission. For instance, PayPal claims to have less expensive conversion rates than its competitors. What does that mean? It means when someone pays you in Euros, you naturally want the Euros converted into dollars (unless you're planning a trip to Europe). There's a fee for the conversion.

International Money Orders

International money orders are available to locals from banks in foreign countries to make payment for eBay auction items. This is a traditional means of payment and is secure. But don't take any counterfeits, and require payment in dollars.

Checks

Yes, they use checks abroad too. And you can accept them. But wait until they clear before shipping. That is, make sure they clear. Don't just wait a certain number of days. This will cause a long delay, of course. And that's not good customer service. But when it comes to receiving payment, export can be a risky business if you're not careful.

If the check is in a foreign currency, you will want it converted to dollars. Between the time it is send to you and you receive it, the conversion rates can change, perhaps a lot for some unstable countries. That's difficult to handle gracefully, and it has the potential to lower your profits.

Fraud

Unfortunately, beyond the payment methods above, it's too risky to sell abroad. International credit card fraud is too widespread, and Americans make good targets. In Indonesia, middle-class college kids make a sport out of Internet credit card fraud. It's a rite of passage. They get credit card numbers when tourists use their credit cards. They also get them online from the Internet, hacking here and there.

Smart business people online refuse to do business with Indonesians, and smart tourists use travelers checks in the islands, not credit cards. Some other countries you will want to avoid in regard to accepting credit cards are listed in Chapter 15 in the International Fraud section. Just refuse to do business with people in such countries who insist on paying with credit cards.

Export

You need to learn the export business just to sell in foreign countries. For instance, you may have to include documents with your shipments to satisfy customs in other countries (e.g., invoice, shipper's export declaration, certificate of origin, and NAFTA certificate of origin). UPS provides information on exporting at its website under International Export (see the UPS Site Guide).

http://www.ups.com/using/services/intl/intl-guide.html

Review it, and you will start to get the flavor of international trade. Also read eBay's International Trading tutorial for background information under Services, Buyers & Sellers. eBay provides currency converters, which you can link to from your auction ad, among other devices.

Make an Alliance

You're always going to have better luck selling abroad when you can sell locally in the local language rather than English and sell via someone who can provide local customer service. If you are a niche seller on eBay, you will very likely be contacted by people from abroad desiring to make an alliance with you to sell your products in their locale. With this sort of an arrangement, you become something of a wholesaler, in effect. This is a great way to increase sales volume abroad, albeit at perhaps a lower sales price than selling directly.

This, of course is not an eBay idea, but your eBay business may generate the contacts that enable you to do business this way.

Buying to Sell

And how about finding lots of cool things abroad—via eBay in a country abroad—that aren't on the market here in the US yet. Fabulous opportunities.

Want to write off your next trip to Paris? Find something in France that you can buy on eBay there and sell on eBay here. Voila! You're in the export-import business. Then go visit the French seller.

What's the catch? You need to speak the language. It's tough to decipher those French eBay auction ads without knowing French.

Figure 21.2   eBay France. ©1995-2003 eBay Inc.

As this book went to print, eBay had auctions in the following countries:

Australia

Austria

Belgium

Canada

China
France
Germany
Ireland
Italy
Mercado Libre
Argentina
Brazil
Chile
Columbia
Ecuador
Mexico
Uraguay
Venezuela
Netherlands
New Zealand
Singapore
South Korea
Spain
Sweden
Switzerland
Taiwan
UK

What a wonderful way to buy exotic foreign goods that you would never see otherwise without a visit! This is a great way to look for merchandise abroad without an expensive plane ticket.

Keep in mind that eBay auctions in the UK and Australia are in English. They may not be the most exotic foreign markets, but you may be able to find something interesting to buy and then resell on eBay in the US.

Make an Alliance

If you can buy in France and resell in the US for a good profit, you can attempt to establish an alliance with a French retailer. She supplies you in quantity at a low price, and you sell in the US on eBay. The possibilities expand.

Buying

You just want to buy merchandise or machinery at low prices for your business, and there are some attractive purchases available abroad that you've heard about. Why not look for them on eBay? Alas, we again run into the language barrier. Buying on eBay in foreign countries requires one to know the local tongue.

Merged Markets

eBay has merged some markets into one. The antique market, prior to eBay fragmented by geographical borders, now stretches across borders like it never did before eBay. It has substantially changed the market for antiques. In the future, this will happen again and again in market after market as eBay emerges as a huge and truly international marketplace.

The old barriers preventing markets from different countries merging were communication, distance, and language. The Internet has provided easy and inexpensive communication. It has also done its part to make distance irrelevant to international commerce. New aggressive shipping companies such as FedEx have made shipping more convenient.

The last barrier still standing is language.

As mentioned above, language works in the favor of those who speak English, the international business language. It works reasonably well when we want to sell something abroad. There are hundreds of millions of people who speak English. Many of them are able to buy on eBay in the US. But it doesn't work perfectly, because hundreds of millions more don't speak English and never will.

The large number of English-speaking people abroad who decide to sell us something on eBay in the US can put up auction ads in English, and we are willing, waiting, and understanding buyers. But we have little control over what they offer.

It's when we go to buy on eBay in another country that the language barrier is the greatest disadvantage. We need to know the language to buy on a foreign-language eBay.

Thus, when you discuss the merger of markets, the question arises, Merger for whom? For Americans buying on eBay in foreign countries, there's little merger. The language barrier is a real obstacle. For English speaking people abroad buying and selling on eBay in the US, the merger is real. The language barrier is of little import.

Consequently, for all we have said about the wonderful opportunities to sell our goods abroad to the vast numbers of English-speaking peoples of the world, we are still at a sad disadvantage when we go to buy abroad on eBay in foreign countries.

New Yankee Traders in Force

Thanks to eBay, the new Yankee traders (eBay businesses) are going international in force. We have lots to sell that the world wants. Don't be left out of the international markets. Be careful and learn to cope. The profits are just over the horizon but will be here soon. For additional information read *A Basic Guide to Exporting*, 3rd Edition, Alexandra Woznik, World Trade Press, 1999. Visit the World Trade Press website for additional information on export/import.

http://www.worldtradepress.com

For an Encore

For more on eBay import/export, check *http://bookcenter.com* from time to time to see what's new. Look for Trade Affiliates (*http://tradeaffiliates.com*), which brings businesspeople from different countries together to do business.

22

Determining Your Profit

Calculating your profit (net income) is more than arithmetic. It's knowing what to include in income, and more importantly what to include in expenses. Then it's knowing what to compare your profit to. After all, you do have other choices; you can get a job or keep the job you already have.

To begin this chapter we're first going to consider the question, to what other opportunities should you compare your eBay business profit? That will make you more sensitive as to what expenses to include in your net income calculations, to be discussed later in the chapter.

How Are You Doing?

You go on vacation to a pleasant beach town in Florida and find a local bike rental company doing a booming business renting the old fat tire bikes from the mid-twentieth century. You inquire where they get the bikes. It turns out they purchase them in bulk from the Kingstown Bike Company in Layton, Oklahoma. Kingstown makes a business of selling these old fashion bikes—adult versions only—in fleet quantities to resort town bike rental places.

Figure 22.1   Beach town in Florida. ©2002 CocoaBeach.com.

You get the idea that perhaps you can sell the bikes one at a time to baby boomers who are starting to reach retirement and may be nostalgic for an old fashion bike to ride around in their retirement resort towns. Kingstown agrees to sell you these bikes individually at wholesale and drop ship them disassembled via UPS inexpensively. You don't like Kingstown's incomprehensible assembly instructions, so you provide them with your own version, to be sent along to your customers.

Then you get on eBay and start auctioning them. You are very successful.

You currently work at a normal eight-hour-per-day job where you make $30,000 a year with two weeks of vacation. This is 2,000 hours a year, a nice round number to use for standard calculations. You are making $15 per hour. As you become more successful on eBay, you have less and less time for yourself. Your eBay operation takes up your evenings and weekends. You start keeping track of the hours you spend on your eBay auctions. When you look at your eBay income, you see that it's getting close to $15 per hour. You anticipate that in two months it will be up to $15 per hour as you streamline your eBay operating procedures. If you quit your job in two months, you anticipate you will be able to work at least 40 hours a week on eBay auctions.

Your plan pans out. You quit your job. You are still making $30,000 per year but now you're doing it retailing on eBay. You are able to work a schedule that suits you, and you don't have to listen to your boss yak at you any longer. Although your sales (auction) revenue has leveled off, you figure that you will be able to find other things to sell on eBay eventually that will provide additional income. How are you doing?

Not Very Well

The benefits on your regular job included some—perhaps all—of the following:

- Health insurance

- Dental insurance

- Disability insurance

- Unemployment insurance

- Life insurance

- Life insurance for spouse

- Profit sharing

- Pension fund

- FICA

Your employer made major contributions to all the benefits while your contributions were minor. Typically the benefits for a good job from an employer's point of view cost about 10 to 40 percent of an employee's salary. Assume the benefits on your job cost your employer 15 percent. Thus, you were really making $34,500 on your job if you include the value of the benefits. So, right now making $30,000 for a 40-hour week on eBay, you are really behind, not even, with your old job.

What's the point? The point here is to compare apples to apples when comparing the profit of an eBay business to the compensation of a job you now have or a job you can get. Don't kid yourself.

Do You Really Need These Benefits?

The benefits that employers typically offer are sometimes perceived as irrelevant by young people. However, when you get married and have a family, these benefits become much more important. Indeed, the benefits that employers offer are based on demand from mature employees who do have families. They offer a greater measure of security than a simple salary.

Health Insurance

Without health insurance, the medical care that you may need one day may not be available to you. If it is available to you, it may bankrupt you. Health insurance is not a luxury item. You need this regardless whether you have a job or are making your living on eBay. Specifically, you need group health insurance that costs less and has fewer restrictions than individual health insurance.

Fortunately, eBay now has a health insurance program in which you can enroll. If that doesn't suit you, there are thousands of business organizations and associations that offer group health insurance plans to their members. Join one and get the group health insurance. Unfortunately, eBay's plan (Marsh Advantage America, available to PowerSellers) is not a group plan although it does offer advantages that you cannot normally get by getting heath insurance on your own.

Dental Insurance

A dental problem won't bankrupt you, but it can sure put a dent in your disposable income. Dental insurance typically pays only half the cost of most dental procedures, but that's a welcome relief when you need a filling, crown, or something more serious. As it is for health insurance, a group dental plan is less expensive.

Disability Insurance

Disabilities come in different flavors. One is an injury incurred while performing your job (e.g., broken ankle). Another is a general disability not caused by your job (e.g., prolonged disease). Some disabilities are temporary, some permanent.

Workers' compensation covers injuries incurred on the job. However, to get workers' compensation coverage, which is state regulated, you may have to be an employee or find comparable non-employee coverage. Workers' compensation insurance is not terribly expensive because most employees don't get injured on the job unless they are in hazardous occupations.

General disability insurance, however, tends to be expensive. It is designed to provide income for people who become disabled as a result of any injury or illness. Since most people are reasonably healthy until they get past retirement age, disability benefits are not as widely offered by employers as other benefits. Self-employed people also tend to overlook the risk until later in life.

Unemployment Insurance

This is provided and subsidized by government. It lasts for a limited time and is available only to employees.

Life Insurance

Life insurance is reasonably inexpensive if acquired via a group policy. When you're young, you need to have enough to bury yourself so as not to be a burden on your relatives. When you have a family, you need to have enough to get them off to a good start financially without you, should you die early. It's not fair to your family to leave them scrambling financially for survival after your early death. So, life insurance is a real need.

Pension Fund

It's impossible to retire comfortably on Social Security. You need to start putting something away early in your career in order to have a decent retirement. The tax laws allow a variety of individual retirement plans that can work well if you start when you're young and don't miss your annual contributions.

If you start when you're older, you're already behind. But it still makes sense. For instance, if you're 50 and have no retirement fund yet except Social Security, you have only fifteen years (until age 65) to salt something away into a tax-deferred retirement fund, right? No. You probably won't be able to afford to retire at 65. Consequently, you will have extra years to contribute to your retirement fund. Suppose you retire at 72. You will have 22 years to contribute to your retirement fund from the age of 50. That's a substantial amount of time.

FICA

Your employer pays a portion of your Social Security and Medicare taxes. When you're self-employed, you pay all. So, your pretax income for your eBay business will have to be higher than your base salary on your job in order to reach the same take-home paycheck.

Expenses

In order to determine your profit, you need to know your expenses. Your expenses are the sum of everything you spend to get products into the hands of sellers. Everything.

Estimating Expenses

Make an estimate. Nothing formal. When you get started, your accountant will help you set up a chart of accounts for your bookkeeping. For now, just make a few estimates to help determine whether an eBay business is for you.

Employees

Wages are a considerable expense when you have employees. Speaking of benefits, if you have employees, you may be expected to provide many of the benefits (above) to them, substantially increasing your employee costs. This is particularly true for loyal long-term employees. Consequently, an employee's wages are not your only employee expense.

If you have no employees, you still need to provide benefits for yourself.

Independent Contractors

These are employee substitutes. You need to pay them for services rendered. Once you get rolling, you can't do everything yourself.

Real Estate

So, you're working out of your home now in your eBay business, and it doesn't cost you anything, right? No. It does cost you, and you should use the value of your real estate use (rent) in your expense calculations. Calculations that include free real estate can be very misleading when it comes to comparisons to other businesses.

You may also be kidding yourself regarding your home. You're now using a bedroom for your office, so you decide to convert the back porch into a room. After all, your mother needs someplace to sleep when she visits. It suddenly appears obvious that the cost of converting the porch into a room is the real cost of having a home office.

Whether it's a bedroom, garage, or study that you use for your eBay operations, take into account the market value of the room.

(Note: This is a different idea than taking depreciation on your home business area for income tax purposes.)

If you are using real estate other than your home, include the rent in your calculations.

Equipment

If you already have the requisite equipment you need to carry on an eBay business, you still need to include it's cost in calculating your profit. You will have to replace it someday. Don't forget software, which is a type of digital equipment.

Supplies

You will start consuming office supplies and other supplies at a greater rate for business than for normal nonbusiness activities at home.

Transportation

If you need to use a vehicle a lot in your eBay business, include the expense at the IRS allowed mileage rate.

Utilities

You need to include electricity, heat, water, telephone, Internet service, and other ongoing services in your expense calculations. For a home office, some of these will have to be prorated. If you leave them out because you're already paying them, you will be kidding yourself.

Advertising

This can be a huge cost for most businesses. Fortunately, for an eBay business, it can be quite low.

Fulfillment

Running a fulfillment operation is almost like running a separate business, and you need to include the costs for that.

General

Other overhead costs that you incur in running a business.

Cost of Goods

This is the wholesale price of your goods plus the cost of transportation and storage.

Direct Costs

This is the cost of selling each item (e.g., eBay fees). Since different items may have different direct costs, this portion of your overhead is tied to what you sell.

Shipping & Handling

Don't forget, you can charge a shipping and handling fee to buyers. Whatever shipping and handling cost you over and above what you charge buyers is an expense. If it cost you less than you charge buyers, it is additional income.

Benefits

Don't forget the cost of benefits discussed earlier in this chapter.

Accounting

It isn't the purpose here to give you a basis for your accounting. Your accountant or bookkeeper can do that and provide more accuracy than this chapter provides. Rather this chapter is intended to raise your consciousness of what to include in your expenses to estimate your profit.

You can make a reasonable estimate of your expenses before you ever get to the point of hiring an accountant or bookkeeper—or before you learn to do the bookkeeping yourself. Write a list of expenses that you learned about in this chapter together with a list that is relevant to your own situation. Estimate them. Add them up. That's what it's going to cost you to operate your eBay business.

Profit

Estimate your income. If your estimated income is greater than your estimated expenses, you've made a profit. Well OK, it's just an estimated profit, not a real profit. Nonetheless, you can compare the estimated profit to your other earning opportunities.

23

Developing a Strategy

There are a number of considerations in building a strategy for creating and operating an eBay business. First is building a product profit model. Finding inventory (finding a niche) follows. Predicting the future and planning for it is important too; you may not have much time before the future comes moving in at a digital-age speed. Finally, handling growth becomes a serious consideration after you become successful. This chapter looks at the big picture.

What's missing from this chapter is what's taken for granted. It is taken for granted that you will run a well-organized and efficient business on eBay by using the requisite digital equipment, auction management services, and ecommerce software. This chapter is not about cost-cutting and becoming more efficient.

Commodity Products

Let's start with a product profit model based on commodity products. These are mass-produced consumer products widely available. A Panasonic VCR is a good example. When you buy this VCR, you're likely to buy it where you can find it at the lowest price instead of a retail outlet to which you are loyal. Perhaps the best value-added a retailer can offer for this product is a satisfaction guarantee.

Building a Product Profit Model

The first profit estimate (Chapter 22) has to do with your personal finances. The second has to do with the ideal product. Both are important to you. This section is about building a product profit model.

Using Numbers

To make comparative calculations use the following:

- 2000 work hours per year
- 50 work weeks per year (2 weeks vacation)
- 250 work days per year

These numbers are not absolutely accurate, but they're close enough. They assume you work a 40-hour week.

Personal Finances

Chapter 22 helps estimate the expenses to be charged against income in order to estimate the profit that you need to live off an eBay business. You also need that information to help you determine what products will help you achieve your desired profit.

For the purposes of discussion, let's say you need income of $40,000 per year to pay yourself and fund your benefits.

The Ideal Product

The ideal product is one you are willing to handle for the profit it generates (see Figure 23.1). Some people will gladly ship and account for 40 items a day to make a profit of $160 ($40,000 per year). Others wouldn't get into an eBay business where they had to handle 40 items per day and didn't make enough money to hire someone else to help. But how can you afford to hire someone else to help you on only $40,000 a year and still have enough left over to make a decent living?

Everyone is different and in different circumstances. Each product is different and requires a different degree of care in marketing and handling. You have to decide what your product profit model is. It's not that you're going to be able to do business exclusively with products that fit your model. Business is not that simple. Nevertheless, your product profit model is something against which you can measure all the opportunities you come across for selling inventory on eBay.

Would you handle 40 prepackaged mass-produced items a day? All you have to do is paste a mailing label on them and have UPS pick them up. Of course you have to do the accounting for them, too, and work with a wholesaler to keep the inventory coming in. In addition, that's 200 auctions a week that you have to run on eBay. But this probably isn't too much. This is probably an attractive business for many people for $40,000 per year. You have to make $4 profit per product (($40,000 ÷ 250) ÷ 40 = $4).

Would you handle 40 antiques (not commodity items) a day? You have to pack them for shipping and have UPS pick them up. You have to do the accounting for them. And you have to keep finding more to purchase for your inventory. In addition, you have to run 200 auctions a week. Antiques are unique and require communication with bidders that's more intensive than average. This seems impossible for one person to do, and you might decide you wouldn't even attempt it for $40,000 per year. You might want to pay at least two people $40,000 a year to help you, and you would want to make at least $60,000 a year yourself to manage such an operation. That requires an average profit of $14 per antique ((140000 ÷ 250) ÷ 40 = $14).

Figure 23.1   The ideal product.

If you have a bad back, you probably don't want to handle large heavy items. If you have an uncle who owns a local trucking company, you may feel perfectly comfortable selling large heavy items, because the family connection (large scale shipping) provides a competitive advantage for you.

If you love accounting, you may be willing to handle 40 items a day or even 80 items a day (with the help of software, of course). If you can't stand accounting, you may be willing to handle only five items a day.

Your garage size may limit what you do. Your working hours may limit what you do. Do you watch after the kids all day and start working only after your spouse gets home from a job?

You must take all things into consideration in building a profit model for the ideal product. You begin by determining how much you want to make per year. Then you decide how many items you can handle per day and under what circumstances. Then you can calculate how much profit you have to make per item.

> The ideal product is the one that makes the most profit for the least amount of work within your notion of what is acceptable.

Example

You need to make $40,000 a year but want to handle only five items a day. Each item can take more than an average amount of communication with bidders, but not a lot more. You're willing to order inventory, but you don't want to have to find inventory. Finally, you want to work a 40-hour week. You need to find products that you can order from a wholesaler and on which you can make an average profit of $32 (($40,000 ÷ 250) ÷ 5 = $32). This calculation gives you a guideline for decision making when considering inventory opportunities.

Another Slant on the Product Profit Model

The product profit model doesn't take into consideration passion. If you are passionate about the cell phone accessories business, for instance, then you might be better off pursuing that business for two reasons. First, your passion will fuel your motivation, and you will be more likely to be successful. Second, cell phone accessories have a bright future.

Nevertheless, doing a product profit model, or multiple models, for cell phone accessories will help you better formulate how to operate profitably in that particular market niche.

Calculating Profit

Calculating the profit on a product is simple yet complex. The ideal is simple. You subtract from the sales price the cost of the product and the amount of overhead allocated to the product. The remainder is your profit. Unfortunately, estimating the amount of your overhead is complex (but not impossible). Here's a simple example:

Sales price	$83
Cost of product	$47
Direct cost to sell product	$5
Overhead allocated to product	$9
Profit per product	$22

Time

Shouldn't the product profit model consider time? Yes. It's assumed that you will estimate the time spent handling each product and include it in your calculations. Still, you might want to take a systematic approach and consider time methodically, even going so far as taking time measurements for the various handling tasks.

What About Your Current Sales Plan?

You are an expert on digital voice recorders, transcription, and creating audio records. You have a current plan to sell voice recorders and related software and equipment on eBay. You perceive that there's a growing market for it. You don't need to do a product profit model, right? Actually, a profit model will give you a lot of insight into what you are doing or are about to do on eBay. Should you create a product profit model, you might come to one of several different conclusions. Here are some possibilities:

1. Your business will be profitable and reasonably easy to manage well.

2. You should sell related software and equipment but not voice recorders.

3. You should sell voice recorders but not related software and equipment.

4. You should look for another niche on eBay.

A product profit model is just another way of looking at the numbers. And each different way you can look at the numbers will bring additional enlightenment.

The Calculation Changes

When you grow, several things are likely to happen. Your overhead will increase because you will need more help both from people and possibly from additional software and equipment. You will need to readjust the overhead component of your profit-per-item calculation to keep it accurate. This is important to do to see where you're headed (see Handling Growth below).

Finding Inventory

Looking for inventory before you determine a product profit model is not going to be as fruitful as looking for it after you have such a model. There's plenty of inventory available. The trick is to find something that will sell and at the same time satisfy your product profit model.

Wheeling and Dealing

There are those who wheel and deal. It's almost a profession. You buy low and sell a little higher. You solve someone's problem by buying something from them at a good purchase price, and you turn around and present it as an opportunity to someone else. eBay is the perfect home for the wheeler-dealer. It's a huge unlimited market. The possibilities are infinite.

Not Derogatory

Wheeler-dealer is not a derogatory term. Most wheeler-dealers think of themselves as honest and straightforward. They pride themselves on putting together deals that help people, just as insurance agents pride themselves on selling insurance that protects people.

Wheeling and dealing is clearly a viable eBay business strategy. Buy whatever you can, wherever you can, at less than market price, and turn around and sell it on eBay at a higher price.

If you're a wheeler-dealer, your biggest problem on eBay is deciding whether to be a generalist or a specialist. Even as a specialist, however, you will not confine your business activities to a niche. Your outlook will always be broader. As long as you're careful and study your markets, you will have great success on eBay.

Unfortunately, most of us are not wheeler-dealers. Most of us cannot tolerate the uncertainty of wheeling and dealing. We look for something more reliable.

If you're not a wheeler-dealer, in order to be successful on eBay you need to pick a niche. That is, you need to restrict your selling efforts to a market that you understand and have confidence in. The trick is to find that niche.

Finding a Niche

Most people find their eBay niche naturally. If you sell voice recorders and related software and equipment as your job, it's a natural to quit your job and go into business for yourself selling the same stuff on eBay. Many people have been successful on eBay in a business based on a hobby, a job, a skill or profession, or an area of interest in which they have acquired some expertise. This is a time-proven way to get off to a good start on eBay. However, it isn't foolproof.

You need to add some hard business judgment to your evaluation of any niche that you consider on eBay. First, the niche must be big enough to make a profit. In other words, the niche must have enough people in it that you can expect enough sales to make money. Second, the niche can't be too big. If it's too big, it will attract a lot of competition. It will contain a lot of people, and the potential sales will be huge. It might be uncrowded today, but it will be overcrowded soon.

In our example, selling voice recorders for dictation and transcription is a large enough niche to potentially make enough sales for a considerable profit. It's not so large that it's likely to attract everyone and their brothers to sell in the niche.

On the other hand, if this niche were to be defined as audio recorders (including tape recorders, digital recorders, and other recorders intended for music), it would be a rather large niche with large potential sales. In fact, this particular niche is large and does attract plenty of competition.

If you can find a way to quantify the niche market you're considering, that will help you make a decision. Both Andale (*http://www.andale.com*) and HammerTap (*http://hammertap.com*) offer software that squeezes statistics out of eBay by categories, products, or sellers. Andale's works on its website and is free (see Figure 23.2). HammerTap's is a program (trial version available).

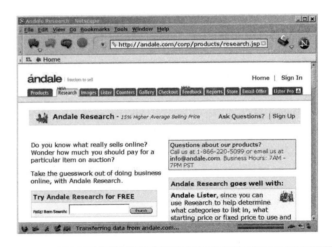

Figure 23.2   Andale free eBay research webpage. ©1999-2003 Andale Inc.

In addition, you need to consider whether your product profit model will work with the products to be sold in the niche. That's an important consideration covered at length earlier. Another consideration is the expertise threshold necessary to sell products in the niche. If extensive medical expertise is required, for example, that will keep most people (sellers) out of the niche.

Let's face it. Picking a niche intelligently is the toughest part of getting an eBay business going, particularly for those who don't naturally fall into a niche based on their hobby or their expertise. Don't take this process lightly. It's worth spending some time on. Pick the right niche, and you'll get off to a solid start on eBay.

Making Arrangements

Once you decide what your niche is going to be, you need to make arrangements to buy low and sell high. You need to find a supplier to keep your inventory replenished. For some sellers this will be a manufacturer. For others it will be a distributor. For some it may even be a discount retailer. And for some it may be a new source for every purchase.

Going to a trade show associated with your niche is perhaps the best way to get off to a quick start. The reference section of your library is another place to get off to a quick start. You can find directories of trade associations, manufacturers, wholesalers, and retailers as well as much other useful information in the massive volumes in the reference library (see Chapter 5).

The Web is another good place to find sources of inventory. Do some intensive searches to see what you can find. Find the contact information for the sales staff at manufacturers and distributors.

When you have identified some sources of inventory, do a few dry runs; that is, make some trial contacts with wholesalers. Call to ask whether you can become a retailer to sell a product. Find out what the requirements are. Each industry is a little different. Find out what special equipment, if any, you need. Learn about the hidden expenses in the industry. When you're ready to get serious about finding suppliers you will be able to put your best face forward. You'll sound like you know what you're talking about. Some suppliers are fussy about who they will sell to.

Sales Tax License

Before you start serious communications with suppliers, make sure you have your sales tax license.

Play the field. Seek the suppliers that offer the best deals. Don't commit to exclusives or take the first deal that you come across. Most industries are very competitive.

If you run into a roadblock, work around it. For instance, if a wholesaler won't sell you the products you need because it has given an exclusive to another retailer in your area, look for other sources. The retailer that has the exclusive might be a source. A retailer three states away might be a source. There may be a wholesale black market for the products.

If you base your selection of a niche on whether you can easily find suppliers, you may miss good opportunities. Base your selection of a niche on other analyses and then make a determined effort to find suppliers.

Predicting the Future

There's a reality to selling on eBay that you need to figure out for your particular business. Let's take the business of selling voice recorders (price range: $39 to $390). You decide to sell them on eBay because most places today sell them at full price on a 40 percent margin. You figure you can make a good business out of selling them on eBay on a 20 percent margin. You are 35 years old and have two children and a spouse to support, requiring you to make a certain minimum income each year. You start your eBay business, and it proves to be successful.

What happens when a 25-year-old with no children and no spouse comes along and decides to sell voice recorders on a 10 percent margin? And let's say that in every respect your business and the newcomer's business are equal except that the newcomer charges less for the products.

What happens when a 65-year-old retiree with no children at home but a spouse to help with the business comes along and decides to sell voice recorders on a 10 percent margin? And let's say that in every respect your business and the newcomer's business are equal except that the newcomer charges less for the products.

Clearly if the newcomers don't put you out of business, they may reduce your profits to the point where the business is no longer attractive to you. It just becomes too difficult to make enough money.

Isn't that what business is all about, including eBay business? It's competitive. To the lowest-cost operator go the spoils. Now, eBay claims to provide a level playing field for individuals and corporations, the little guys and big guys alike. It's supposed to be a "democratic" marketplace. And I think that's right. It is a level playing field today. Logically that means that eventually the lowest-cost operators will sell almost everything. And a 25-year-old or a 65-year-old can sell at a lower cost than you because they don't have dependents and require less income.

Theoretically, every niche on eBay will eventually belong to 25-year-olds, 65-year-olds, or perhaps 18-year-olds. The question for you (assuming you're not an 18-year-old) is, What happens when this trend comes your way? Here are some possibilities:

1. You are waiting for it. You spot it quickly. And you close down your business and cheerfully move on (perhaps to another eBay business).

2. It takes you by surprise, and your business falls off a cliff. You are devastated psychologically, and your finances aren't in

such good shape either. A real bummer and not an experience you would intentionally seek.

Of course it has happened already. Hardy businesses offline have been replace by small businesses on eBay. Hardy businesses on eBay have been replaced by lower-cost operators on eBay. It's not a new story. For instance, how many collectibles dealers have been put out of business by eBay since 1995? Quite a few. The ones who have survived are the ones who have learned to integrate eBay into their businesses enough to keep afloat. But business isn't what it used to be. The new collectibles dealers are individuals on eBay, many quite young.

Future Shock

You need to develop a strategy for the future when the lower-cost operators on eBay affect your eBay business adversely. First, you need to recognize what's happening as soon as possible when it starts to happen. You have to have planned your business response. And you need to have an exit strategy in the event that the most prudent course is to close down your business. Events tend to move fast in a digital environment, and without a strategic plan, you may not be able to respond quickly.

There is not a certainty that this will happen to you and your niche. Every market is different. Every product is different. Some niches last a long time for some people. But you have to keep your eyes and ears opened to the possibility that your niche will be invaded someday, and you need to be ready for the consequences.

Customer Service Again

Certainly first-rate customer service can go a long way toward protecting any business in a competitive environment. Providing good customer service on eBay can extend your profits in your niche for the longest possible time. Make customer service part of your strategy.

The Ultimate Strategy

Perhaps the ultimate eBay strategy is to always be ready to change niches. There will always be new products and new opportunities. For instance, when digital cameras first used flash memory (SmartMedia and CompactFlash), there were a few sellers on eBay selling a large volume of upgrade memory modules. Cameras typically came with 8 MBs of memory, and the upgrades contained 32 MBs, 64 MBs, or 128 MBs. It was a great market. Today that market is spread pretty thin among many sellers. It's a mature market now, but for perhaps a year it was a good opportunity for the quick and nimble.

Jumping from niche to niche can be devastating psychologically as well as financially unless you prepare for it. For instance, you can think of yourself as a voice audio expert. When your eBay business selling voice recorders dries up, you might easily be devastated. On the other hand, if you think of yourself as an eBay business expert, your attitude will be a lot different when the voice recorder business is taken over by lower cost operators. You'll think, "Boy, it was a great run and I'm glad I was able to start my selling career on eBay in a field I know, but now it's time to move on to another eBay business." If you can spot new niches and move into them quickly, you will always have opportunities on eBay. In order to do so, however, you must have a great curiosity about things in general and about new industries and new products in particular. That's why I believe going to regional and national trade shows is so important. That's where you see what's coming own the road. Indeed, there might be something coming down the road in your own niche that will enable you to stay in it profitably for a few more months or a few more years. If so, you'll probably see it first at a trade show. And if you don't see it, eventually someone else will.

And who is to say that you can't go back to working for someone else again as an employee for a year or two until you find your next eBay niche. Your strategy doesn't have to be 100 percent eBay.

Handling Growth

Growing larger is usually a sign of success. Thus, it's thought to be good to grow as large as possible. However, you need to look at growth cautiously in light of some of the issues covered above. The bigger you are the harder you will fall on eBay should your business be undermined by a lower-cost operator.

Don't get me wrong. I'm not antigrowth. You should grow as fast as you can and as large as you can on eBay under most circumstances. But do it smartly.

How do you grow smart? You maintain flexibility and keep fixed costs as low as possible. For instance, if you can grow to the point where five people are helping you but all five are independent contractors, it will be easier for you to cut back operations when sales slow down in your eBay niche, easier than if you had employees. If you maintain two weeks of inventory, you will be able to cut back easier and faster than if you have four months of inventory. If you have a month-to-month rental arrangement for your warehouse instead of a two-year lease, you will be able to cut back without a huge loss.

Unlike most offline businesses, many eBay businesses are vulnerable to being hurt immediately by new lower cost operators. That means to operate smart and to grow smart, you must be smartly flexible to the point where you can expand and contract your retail operation like an accordion.

Growth and Profits

The product profit model is handy to analyze growth. If you can grow and increase your profit per item, you have a potentially great business. If you can grow and keep your profit per item the same, you will make more money even after paying others to help you or after buying more software and machines. If your profit per item decreases as you grow, you can still make more money, but there's a limit on your growth. You better find out what that limit is before you grow so much that the risk and effort to run your business is no longer worth the profit.

Value-Added Products

For discussion purposes, a product to which a retailer can add substantial value is not a commodity. Value can be added in simple ways. It can even be automated. Or, value can be added in more complex or labor-intensive ways. Adding value provides you an opportunity to develop a stable market of customers that a low-cost operator cannot take away from you.

Mass-Produced Products?

Is it possible for mass-produced products to be value-added products? Sure. Products that require expertise to purchase, operate, and eventually sell have the potential to be value-added products where the retailer provides expertise and after-market services. For instance, a mass-produced $2,000 violin is less likely to be a commodity than a $69 Sony Walkman. Why?

First, the market for Sony Walkmans is much bigger. Sony Walkmans are inexpensive. People purchasing a Sony Walkman are likely to purchase it without getting any advice (from a retailer) and will seek the lowest price. People buying a $2,000 violin, however, are likely to seek advice on the purchase. Often the best source of such advice is the retailer. There are a limited number of places one can buy a $2,000 violin because the market is small. So, it is more difficult to find a wide range of sellers competing on price.

Second, usually the only aftermarket relationship between buyer and seller for a Sony Walkman is the manufacturer's guarantee. If the item fails, the retailer replaces it and returns the defective item to Sony. In some cases, the retailer simply instructs the customer to return the item to Sony directly. Can you get a Sony Walkman repaired? Unlikely. Any substantial repair would cost more than the original purchase price. A Sony Walkman is susceptible to being instantly obsolete. Next year's model is better and less expensive. Then too, when you're ready to sell your used Sony Walkman, you won't find a retailer to do it for you. Most likely it will end up in your closet or the trash unless you take the trouble to sell it yourself.

The aftermarket relationship between buyer and seller of a violin is likely to be more complex and enduring. A violin is unlikely to fail but more likely to get damaged. A retailer that can provide musical instrument repair services is a valuable resource. A violin, theoretically, will never become obsolete. When you are through using the violin, you will probably try to sell it. It's too valuable to keep in the closet. A retailer that deals in used musical instruments, again, is a valuable resource.

Thus, you can see that some mass-production items are not necessarily commodities. If they require extensive information to purchase, can be repaired, don't become instantly obsolete, and can be sold eventually, they can become value-added products in the hands of a competent retailer.

Unique Products

Unique products tend to be one of a kind (not mass-produced), are made in small production runs, or are the survivors of old mass-production runs (e.g., antiques). They are often repairable, expensive, and sometimes encourage an ongoing relationship between buyer and retailer. Unique products tend to be value-added products. In other words, unique products are the opposite of commodities.

To Add Value Takes Resources

Adding value to products requires your resources. Take a cello for example. To sell expensive hand-made (not mass-produced) cellos credibly, you have to know something about music and something about cellos. That experience and expertise is one of your resources. It's a resource that few people have and one that takes a lot of time and energy to acquire. Your expertise adds value to the product when you give customers advice on what to buy and then assist them to use the product effectively. As a musical instrument retailer (dealer), you will have contacts with competent and reliable instrument repair people to whom you can refer your customers. This is valuable to a customer who needs to repair an expensive instrument and wants it repaired properly.

When your customer stops using an instrument and wants to sell it (her son graduates from high school, goes into the Marine Corp, and doesn't need the cello any longer), you provide a market for it by buying it from your customer and then selling it.

In fact, you provide a choice for your customers in the first place by offering them new or used instruments. Moreover, you arrange with the local high school music department a long-term musical instrument rental program for those who cannot afford to buy high-quality instruments.

In other words, this business is not just a matter of getting some inventory and selling it on eBay. It's creating a retail environment that accommodates the customer from purchase to sale. It takes extra time, effort, and even money.

The musical instrument business is one that is likely to have a presence offline as well as on eBay. That's why businesses that sell unique products in a physical location can go online and increase their business on eBay. No one can drive them out of the market with low prices because the typical customer needs the value-added features or services.

Businesses that sell commodities in a physical location may find, conversely, that they can't compete effectively in the low-price wars on eBay.

Don't Neglect the Cost

When you create the product profit model, you generally don't consider your own time and effort as part of the expense. The profit is your reward. And that's as it should be. However, when you add value that costs money, plug such cost into your product profit model as an expense.

Predicting the Future Again

With unique products, ones to which you can add value, anticipating the future takes a different twist. The dire prediction above that the 25-year-olds and 65-year-olds will take over eBay suddenly doesn't seem so threatening. That's more likely to be a phenomenon of the commodities markets rather than a phenomenon of the markets for unique products.

What's Your Thing?

If you can combine your interests with your eBay retailing, that's likely to be a satisfying business for you. Unfortunately, if your interests dictate that your retailing effort consists of selling commodity products, you may eventually find yourself in price wars that may not be profitable. On the other hand, if your interests coincide with retailing unique products, you can add value, avoid price wars, and build an enduring business.

I encourage you to pursue your passion in regard to retail rather than to strictly seek a product that meets your product profit model criteria. Your passion will bring a sense of enthusiasm and authenticity to your retailing that will be an added value by itself. At the same time, be warned that the merchandise commodities markets are extremely competitive and ultimately may not produce a level of profit you can live with. In such cases, you are better off seeking unique products to which you can add value and sell profitably now and many years from now.

Add Value

Unlike the commodities markets where the 25-year-olds and the 65-year-olds will win the price wars, retailing unique products to which you can add value makes a great business strategy. It's a great strategy because it enables you to build a durable business on eBay and it potentially enables you to follow your passion permanently. The catch is that you have to be willing to apply your passion to add value to your products for the sake of your customers.

Customer Service

Can you sell Sony Walkmans and add value? Sure. You can provide great customer service. If you build your brand (reputation) on eBay for providing solid customer service, bidders will be willing to bid a little higher on your eBay items.

Whatever Helps

What is great customer service? It's whatever helps the customer make a good purchase decision and helps the customer use the product effectively. In a market where price competition is fierce, good customer service doesn't get you much more, but the little bit extra it does get you might be the business edge that enables you to win out over your competition.

Guarantee

Perhaps the best customer service to offer on commodity products is a satisfaction guarantee. The mail order business has done very well by offering satisfaction guarantees. People feel more comfortable buying with a satisfaction guarantee than they do without, particularly when purchasing from a distance.

Product Profit Model

With unique products, do you still use the product profit model? Sure. It's more difficult to do because unique products tend to encompass a wider range of time commitments (i.e., your time) than commodity products. This points out, again, that you may want to systematically consider time requirements for your product profit model, particularly when the way you add value is by contributing your labor. That is, rather than guessing how much time it will take you to handle a product, you might want to ascertain how much time it will take by systematically reviewing and timing each step in the process of handling the product.

The product profit model does work for noncommodities. Remember that the product profit model is based on your goals and management style. It's handy for unique products as well as for commodities.

Not the Same

Dividing products between commodities and value-added products is artificial. Every market is unique. Within every market, every product has its differences. eBay consists not of millions of similar products, but of millions of products different from each other. Few products are purely commodities just as few products are purely unique. Many products and their markets have attributes of both commonality and uniqueness. The point of this chapter is to help you analyze your own situation and match your aspirations to products with which you can carry on a satisfying and profitable eBay retail business.

24

Education

Education is the key to success for an eBay businessperson just as it is for other endeavors. Fortunately, there is much eBay education from which to choose. I am writing this chapter in Oklahoma City during a holiday visit to my in-laws' home, and I have been informed that a local community college now offers two courses on eBay. But you don't have to go to college to learn about eBay. There are other opportunities.

Keep in mind that eBay is here to stay. It's a permanent commercial institution like the New Your Stock Exchange. Dave Barry, the *Miami Herald* columnist, has described the national economy as a horse with four legs (December 2002):

1. Government spending

2. Business spending

3. Consumer spending

4. eBay

And so it is. Thanks Dave. I like getting insightful information from easy-to-digest business columns in the newspaper. But the academic side of me requires that I also cite other authoritive sources.

Fortunately, a graduate student at my alma mater (Go Wolverines!) has already done research about eBay as part of the PhD program in the School of Information.

Read *Pennies from eBay: the Determinants of Price in Online Auctions,* January 2000, *http://www.vanderbilt.edu/econ/reiley/papers/ PenniesFromEBay.pdf,* and note that Daniel Reeves is one of the authors. Daniel referred me to Axel Ockenfels (*http://www.uni-magdeburg.de/vwl3/axel.html*) who has done a research paper about eBay. Try *Late and Multiple Bidding in Second Price Internet Auctions: Theory and Evidence Concerning Different Rules for Ending an Auction, http://www.uni-magdeburg.de/vwl3/axel/uni/paper/ ockenfels-roth.pdf,* a paper on sniping? Read it and find out. (See another academic reference in Chapter 18 in the Feedback section.)

There will be more and more academic education available about eBay as the years go by. And more PhD papers. Gadzooks, I hope my editor doesn't require me to read them.

eBay University

eBay University, sponsored by eBay, gives seminars at major cities all over the country. Check the eBay website for the schedule. Recent offerings included the following topics:

- Basic Selling
- Technology for Becoming a PowerSeller
- Improving Your Fixed Price Listings
- eBay Payments
- Advanced Selling
- Turbo Lister
- Selling Manager
- eBay Stores

The seminars are inexpensive, but be sure to sign up well in advance on eBay's website.

eBay Live!

This is the annual eBay conference (inexpensive) held in June. It offers a healthy list of seminars and other educational events. Many vendors exhibit, and a lengthy meander through the exhibits can be a premier educational experience. Then too, you will meet a lot of people from around the country who can provide you with practical experience beyond your own. And it's fun as well. This is a "must attend" event for serious eBay business people. Go to the eBay sitemap and look for the conference announcement.

Books about eBay

Now here's a subject dear to my heart. There are a variety of eBay books, and most are reasonably inexpensive. In the future they will get more specialized, and you will have the opportunity to learn more and more about less and less, as the wags say.

I am an avid reader of nonfiction books, including business books. If I can find just a few new ideas in a book or even reinforce a few old ideas that have proven successful, I think the book is worth reading. There will be more books about eBay worth reading in the future, and there are a few in print already. Here's my recommendation, of course. Look for my book *eBay the Smart Way*, Third Edition, AMACOM, to be published in the fall of 2003, a general book about eBay.

eBay Tutorials

Web-based training (WBT) is the wave of the future, and some of it is compelling. Barnes & Noble University offers free WBT tutorials on a variety of topics. eBay has been included in the past (my WBT course). Look for other online tutorials about eBay. They are generally free. Of course, don't overlook eBay itself. eBay offers a variety of WBT tutorials on the eBay website under at Help, Basics on the menu bar. eBay also sponsors online workshops on specific topics. You can attend them live (about two hours) or read them in the archives.

Business Seminars

The commercial seminars given in every field in these United States are some of the great invisible assets of the nation. The universities have a high profile, but commercial seminars cruise in below the radar. They have to be good for two reasons. They're often pricey, and they operate to make a profit. If they weren't good, they wouldn't exist.

Look for national business seminars given from time to time in your nearest major city. Spend the money and take the time to attend. Look for topics that will help you improve your business today. You will often learn more than you expected to.

Many of these seminar series are sponsored by professional organizations. Get a list of professional organizations that serve your segment of retailing or just business in general, and visit the websites. Often you will find seminars coming to a city near you. In the library you can find:

- *National Trade and Professional Associations*, Columbia, Washington, DC, *http://www.columbiabooks.com*

- *Encyclopedia of Associations*, Gale, Detroit, *http://www.gale.com*

The publisher of this book is a division of the American Management Association (AMA). You can find AMA's offering of business seminars at:

http://www.amanet.org/seminars/index.htm

Some are of interest to eBay businesspeople.

Business Books

Most bookstores have a robust business book section where you can find books on specific business matters about which you worry everyday. Buy a book and relieve your worries. And find new things to worry about. If you don't happen to have an academic mind, you will find many of the books easy to read. Most are not written for college courses. Of course, you will want to consider my book, *eBay the Smart Way* Third Edition.

Web Development Tutorials

Many eBay businesspeople do much of the busy work themselves required for eBay business success. If you want to learn a little HTML (Web development) to brighten up your auction ads, find one of the many free HTML tutorials on the Web. Here are a few:

- *A Beginner's Guide to HTML* (National Center for Supercomputing Applications), *http://archive.ncsa.uiuc.edu/General/Internet/WWW/HTMLPrimerAll.html#GS*

- *Getting Started with HTML* (World Wide Web Consortium), *http://www.w3.org/MarkUp/Guide*

- *HTML Basics* (WebMonkey), *http://hotwired.lycos.com/webmonkey/teachingtool*

- *HTML Primer* (HTML Goodies), *http://www.htmlgoodies.com/primers/basics.html*

- *Introduction to HTML* (Case Western Reserve University), *http://www.cwru.edu/help/introHTML/toc.html*

HTML is easy to learn, and you don't need to know much to make better auction ads. See Appendix 5, 6, and 7 for tutorials on Web development.

Web Books

If you insist on paying for your Web development education, there are also good books available on HTML and Web development many of which are very easy to read. Browse through you local bookstore and find one you like. My recommendation is my book: *Web Pages the Smart Way*, AMACOM, now out of print. However, publication of this entire book on the Web is planned for late 2003.

VII

Something for Business Buyers

25

Buying on eBay

Now is the time for all good buyers to come to the aid of their company. Finally, we get to the buyers' portion of this eBay business book. Can buyers save money for their businesses by buying on eBay? Absolutely!

Certainly, there are bargains on eBay, even for businesses. The real test of buying for business on eBay, however, is to do it consistently and efficiently. Whether that's possible for your business will depend on some of the considerations covered below.

Normal Buying

Normal nonbusiness buying on eBay is part recreation, part frugality, and part convenience. Time is seldom the prime consideration. Normal buying is casual.

When you're in business, however, casual work is usually not cost-effective, and time is money.

Buying for Your Business

When you buy for your business, the considerations are different from normal buying. It's not recreation. It needs to be cost-effective. Furthermore, it needs to be effective. The business reasons to buy on eBay are usually to buy inexpensively or to buy something you can't find anywhere else.

Cost of Buying

When you buy on eBay for business, someone has to do the buying. If that's you, you need to be able to put a price on your hours so that you can calculate exactly what the process of buying on eBay is costing you over and above your normal buying practices. If an employee does the buying, you can use her hourly pay to calculate the price per hour.

First, you need to make the simple calculations explained in all basic eBay books to determine whether you're getting a bargain when you buy something for your business. For example, did you include the cost of the shipping in your calculation? Do you have to pay sales tax?

In addition, for business you need to take the price-per-hour for your time or an employee's and apply it to the extra time, if any, it takes to purchase on eBay. In other words, is the savings you get by purchasing goods on eBay enough to pay for the extra time you or your employee spends on eBay doing the buying?

Extra Time?

Does eBay take extra time to buy something compared to normal buying? Until you analyze your buying practices, you don't know. eBay might save you time.

Whatever is bought from any source has to be bought by someone. For business, it's common for an employee to buy out of a catalog, from an office supply store, or from a salesperson who comes calling. This process is what you compare to buying on eBay. One has the notion that eBay can potentially take more time. After all, tending your bidding can be time consuming; and when you lose an auction, it's wasted time. You have to start over again. So, you need to do a cost analysis to determine the portion of time spent buying on eBay that exceeds normal buying time, if any.

Once you've estimated the difference between buying on eBay and normal buying, apply the price-per-hour to the excess time. That's the extra cost of buying via eBay.

Average time to buy normally	12 minutes
Average time to buy via eBay	19 minutes
Difference	7 minutes
Items per week	18
Total extra time per week1	26 min (2.1 hrs)
$ per hour employee cost	$14
Total extra cost	$29.40

If you saved more than $29.40 by buying the 18 items on eBay, then buying on eBay starts to make sense.

If you or your employee has to drive somewhere to buy or pick up goods, eBay will probably take less time rather than more time.

The real opportunity lies hidden in the way we think of buying on eBay. If there is a way you can set up guidelines to make buying on eBay more efficient, it's possible that buying on eBay might be significantly less expensive than buying via other means.

Minimizing the Cost of Buying

Here are a few guidelines you may want to consider:

1. Have one person do all the buying on eBay. She will presumably hone her skills and be able to do it more efficiently than other employees without well honed skills.

2. Don't play the bidding game. Use proxy bidding. You put in one bid. You will be notified by email whether you won. You have as good a chance to win the auction as anyone.

3. Set up an easy-to-use payment procedure.

4. Use auction management software for buyers, if available.

5. Use Buy it now! (fixed price) when it provides a significant savings.

This not only keeps your costs down but gives you a shot at making your eBay buying cost even less than normal buying.

Business to Business

eBay has a business-to-business (B2B) section that may make eBay buying even more attractive if your industry happens to be well represented. The B2B auctions have developed more slowly on eBay than consumer auctions, but they are growing. Someday soon eBay will be an effective B2B marketplace for small businesses. (See Chapter 11 for more information on B2B auctions.)

Many businesses get a huge savings buying expensive equipment on eBay. This is one type of eBay buying that makes sense on its face without any analysis.

Local Auctions

eBay auctions where the sellers are in your area are fertile grounds for business purchases. For instance, it's difficult to buy a $150 desk in Omaha from 600 miles away in Louisville. The transportation cost renders such a transaction expensive. If you're in Omaha, however, the desk may be a real bargain.

Bulk Supplies

Although the bulk sales auctions (a type of B2B auction) are also growing slowly on eBay, they continue to offer more and more possibilities. A metal fabrication business owner in Alabama, was able to buy drywall for a new metal building cheaper (even after shipping cost) in Tennessee via eBay than locally. It pays to check eBay first before buying elsewhere.

For Inventory

Buying via eBay is not confined to goods you need for your business. You can also buy for your inventory. If you can buy cheap on eBay and turn around and sell for a profit on eBay, there's nothing wrong with that. Although eBay is an efficient marketplace, it's not a perfect marketplace. Opportunities for buying and selling at a profit strictly on eBay certainly exist.

International

The international markets for business have tremendous potential. They are big now and will get bigger. You may be able to enjoy great savings by buying abroad. Unless you are in the import-export business, however, there is no simple way to buy abroad other than to travel. eBay is an exception. You can buy in the UK quite easily because the eBay website is in English. For the other foreign eBay auctions, you will have to use the local language.

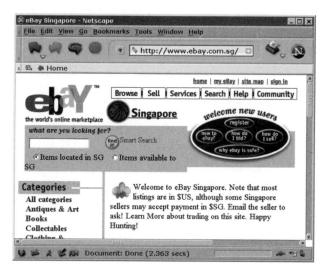

Figure 25.1   eBay in Singapore. ©1995-2003 eBay Inc.

You can use PayPal, BidPay.com, etc., to pay abroad as well as your credit card (see Chapter 13).

Euros Anyone?

PayPal now pays in several foreign currencies, as of early 2003. Want to buy something in Europe with Euros? Pay via PayPal, and it's not a problem.

Buy It Now!

eBay's fixed price device can be helpful for buying in two situations. First, if you're in a hurry, you can buy immediately. Second, if the fixed price represents a reasonable savings for you, you can purchase cost-effectively. It's just like buying out of a catalog.

Organizing Your Buying

Beyond determining whether eBay is a cost-effective means of purchasing for your business, you also need to set up your buying in an organized manner.

Accounting

You need to work with your bookkeeper or accountant to account for your purchases without regard to eBay. Whatever system you use is likely to work with eBay purchases too. In addition, you need to manage and account for your payments and your bidding.

Payment

It's essential that a practical payment procedure be set up for purchasing on eBay. If you are doing this yourself, it's nice to have a routine so you don't have to think how you're going to pay with each auction. It's also easier for accounting purposes, after the fact.

But a payment procedure is most essential when an employee does the purchasing.

The payment method needs to be widely acceptable (e.g., PayPal) and easily auditable. This will give you confidence that an employee is not embezzling (small-time embezzling is much more wide spread than most small businesses realize), and it will also give the employee the confidence to buy flexibly, aggressively, and in a timely manner.

We bought about $10,000 of fiber optic network cable on eBay for our charter high school for $1,200. This would not have been possible without using a credit card. Public school accounts payable systems, holdovers from the Civil War era, are not supportive of online purchasing. Fortunately, I had insisted (as a board member) that our school get a credit card. The school saved about 88 percent ($26,500) on just one purchase.

Being able to pay in a practical way seems like a small matter, an obvious requirement. Nonetheless, it's an important key to successful buying online and particularly on eBay. Think it through. Make it easy for an employee to pay.

What happens when the seller requires a method of payment outside your immediate capability? You need to have a policy in place for this. The obvious policy is not to buy from buyers who do not accept the means of payment you use. You might consider modifying such a policy with two additional procedures. First, contact the seller to see if she will make an exception and accept another method of payment from you. Second, set up a special in-house procedure for handling payments in a way that's outside your normal payment practices.

Tracking Purchases

Many sellers ship via shipping that you can track, such as Federal Express. If you have the tracking number (obtained from the seller), you can look up the package on the FedEx website and find out where it is in transit. This is usually a waste of time and is not necessary. Occasionally, though, tracking may be important for a purchase, and it's helpful to be able to do it. If it's important to your purchasing efforts, make a point to deal with sellers who use shippers that provide such a capability.

Figure 25.2   FedEx package tracking via its website. ©1995-2003 FedEx.

Auction Tracking

You need to account for purchases on eBay, just like you do for any purchases. Since buying on eBay does not necessarily happen instantly, however, you have additional accounting to do; that is, you need to manage your bidding and your transaction arrangements. If you can find an auction management service that will do this for you, that might be your best bet. Otherwise, you'll have to devise a system of your own.

Buying Details

There are number of bidding techniques listed in my *eBay the Smart Way* book. Most are for active bidding. Active bidding is perhaps cost-effective for big-ticket items, but it isn't for normal business buying. Your best bet to make eBay business buying cost-effective is to automate the buying process as much as possible.

Bidding Technique

Use proxy bidding to buy for business. It's easy. Just enter your bid once. It's effective. It will never bid more than you want to pay, and it will always bid as low as possible to win an auction. It's built into the eBay system, and you don't have to do anything to activate it other than enter as your bid the highest amount you're willing to pay. It's automatic. You bid once and wait to know the results when the auction is over.

This is the ideal bidding for a business buyer and perhaps the best bidding technique for anyone. Keep in mind, that if someone is willing to pay more for the item than you are, all the bidding techniques in the world aren't going to help you much to win the bidding. Don't waste your time or your employee's time with numerous bidding strategies for business buying. Just use proxy bidding.

When you bid on expensive items, of course, it might be cost-effective to spend some time using other bidding techniques that require ongoing attention to the bidding. For instance, if you're bidding on a milling machine you think is worth $19,000 and you think you can buy it for $14,000 via active bidding, then risking your time or an employee's time to bid actively might be worth the chance to save $5,000.

Feedback

Feedback, as always, is a two-way street. First, you need to check the feedback of every seller. It takes only a few seconds, and you never know what you might find. Occasionally, you will find sellers that seem too risky to bother with. Second, you need to tend to your own feedback. You can't afford to have significant negative feedback. Some sellers will refuse to sell to you.

Think carefully whether you want to use the same eBay account (eBay ID) to both buy and sell for your eBay business. The considerations are as numerous as there are eBay businesses. Weigh the pros and cons and make a choice. If you are an eBay seller and you make a lot of purchases on eBay too, there might be reasons to keep your buying and selling separate for not only feedback purposes but accounting purposes as well.

Let the Seller Manage

Don't go to the trouble of trying to manage individual auctions. This will not only take extra time and energy but will also confuse the seller or upset the seller's operations. Let the seller manage the transaction. That's part of the seller's job. Wait for the seller's communications and answer them in a timely manner.

Then again, if the seller doesn't do his job properly, you may have to step in and make a request. For instance, if the seller doesn't provide a receipt, you may have to ask for one.

Services

Can you buy services on eBay? Your best bet is Elance, eBay's auction for professional services. In times when the national economy is depressed, you can find a lot of bargain services via Elance. Even when the economy is hot, there are always plenty of independent contractors ready to do short-term and even long-term work.

For Your New eBay Business

When you're starting out, need some professional work done, and can't afford to hire an employee or a local firm, you might be able to find an inexpensive freelancer on Elance to get the job done.

We Have Stories

We've all heard stories about who bought what on eBay and saved a ton of money. Many of those stories are about expensive items purchased for business. They tend to make it seem like buying on eBay is a no-brainer; that is, you can always do better buying on eBay. When you're running a business, though, you have to establish your purchasing operations on facts and projected costs that make sense.

For ordinary business buying, the jury is still out on whether a business can buy on eBay more cost-effectively. Indeed, many corporations are reducing their traditional purchasing programs and giving employees credit cards to do the buying ad hoc for a wide range of supplies and even equipment. It's more cost-effective than using a managed purchasing operation. So, there are no easy answers as to how eBay purchasing compares. Experiment with your own business to find an answer that fits your operation.

Again, it should be acknowledged that for expensive items, many businesses have saved money buying on eBay. It seems to be worth it to put in the time and energy to buy (bid) carefully and actively for potentially large savings.

Matters of Interest

As this book ends, I appreciate your interest in my book and hope it has assisted you to reach your eBay business goals. For more information in the future, check *http://bookcenter.com* where matters of interest to eBay businesses will be posted from time to time.

Appendix I The Top 10 Tips for Beginning Sellers

Top 10 tips for beginning sellers; that is, people who intend to establish and operate a business on eBay.

1. **Trials** Run some trial auctions.

2. **Financial Needs** Determine your personal financial needs.

3. **Profit Model** Think through a product profit model.

4. **Niche** Find a niche market with products that satisfy your product profit model and, if applicable, your personal passion. Line up some wholesalers.

5. **Name** Decide your business name and use it everywhere.

6. **Business Form** Choose a business entity and get a sales tax license.

7. **Accounting** Get your accounting set up.

8. **Auction Management** Subscribe to an auction management service and set up your business from beginning to end. Integrate your accounting with your auction management.

9. **Help** Find people to help you (as independent contractors) with your business tasks.

10. **Customer Service** Plan overall and specific customer service policies and programs.

Appendix II The Top 12 Tips for Seasoned Sellers

Top 12 tips for existing eBay businesspeople who want to expand their sales on eBay.

1. **Analysis** Analyze your existing eBay business using the product profit model to see where you can improve efficiency, profits, and personal satisfaction.

2. **Auction Management** Start using an auction management service to run your business from beginning to end, unless you are already using something comparable.

3. **Accounting** Integrate your accounting with your auction management service.

4. **Name** Coordinate all the business names you use (name on eBay, eBay ID, domain name, AOL name, email name, etc. That is, make them all the same. Start with a new name if necessary.

5. **Top 10** Review the Top 10 Tips for Beginning Businesses to make sure you've covered all the bases.

6. **Delegate** Start delegating more work to others (independent contractors) and take the time to develop strategies to improve your business.

7. **Customer Service** Expand your customer service effort. Invent a new online customer service technique.

8. **Copy Writing** Read a book on copy writing to improve your auction ads.

9. **Conference** Attend the annual eBay conference.

10. **Website** Evaluate your ecommerce website objectively, if you have one, and make a determination as to whether it's cost-effective or otherwise beneficial to continue operating it.

11. **International** Learn about exporting and international finance. Review PayPal's international services.

12. **Expand** Expand your business internationally a few countries at a time.

Appendix III The Top 8 Tips for Business Buyers

Top 8 tips for businesses that want to buy equipment and supplies on eBay to save money.

1. **Employee** Have an employee (or yourself) start buying routine equipment and supplies on eBay and keep detailed records including time records.

2. **Cost-Effective** Do a study to determine whether buying on eBay is more cost-effective than other means of purchasing.

3. **One Person** Designate one employee to do the buying on eBay.

4. **Easy Payment** Set up an easy, practical, and accountable means of payment for the employee doing the buying.

5. **Procedures** Develop accounting procedures for eBay buying, including auction management procedures.

6. **Categories** Take the time to match your buying needs to the corresponding eBay categories. Don't overlook eBay's B2B auctions.

7. **Equipment** The next time you need to make a major equipment purchase investigate the possibilities and ramifications of buying such equipment on eBay.

8. **Professional Services** Check eBay's Elance when you need professional services.

Appendix IV Custom Database System

Usually to do a bulk upload of information, you use a data file; that is, you export data into a file from a desktop database manager (e.g., Microsoft Access). Then you import the data file into the application in which you need to use the data.

Database

Many people keep all their inventory data in a desktop database manager (e.g., Access) where they can easily and quickly maintain the data. You will find Access and its competitors, such as Paradox and FileMaker, easy to use. From a database manager, you export the data into a data file (i.e., a delimited data file). You can then upload the data file into a ecommerce program at your website. The ecommerce program includes a catalog (essentially a database). The data file provides all the information to fill in the catalog. This process takes only a short time, three to five minutes depending on the size of the data file. The result is that the catalog blooms. It suddenly has hundreds or thousands of items in it. It works pretty slick.

eBay had not permited this straightforward process for auction ads until Turbo Lister. Turbo Lister will accept data in a delimited file.

Why does this matter? I have taken the point of view in the book that you need to use an auction management service. Such a service does everything for you. You don't have to concern yourself with how it works. Nonetheless, some people who have physical retail stores use traditional commercial retail software to run their businesses and don't want to switch to a new system. Such retail software inevitably has a database core and can normally export data in a delimited file. If such retail systems enable custom database use, and many do, a retailer can easily build in the columns for data that supports eBay auction ads. Then they can export such data to Turbo Lister.

Some other people have constructed database systems of their own using Access or a comparable desktop database manager. They don't want to give up such applications. Such database applications can export data in a delimited file to Turbo Lister.

It all starts with the database. You can create a database—a simple table—that includes both data for inventory control and data for creating eBay auctions. You extract the data (subset) for eBay auctions by using a query (the eBay Query). The result is a data file that contains a subset of all the data. Such a subset is designed especially to provide the data for your eBay auction ads.

Only eBay

You can, of course, create a database that is only for eBay auctions and nothing more. In that case, you export the data from the entire table for eBay auctions because the table does not contain any other data.

Why a Database?

Why maintain your data in a desktop database manager such as Access? It's simply easier. Desktop databases like Access are easy to use. That means that you can add, subtract, and change data easily, quickly, and conveniently on a desktop (or laptop) computer. You do this with the table open—where you can go directly to each column entry (field). Maintaining large amounts of data any other way is invariably more difficult. You can manage small amounts of data perhaps more easily in other ways, but desktop databases make managing large amounts of data easy even for untrained personnel.

eBay's new Turbo Lister enables you to work in a database-like table. Andale's Lister Pro enables you to do the same. So, unless you already have a eBay database application you like to use, there's no reason not to use Turbo Lister, Lister Pro, or a comparable program.

Developing a System

If you want to create a system to store your auction ads in a database, you might use 12 fields (columns):

Title (one-line title for auction)

Category (get category numbers from eBay)

Bold (**y** for yes, **n** for no; costs extra)

Category featured (**y** for yes, **n** for no; costs extra)

Featured (**y** for yes, **n** for no; costs extra)

Location (location of seller)

Picture (URL for photograph)

Quantity (number of items being auctioned)

Reserve (a decimal is required even for zero)

Minimum bid (a decimal is required even for zero)

Duration (**3**, **5**, **7** or **10** days)

Private (**y** for yes, **n** for no)

As you see, eBay wants you to enter this information much as you would fill in the input form at the auction entry in the Sellers section on the eBay website.

If you have all this information in a database, you can export it in a delimited file. If you are using traditional retail software, the eBay auction ad data can be stored together with other data in a table. For instance, it might be stored with your inventory data in an inventory control application. If it is, you might get a table full of data similar to the example, which follows. From that table, you extract (via query) a subset of the data just for eBay auction ads and export it in a delimited file.

Entire Table		eBay Query
product		
manufacturer		
cost		
shipwt		
received		
sold		
instock		
title	—>	title
ebaycat	—>	ebaycat
bold	—>	bold
featurecat	—>	featurecat
feature	—>	feature
location	—>	location
quantity	—>	quantity
reserve	—>	reserve
minbid	—>	minbid
duration	—>	duration
private	—>	private
open	—>	open
ad	—>	ad
shipcost	—>	shipcost

boilerplate	—>	boilerplate
weburl	—>	weburl
imageurl	—>	imageurl

In other words, you export only part of the data, the part that eBay needs to create an auction ad.

Database —> eBay Query (delimited file) —> Turbo Lister

Benefits and Disadvantages

What are the benefits and disadvantages of the eBay bulk upload system, Turbo Lister?

Benefits

A primary benefit is that you can save a lot of time if you run a lot of auctions. Entering the information for each auction online manually is tedious if you run more than just a few auctions each week. A bulk upload is quick and relatively painless.

Another benefit is that you don't have to be a programmer to use Turbo Lister, either by itself or in conjunction with a database application or retail software. You can learn to do it yourself if you feel comfortable operating a personal computer. In addition, if you hire someone to set up your system, that person doesn't have to be a programmer or a database programmer.

Yet another benefit is that you can expand the number of your eBay auctions with the confidence that you can repeat your bulk upload week after week with little effort. This will enable you to start thinking about your eBay business with a larger vision for the future.

Disadvantages

Turbo Lister itself is not difficult to use. However, if you want to create your own custom database application and have never used a desktop database manager, you will have to learn how to use one before this system will work for you. It's not difficult to learn, but you do have to learn how to build a table, enter data into it, and change the data in it. Likewise, you will have to do the same in your retail software, which may be more difficult to learn than a desktop database manager. The alternative is to hire someone to do it for you.

Finally, you probably recognize that you can't do it all. To get set up to do bulk uploads with your own custom database system, you may have to hire someone knowledgeable in databases rather than take the time to do it yourself.

Moreover, many people reading this book are probably unlikely candidates to perform the tedious data-entry work that it takes to enter and maintain the data in a database. You need to hire someone who can type well and who is comfortable using a computer to do the routine data-entry and data-maintenance work.

Alternatives

What's the alternative to setting up a system covered in this appendix? Use an auction management service; that is, software used online and made especially for managing an eBay business operation. I recommend this alternative. An auction management service enables you to manage your eBay business from beginning to end without anyone's assistance. Priceless! The data entry is the only part of the job you may not be able to do (too tedious). Hire someone to do it.

Summary

Use an auction management service. Don't start a database application from scratch. Why reinvent the wheel?

On the other hand, if you've already created a system using a desktop database manager, you can now, for the the first time, upload your auction ads simply by exporting data to the new Turbo Lister. Or, if you use traditional retail software, you can add columns (fields) to your inventory control system to store the data necessary for auction ads, and then export the data to the new Turbo Lister.

Appendix V Using Web Authoring Software

An authoring software program is one that takes media and arranges them into a presentation. You can think of a word processor as a text authoring program. For the purpose of this book, you will be interested in Web authoring programs. Because the Web is a multimedia medium, Web authoring programs are multimedia-authoring programs, which means they handle a variety of media.

Multimedia and the Web

The media generally used on the Web are text, color graphics, animation, streaming sound, streaming video, MIDI music, and embedded programs (e.g., Java applets). Of the greatest interest for running auctions on eBay are text and color graphics (digital photographs). Anything more may interfere with the efficient functioning of your auction ads.

Implied in digital multimedia is interactivity. The primary interactive device is the link. The link enables you to have choices: The simplest is stay where you are or click a link and go somewhere else. Links can be important for eBay auctions. With these simple ideas in mind, you can learn to author your own eBay ads, and even webpages, using a Web authoring program.

Netscape offers Composer as its Web authoring program, and it comes free with the Netscape browser. Microsoft's FrontPage is its authoring program, and it comes free with certain versions of Microsoft Office; otherwise you can purchase it separately.

These two Web authoring programs are not only easy to use but quite similar to each other. In fact, they were both designed as Web word processors, albeit word processors for Web text. But remember, the Web is a multimedia medium. Both of these Web authoring programs handle other media competently too.

You will find using these programs about the easiest way you can do Web work without knowing HTML. Nonetheless, it always pays to know HTML. You never know when you might have to fix some little thing that the Web authoring programs can't seem to get quite right.

I do not encourage you to use both of these programs on the same webpages. You're just asking for trouble. Chose one or the other and stick with it. Because the two are so much alike, this chapter covers only one, Composer. If you can understand Composer, you won't have any trouble using FrontPage .

You will also find that using these authoring programs is incompatible with hand coding and editing. If you can code HTML, you can work more efficiently using an editor, such as Macromedia's HomeSite, that does not change your HTML (except what you change). Composer and FrontPage, however, do change your HTML (beyond what you change), and that makes subsequent editing both tedious and inefficient. Do not use either of these if you want to do your own HTML coding. You will be disappointed.

Basic Assumption

This appendix assumes that you will be using Composer to create an eBay auction ad. This is a basic assumption about a special purpose, and some of the things this appendix covers may not apply to general Web development work.

Composer

Open Composer and start typing. It doesn't get any easier. It's just like using a word processor (see Figure A5.1).

Authoring

Think of a word processor as a "text authoring" program. Then think of Composer as a "webpage authoring" program or a "Web authoring" program.

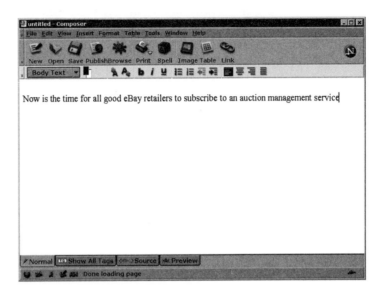

Figure A5.1   Open Composer and start typing.

Want to add some headings? Do it. It's just as easy as using a word processor and virtually identical (see Figure A5.2).

Unless you know something about HTML, however, you may not fully understand how to format your headings and other typographical devices. For instance, <h1> is the largest heading, <h2> the second largest, <h3> the third largest, and <h4> the fourth largest. Few Web developers use <h5> or <h6> because you never quite know what you will get. Just understanding this HTML heading scheme will enable you to use Composer better, even if you never do any HTML coding. When you use Composer with templates, it helps to know a little HTML too.

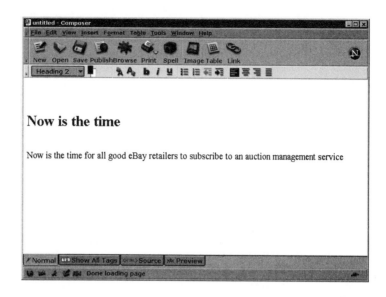

Figure A5.2   Add a heading.

Text

Don't do funny things with text. Keep it simple, readable, and well organized. Unless you have something unique (e.g., a work of art), potential bidders just want to read quickly and move on. If you have what they want at a reasonable price, they will be likely to bid. If you don't, they won't. No amount of jazzing up your eBay auction ad is going to change that. Help potential bidders to quickly get the facts and information that they need from your auction ad.

Typesetting

Typesetting is pretty straightforward for an eBay auction ad. Browsers have Times New Roman or Times (serif fonts) for their standard font; they have Arial or Helvetica for their sanserif font; and they have Courier for their monospaced font. Beyond those, you're kidding yourself; only a percentage of people will see anything else you use because the remainder don't have the requisite fonts installed on their computers. If you want to do some fancy typesetting on your website, read my book *Typography on the Web* (AP Professional, 1998). If you want to do some fancy typesetting for your eBay auction ad, forget it. It's not worth the trouble because few will see it as you see it, and you lose control over the typesetting process when you don't use the standard three fonts.

Chapter 8 discusses readability. Typesetting is about readability. Good typesetting is easy to read. Lousy typesetting is hard to read. And guess what? If a potential bidder cannot read your ad easily and quickly, he or she is apt to move on without finishing it. Better pay attention to your typesetting. Chapter 8 provides some brief readability and typesetting guidelines. Review them before you do the typesetting for your eBay auction ad.

Graphics

You can easily place color graphics (e.g., digital photographs) in your eBay auction ad. Just place the cursor where you want the photograph to go, and click on the graphics button (see Figure A5.3). After you enter the URL of the graphic, the graphic will appear.

The image markup is *<img src="[URL]">*. You will need to enter the URL of the photograph as the value for the *src* attribute, and the image will magically appear.

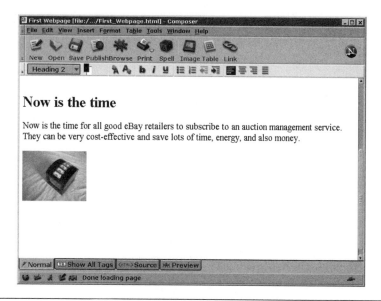

Figure A5.3   Inserting a photograph.

Unfortunately, the photograph will not necessarily appear on your computer screen. You may have to test your eBay ad on the Web (but not necessarily at eBay). Upload the ad to a website and test it with your browser while you're connected to the Internet.

Links

You place a link (correctly called a hyperlink) just as you do a photograph. Click on the link button (see Figure A5.4). Then add the URL of the link target. Links connect webpages within a website and thereby give the website its structure.

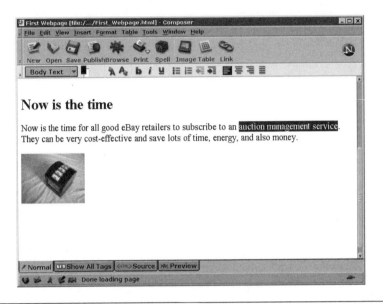

Figure A5.4   Inserting a link.

In this case, however, the link has a beginning markup *<a href="[URL]">* and an ending markup *</a>*. Whatever is between these markups is the hot spot of the link. When someone clicks on the hot spot, she goes to the URL specified in the link markup.

You need to enter the URL for the link. Notice in your Web browser that the text that is in the hot spot of the link is a different color. That's how people find links.

Background Color

Changing the background color can prove attractive, but only if you are careful. The background color should not impair readability. That means light background colors with black type, or dark background colors with light-colored type. The background color and type color must contrast too. A medium background color with medium type color that does not contrast is essentially unreadable.

Keep in mind that you do not want to set the background color with the *<body>* markup for the entire webpage for your eBay auction ad. It will interfere with eBay's color scheme. That's practically suicidal. Use a table, and set the color background for the table.

Tables

To avoid changing the color of the entire webpage and to keep your text in a column that will fit in every browser, you can create a table. The background color of the table becomes the background color of only your portion of the eBay auction ad (webpage), and a column will confine text to within the column boundaries. Click on the table button to start a table (see Figure A5.5).

Make your table one column and one row. Then make the column exactly 500 pixels, align the table to the center, set the table border to 0, and set cell padding at 20. Although the table is outlined in your Composer window with dashes, the dashes don't show in a browser window.

Are you making a table here? No. You're using the table-making capability of HTML to create a usable layout for your webpage. This was a use of tables that may not have been anticipated, yet many Web developers have found tables useful for layout.

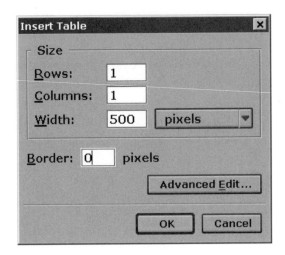

Figure A5.5   Installing a table.

Now within the column, do all your authoring (see Figure A5.6). The result will be an attractive and readable column of text with an appropriate margin on each side (see Figure A5.7).

You can have tables within tables. With different background colors, tables can provide a polished appearance to a webpage (see Figure A5.8).

Real Tables

You can use HTML tables to make real tables too. Many of us use a table occasionally in our text documents. But not often. Indeed, the primary use of tables is for webpage layout.

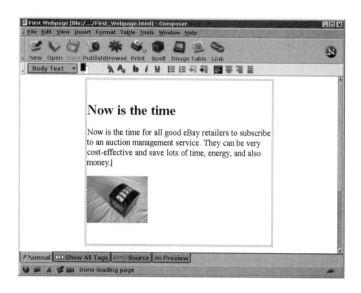

Figure A5.6   Filling in the table in Composer.

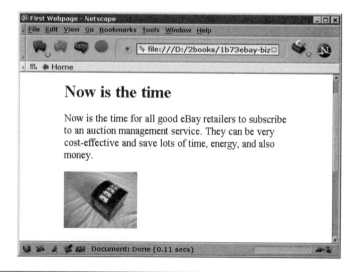

Figure A5.7   Table in Web browser.

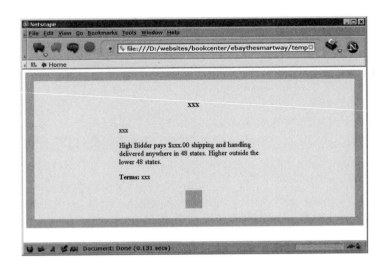

Figure A5.8   Two tables—one inside the other—with different background colors in the template. A third table (same color) contains the text.

Browser

You can check your work at any time with your Web browser. Just open the auction ad HTML file in the browser. Before checking your work, *first*, save the HTML file in Composer, and then *second*, reload the webpage in your browser. You will see your latest up-to-the-minute work.

Chop It Off

When you're done with your authoring, you have to chop off the head of the document. Composer makes webpages. You need only a portion of a webpage. Therefore, you need to chop off the head and foot of the webpage before you can submit it to eBay as the body of your auction ad.

The beginning of the auction listing webpage is reserved to eBay. The end of the auction listing webpage is reserved to eBay. The middle of the auction listing webpage is where your auction ad goes.

This is your last act of webpage developing. Don't do this before you're ready to submit your work to eBay. Save your webpage file and close Composer. Open Windows Notepad or any other plain text editor. Load your webpage. Highlight the *<body>* markup and everything above it. Then delete it. Next go to the bottom of the webpage and highlight the *</body>* markup and everything below it, and delete it. Now you've got something you can copy and paste into the eBay auction input (*Sell Your Item, Description*) in the Sell section on the eBay website.

eBay passes on to you some formatting for your portion of the webpage by using the *<blockquote>* markup. This puts a thin margin on the left and right of the webpage. You can ignore this, and all your Web development will take place inside the margins. Or, you can nullify the markup by starting your portion of the webpage with the *</blockquote>* markup. If you do this, end your portion of the webpage with the *<blockquote>* markup to restore eBay's webpage format.

Summary

Webpage authoring programs are easy to use. Use one to make a webpage. Chop off the top and bottom (markups) and enter it via copy and paste as you would any description of a product to be auctioned. The result can be a nicely formatted presentation that can be better and *easier to read* than the presentation resulting from the normal entry of text in the eBay auction listing form.

Appendix VI HTML Tutorial

You can learn Hypertext Markup Language (HTML) easily. It's not programming, although many Web developers now call it *coding*. This tutorial does not attempt to give you a comprehensive grasp of HTML. It does give you a good start on using HTML to do the basics.

Sometimes using a Web authoring program you just can't get things quite the way you want them. If you know HTML, you can tune up your Web pages more precisely. Sometimes you see a Web page you really like on the Web. You can copy it to your hard disk. If you can read HTML, you can look at the markups to see how the Web page is constructed. Although copying the content of someone else's Web pages may be a copyright infringement, copying layout and typesetting is not.

For a more thorough introduction to HTML, you might try *Web Pages the Smart Way* (AMACOM, 2001), or any one of a number of similar books readily available in many bookstores.

The angle bracket characters (< >) indicate markups. The markups instruct the browser how to display the content (text, graphics, etc.). The markups also enable some interactive functions such as links. Markups are not case-sensitive; that is, you can use either upper- or lowercase characters inside the angle brackets. As you can see, I prefer lowercase markups; I can read them faster.

Terms

Some people call the markups tags. Some people call using the markups coding just as they would call writing a program with a programming language coding. Tags and coding are misleading terms, but we're stuck with them.

Some markups stand by themselves.

```
<br>
```

Most require a closing markup.

```
<b>content</b>
```

The forward slant indicates the closing markup.

Spaces

HTML doesn't like spaces unless you specify them. Therefore, it will change two or more consecutive character spaces into one space. It will change redundant line spaces into one line space. See the   markup later in this appendix for a way to increase spaces.

Defining a Web Page

You use markups right from the beginning to define a Web page. This is just perfunctory work. The real job is marking up your content which falls between the *<body>* markups.

<html> </html>

The entire Web page falls between these markups. This markup tells the browser that this plain text document (ASCII file) is an HTML page.

<head> </head>

This markup designates the head of the document. The head of a Web page can contain all sorts of information that is well beyond the scope of this book, but the head need not contain anything. The browser does not display the information in the head.

<title> </title>

Whatever you put between these markups will show at the very top of the browser.

<body> </body>

The browser displays the content between these markups. This markup sets the specifications for the entire body of the Web page such as background color and text color. To set the specifications, you can use attributes which fall inside the markup itself.

```
<body bgcolor=#ffff00>
```

Attributes are beyond the scope of this tutorial, but you can learn about them in any basic HTML book.

Typical Web Page Setup

You can use the typical Web page setup that follows, without anything additional. You put your content between the *<body>* markups.

```
<html><head><title>Name of Page</
title></head><body>

content

</body></html>
```

Use the above as a template for doing basic Web pages. For instance, the following Web page is simple. All you need to do is provide the content.

```
<html><head><title>The Slickhorn
Trek</title></head><body>

Don't underestimate the ruggedness and
remoteness of this area. Inexperienced
canyon hikers will find the terrain
demanding, and you won't see many
people, if any. This is not as rugged
as many off-trail places in the Grand
Canyon, but some portions are nearly
```

```
as strenuous. Plan your water
carefully. If you find yourself about
to depart on your trek during a
drought year or during a dry spell,
you should first undergo a psychiatric
evaluation! Follow the advisory
published by the Monticello BLM
office.

</body></html>
```

The browser shows the one-paragraph Web page as indicated in Figure A6.1.

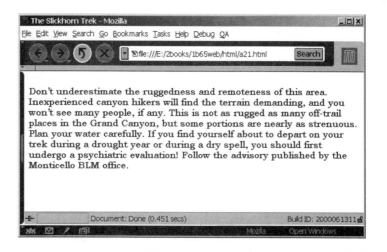

Figure A6.1   The browser displaying a simple Web page.

Markups Alphabetically

This section presents the remainder of the basic HTML markups in alphabetical order.

<b></b>

This is the markup which creates bold type. The browser will render the text inside the markups as bold. Consult Chapter 8 for the proper use of bold in typesetting.

<blockquote></blockquote>

This handy markup enables you to put a margin on both sides of a block of text (see Figure A6.2). If you want to use it to do a real block quote (a long quotation), you may want to reduce the size of the type one increment. But otherwise it makes a good layout tool.

```
<p>We had started out of Mexican Hat
about 3:30 PM. By the time we started
down the trail off the mesa, it was
about 6:00 in the evening. The shuttle
of vehicles between the trailheads at
Slickhorn Canyon and East Slickhorn
Canyon is about four or five miles,
and you can make good time driving it
in good weather. We carried ten
gallons of water in each vehicle (five
in each of two containers) as
recommended in my pamphlet Desert
Hiking Essentials.</p>

<blockquote> It is essential to have
extra water in your vehicle both for
off road and back road travel and as a
replenishing source at the end of the
hike.  Two five gallon containers per
vehicle (four people) is adequate for
many situations.</blockquote>

<p>We took one five-gallon container
```

```
out of the vehicle at each trailhead
and stowed it in the bushes. This is
an arid area. If your car is stolen at
the trailhead, you don't want to come
out of the canyon to find no water.

</p>
```

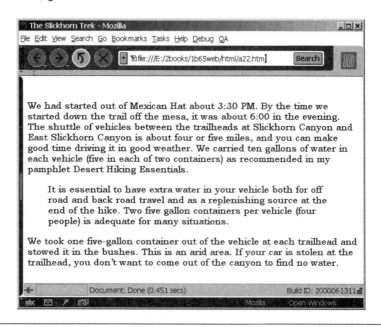

Figure A6.2   A quote in the text.

Double *<blockquote>* will double the size of the margin on each side of the content.

```
<blockquote><blockquote>content

</blockquote></blockquote>
```

This is a case where knowing some HTML will enable you to author more effectively. For instance, if you use *<blockquote>*

with the Web page illustrated earlier, you will create margins on both sides of the text block (see Figure A6.3).

```
<html><head><title>The Slickhorn
Trek</title></head><body>

<blockquote><blockquote>Don't
underestimate the ruggedness and
remoteness of this area. Inexperienced
canyon hikers will find the terrain
demanding, and you won't see many
people, if any. This is not as rugged
as many off-trail places in the Grand
Canyon, but some portions are nearly
as strenuous. Plan your water
carefully. If you find yourself about
to depart on your trek during a
drought year or during a dry spell,
you should first undergo a psychiatric
evaluation! Follow the advisory
published by the Monticello BLM
office.</blockquote></blockquote>

</body></html>
```

Figure A6.3   The *<blockquote>* markup creates left and right margins.

*
*

Use this markup to create a line break. This differs from the <p> markup in that a blank line does not follow the line break.

```
Charlie Craft<br>

Wilderness experience: 21 years<br>

Canyon experience: 10 years<br>

779-341-8533 Ext. 409<br>
```

See Figure A6.4 to see how this looks in a browser.

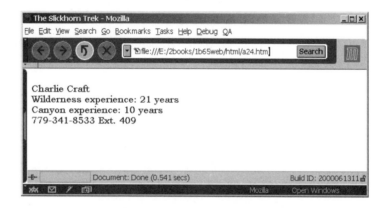

Figure A6.4   Use *
* for line breaks not followed by a blank line.

<dl> </dl>

This markup makes a list of terms and definitions like a dictionary with words and definitions. The <dl> markup creates the list. The <dt> markup marks the term. And the <dd> markup marks the definition of the term.

```
<dl>

<dt>term

<dd>definition

<dt>term

<dd>definition

</dl>
```

The term is displayed flush left. The definition is displayed indented (see Figure A6.5).

```
<dl>

<dt>Petroglyph

<dd>A design made on rock by pecking,
scratching, or carving.

<dt>Pictograph

<dd>A design painted or drawn on rock.

</dl>
```

Figure A6.5   A list of terms and definitions.

This makes a good markup to use for general layout purposes too. For instance, suppose you want to make an unnumbered and unbulleted list. You can use the <dl> and <dd> markups (see Figure A6.6).

```
You will need the following 7.5 minute
topographical maps for the Slickhorn
trek.

<dl>

<dd>Slickhorn Canyon East

<dd>Slickhorn Canyon West

<dd>Pollys Pasture

</dl>

You can obtain these maps at your
nearest US Geological Survey office.
```

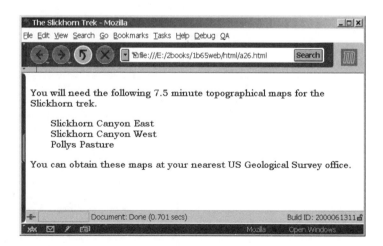

Figure A6.6   An unnumbered unbulleted list.

Note that the indent is on the left side only, not on the right side.

<dt>

This markup creates a term in a *<dl>* list. It is flush left. It must be used with the *<dl>* markup.

<dd>

This markup creates a definition in a *<dl>* list. It is indented. It must be used with the *<dl>* markup.

<div> </div>

This division markup by itself is not much use. Its attributes make it useful. Use this markup (with attributes) to lay out a section of text. The section can be a heading, a paragraph, or multiple headings and paragraphs. For instance, one attribute is *align*. You can use this to center a heading or other text (see Figure A6.7).

```
<div align="center">Slickhorn - East
Slickhorn Loop, Utah</div>
```

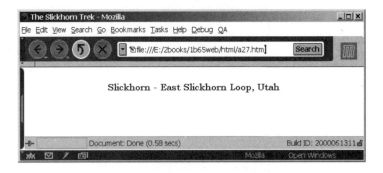

Figure A6.7   A heading centered with the *<div>* markup.

For other attributes of the *<div>* markup, consult an HTML book. Note that for the above example, you can also use the *<cen-*

ter> markup. But the HTML standards committee wants to discontinue the <*center*> markup, so use the <*div*> markup instead with the *align* attribute.

<font> </font>

Like the <*center*> markup, this markup is on the way out. But in the meanwhile, you may find it handy to use because there is no substitute except Cascading Style Sheets (CSS), another markup language for advanced Web typesetting. Use the <*font*> markup to change a typeface or a type size. Chapter 8 indicates the limitations of simple Web page typesetting. You can use the <*font*> markup to create a heading (see Figure A6.8).

```
<font face="Arial,Helvetica"
size="+1">Slickhorn - East Slickhorn
Loop, Utah</font>
```

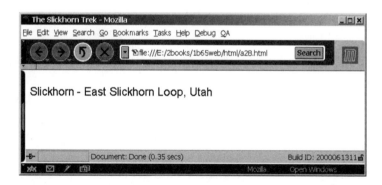

Figure A6.8   Use the <font> markup to change the typeface and type size.

Note that the attributes such as *face* (typeface) and *size* make the <*font*> markup useful.

<h1></h1>

Use this markup for headings. It comes in six sizes: 1-6. For most uses, only sizes 1-3 prove useful (see Figure A6.9). Sizes 4-6 are too small for normal use.

```
<h1>Slickhorn - East Slickhorn Loop,
Utah</h1>
```

```
<h2>Slickhorn - East Slickhorn Loop,
Utah</h2>
```

```
<h3>Slickhorn - East Slickhorn Loop,
Utah</h3>
```

```
<h4>Slickhorn - East Slickhorn Loop,
Utah</h4>
```

```
<h5>Slickhorn - East Slickhorn Loop,
Utah</h5>
```

```
<h6>Slickhorn - East Slickhorn Loop,
Utah</h6>
```

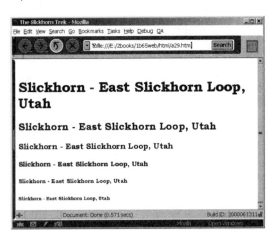

Figure A6.9   Six different headings.

The headings display in bold with a blank line before and a blank line after. The <*h1*> markup is convenient to use, but you can also use the <*font*> markup to make a line of text (heading) larger and the <*b*> markup to make it bold.

<hr>

Use this markup to make a line (a rule) across the page. The attributes control how the rule looks (see Figure A6.10).

```
<hr align="center" size="2"
width="300">

We took one five-gallon container out
of the vehicle at each trailhead and
stowed it in the bushes. This is an
arid area. If your car is stolen at
the trailhead, you don't want to come
out of the canyon to find no water.
```

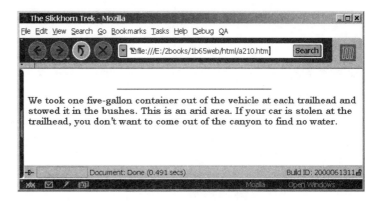

Figure A6.10 Use the <*hr*> markup to create a rule.

The rule shown in Figure A2.10 is 300 pixels wide and 2 pixels thick.

<i> </i>

This is the markup which creates italic type. The browser will render the text inside the markups as italics. Consult Chapter 8 for the proper use of italics in typesetting.

<img scr=" ">

To include an image in a Web page, use this markup. Place the URL of the image file in the *scr* attribute. The URL can be local or somewhere else on the Web. The image displays at the location of the markup.

```
<img scr="slickhorn23.jpg">
```

The *src* refers to an image file, which must be a GIF or JPEG. (The relatively new PNG graphics file format is also acceptable.) Use the attributes of the *<img>* markup to control how the image displays in a browser (see Chapter 5). Note that the URL for the image file can be anywhere on the Web. It doesn't have to be at the same URL as the Web page.

<ol> </ol>

This markup makes a list of numbered items. You do not specify the numbers. The items are numbered in order. You must use the *<li>* markup to designate the list items.

```
<ol>
<li>item
<li>item
<li>item
</ol>
```

The list is indented. For example, the earlier unnumbered list displays with numbers when you use the $<ol>$ markup (see Figure A6.11).

```
You will need the following three 7.5
minute topographical maps for the
Slickhorn trek.

<ol>

<li>Slickhorn Canyon East

<li>Slickhorn Canyon West

<li>Pollys Pasture

</ol>

You can obtain these maps at your
nearest US Geological Survey office.
```

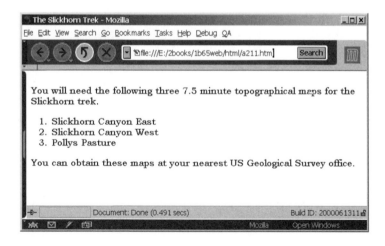

Figure A6.11 A numbered list.

<li>

This markup creates a list item in a numbered or bulleted list. It must be used with the *<ol>* or *<ul>* markups.

<p> </p>

Use this markup for all your paragraphs. The difference between this and the <br> markup is that the <p> markup adds a blank line of space before and after (see Figure A6.12).

```
<p>To find the ruins, you have to
speculate. (It helps to know they are
there.) Look for a place where there
might be ruins (under an overhang).
Then climb up and look. In most cases,
you will not be able to spot the ruins
from the canyon floor.</p>

<p>We traveled about three and a half
miles for the day, not exactly a
death-defying pace. The wet potholes,
although still small, appeared more
often. It's evident that without
recent rain, and particularly in a
drought year, there would be no water
in the canyon. Even with water
present, we topped off at almost every
wet pothole not knowing whether it
would be our last.</p>

<p>We camped at another wide place in
the streambed with flat rock and small
potholes with fresh water. Ravens and
lizards seemed to be the only wildlife
in the canyon.</p>
```

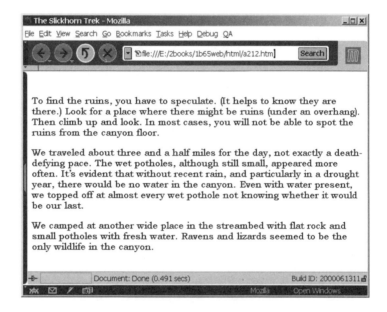

Figure A6.12 Use the *<p>* **markup for all your paragraphs.**

Note that today just the beginning markup *<p>* is enough, and you don't need the end markup *</p>*. But soon the browsers may require the end markup, too, and you don't want to have to go back and add the end markups.

**

This markup makes a subscript, such as in scientific notation (see Figure A6.13).

```
<p>The handiest solvent is H<sub>2</
sub>O (water).</p>
```


This markup makes a superscript, such as in mathematical notations (see Figure A6.13).

```
<p>The equivalent of 4<sup>5</sup> is
1,024.<p>
```

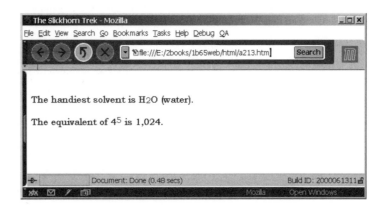

Figure A6.13 Use HTML to create subscripts and superscripts.

<table> </table>

Use the <table> markup to create a table. The <tr> markup (table row) indicates a row (record), and the <td> markup (table data) indicates a column (field). The following is a two-column table with three rows.

```
<table>
<tr>
<td>data</td>
<td>data</td>
</tr>
```

```
<tr>

<td>data</td>

<td>data</td>

</tr>

<tr>

<td>data</td>

<td>data</td>

</tr>

</table>
```

For example, the following table shows three products (topographical maps) and their current prices (see Figure A6.14).

```
<table cellpadding="10">

<tr>

<td>Slickhorn Canyon East</td>

<td>$4.00</td>

</tr>

<tr>

<td>Slickhorn Canyon West</td>

<td>$4.00</td>

</tr>

<tr>

<td>Pollys Pasture</td>

<td>$4.00</td>

</tr>

</table>
```

Note that to create some space between the data of this table, you
need to use the attribute *cellpadding* to add 10 pixels of padding
within each cell. The default use of *<table>* uses no border as
Figure A6.14 shows. To add the border, add the *border* attribute set
to *1* (see Figure A6.15).

```
<table cellpadding="10" border="1">
```

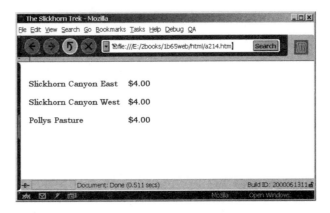

Figure A6.14 The <table> markup makes attractive tables.

Figure A6.15 A table with borders.

As you can see, the <table> markup is handy for tables, but most of us don't use tables very often. However, tables provide another tool in creating attractive layouts. Although CSS does a better job of layout than tables, until you learn CSS, you can use tables for layout purposes.

As Chapter 4 explains, you can use tables to lay out a readable text column. The following one-cell table 480 pixels wide creates a convenient reading environment (see Figure A6.16).

```
<table width="480"
align="center"><tr><td>

<p>To find the ruins, you have to
speculate. (It helps to know they are
there.) Look for a place where there
might be ruins (under an overhang).
Then climb up and look. In most cases,
you will not be able to spot the ruins
from the canyon floor.</p>

<p>We traveled about three and a half
miles for the day, not exactly a
death-defying pace. The wet potholes,
although still small, appeared more
often. It's evident that without
recent rain, and particularly in a
drought year, there would be no water
in the canyon. Even with water
present, we topped off at almost every
wet pothole not knowing whether it
would be our last.</p>
```

```
<p>We camped at another wide place in
the streambed with flat rock and small
potholes with fresh water. Ravens and
lizards seemed to be the only wildlife
in the canyon.</p>

</td></tr></table>
```

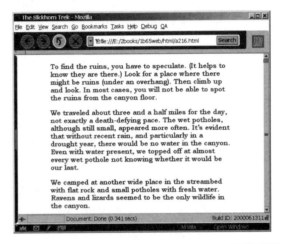

Figure A6.16 Use the *<table>* markup for special layouts such as a text column.

This is a good example of how with a little imagination you can use the *<table>* markup creatively to concoct a variety of layouts.

<tr> </tr>

This markup creates a row (record) in a table. It must be used with the *<table>* markup.

<td> </td>

This markup creates a column (field) within a table. It holds the data (content) for one table cell. Used with the *<table>* markup.

<ul> </ul>

This markup makes a list of bulleted items. You must use the *<li>* markup to designate the list items. Figure A6.17 shows how the browser displays this list.

```
You will need the following 7.5 minute
topographical maps for the Slickhorn
trek.

<ul>

<li>Slickhorn Canyon East

<li>Slickhorn Canyon West

<li>Pollys Pasture

</ul>

You can obtain these maps at your
nearest US Geological Survey office.
```

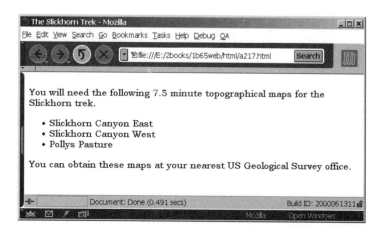

Figure A6.17 A bulleted list.

A browser eliminates redundant spaces between characters or between text blocks. In other words, a browser allows only one space between characters and only one blank line between text blocks. This particular markup establishes a space that will not be eliminated by a browser (see Figure A6.18).

```
Charlie Craft<br>

Occupation:   Wilderness
Trekker
```

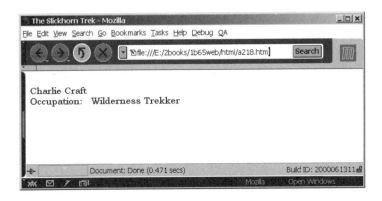

Figure A6.18 Use   to extend spaces.

To use this markup effectively for blank lines, use it with the *
* markup (see Figure A6.19).

```
Charlie Craft<br>

Occupation: Wilderness Trekker

<br> <br>

Topper Craft<br>

Occupation: Wilderness Trekker
```

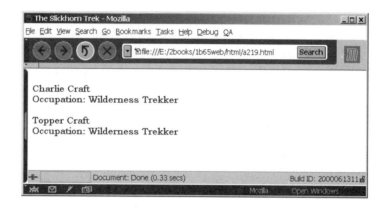

Figure A6.19 Use the * * and *
* markups to create extra blank lines.

<!-- -->

You can put this markup to good use. It marks text that does not display.

```
<!-- Change the color of this page to
offwhite when using it to display
photos. -->
```

You can leave instructions (reminders) to yourself or to others who will be working on the authoring of your Web pages.

```
<!-- This article is not part of the
series of articles by the same author
that appear in the 4/97 archive. This
article belongs in the 2/99 archive. -
->
```

You can use the comment markup for almost anything, but it's not a good idea to use any other markups inside this markup.

Anchors & Hyperlinks

Anchors and hyperlinks (links) have the same markup but different attributes. This is sometimes a little confusing, but knowing that will help you to keep these uses straight.

<a name=" "></a>

This is an anchor. The anchor is a destination. You must give each anchor in a Web page a unique name. You might put the following anchor at the top of a Web page.

```
<a name="top">Slickhorn - East
Slickhorn Loop, Utah</a>
```

This anchor makes the title of the article the anchor. With a link, you can go to this anchor. For example, a link placed anywhere in the Slickhorn trek article will take the reader to the *top* of the Web page where the title line is located.

Keep in mind that it is the attribute *name* that makes this anchor a destination.

<a href=" "></a>

This is another anchor, but it's not a destination. It takes you to a destination. The attribute *href* makes it different than an anchor that has the attribute *name*. This anchor is commonly called a link. For instance, to go to the anchor named *top*, you use the *href* anchor as follows.

```
<a href="#top">Go to top of page</a>
```

Notice that the name of an internal anchor is preceded by the character # in a link. In this case, the markup turns the words "Go to top of page" into a link. The words will change to the link color and will be underlined to indicate that they comprise a link. When you click on this link, it will take you to the top of the page (to the title line).

You use links to go to other Web pages anywhere on the Web. For instance, supposed you want to go to the *Hike-Utah* website to support something mentioned in the Slickhorn trek article. You might use the following link.

```
<a href="http://www.hike-
utah.com">canyon trail maps</a>
```

This link will take you directly to the Hike-Utah website which features information on hiking and backpacking in Utah. Notice that in this case the destination is not an anchor *name*; it's a normal *URL*.

You can use both a URL and an anchor destination in the same link. The following link will take you to the *1959* anchor in the *Models* Web page at the *Cars USA* website.

```
<a href="http://www.carsusa.com/
models.html#1959">1959 Models</a>
```

As you see, anchors can be destinations or they can be links depending on which attribute you use with them.

Example Web Page

The following is an example Web page which includes many of the markups this Appendix covers (see Figure A6.20).

```
<html><head><title>The Slickhorn
Trek</title></head><body
bgcolor="#00ffff">

 <br>
```

```
<div align="center"><h3>In Slickhorn
Canyon</h3></div>

<table width="400" cellpadding="10"
bgcolor="#ffffcc"
align="center"><tr><td>

<p>Don't underestimate the ruggedness
and remoteness of this area.
Inexperienced canyon hikers will find
the terrain demanding, and you won't
see many people, if any. This is not
as rugged as many off-trail places in
the Grand Canyon, but some portions
are nearly as strenuous. Plan your
water carefully. If you find yourself
about to depart on your trek during a
drought year or during a dry spell,
you should first undergo a psychiatric
evaluation! Follow the advisory
published by the Monticello BLM
office.</p>

</table></tr></td>

</body></html>
```

Viewing the Web Page Source

Want to see the HTML in a Web page? You can do so with any Web page. In your browser go View, Page Source. You will be able to see the HTML markups together with the page text.

Viewing the HTML in Web pages that you find attractive is a great learning technique. The next step is to use these Web pages to help create your own templates for your own Web pages. One can copyright content but generally not typesetting and layout.

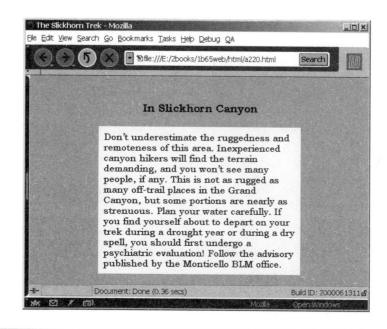

Figure A6.20 An example of a readable Web page.

Summary

This basic tutorial is designed to whet your appetite for understanding and using HTML. It doesn't include much information on attributes for the markups covered, and it doesn't include all the HTML markups. But it will get you off to a good start.

Appendix VII Using Easy Image Software

Why have a graphics software tutorial in an eBay book? Hey! It's fun to touch up your digital photographs for your eBay auction ads. And you will find a few other techniques useful too. Graphics programs range from Adobe PhotoShop at over $700 to freeware or shareware programs you can download from the Web. Some are quite easy to use. Some are incomprehensible. But I will attempt to show only a few simple things and leave the more incomprehensible programs to those who want to learn a lot more.

In fact, many graphics programs make easy-to-use darkrooms. Before you use a graphics program, however, you first have to digitize your photographs.

Digitizing Photographs

Chapter 9 covered digitizing photographs. If you have questions, review Chapter 9. This appendix will assume that you have the photographs on your hard disk or on a Kodak Picture CD. However, know something about those darn photographs? They're never quite like they should be.

The more photographs you take, the more you start to emulate a professional photographer. Where you might take one roll of film, a professional will take six or eight rolls. No wonder professionals get better pictures. But taking all those photographs takes time and even money (if you use film). All you really need are a few simple photographs to use for your eBay auction ads, and you only have the time and money to take a few shots. It's not easy to always do your best photographic work with such time and money restrictions. That's where the graphics editing program comes in; it's a digital darkroom.

The Digital Darkroom

You can do amazing things with graphics editors. Using color graphics is highly complex technology that's impossible to understand without a lot of study. The top programs have extensive and robust capabilities. Using Adobe PhotoShop proficiently, for instance, entails applying it to specific graphics projects. You can spend months, or even years, learning how to use it with photographs. Then, if you want to use it to create digital watercolor paintings instead of photographs, the learning begins all over again.

In contrast, this chapter will simply cover four things you can do quickly and easily to improve your digitized photographs. The program is the freeware IrfanView, (*http://irfanview.com*).

IrfanView

This program was picked because it is a freeware program that you can download from the website mentioned. It's a capable program, but there are commercial programs that offer additional functionality and convenience. If you do a lot of image preparation work, you might consider buying a program like PaintShop Pro (*http://www.jasc.com*) for about $100.

Some versions of Microsoft Office come with image editing programs. Microsoft has had so many different image editors over the years, however, that I won't even attempt to give you a current name.

Today a computer or a video card (powers your monitor) when purchased usually comes bundled with an image editor as does a digital camera or a scanner. If you know you have an image editor, try it on some digital photographs. If you don't know whether you have one, look around your hard disk for an unfamiliar program. You may just find an image editor. Image editors usually have the word *photo*, *picture*, or *paint* somewhere in their name.

Contrast

When shades of black and gray are similar and when colors are similar, a photograph tends to have a flat, dull look. When you digitally increase the clash of the blacks, grays, and whites, particularly around the edges of objects and when you digitally increase the clash of the colors, a photograph comes to life. This is contrast. You have to be careful, however, that you don't introduce too much contrast, or the photograph will look unnatural. But increasing the contrast just the right amount in a photograph will often make it look sharper.

How do you know what the right amount is? You can see it. As you apply the contrast, you will see the photograph change before your eyes. Not all image editors will do this, but you want to use one that does. It's hard to find a photograph that doesn't seem to improve with added contrast. You will probably find yourself adding contrast to all your eBay product photographs.

For IrfanView go *Image, Enhance colors*. The contrast, brightness, and gamma controls are together.

Brightness

Increasing brightness is less straightforward than adding contrast. Sometimes it works, and sometimes it doesn't. If you have a particularly dark photograph, you may want to increase the brightness. However, as you increase the brightness, the colors start to look increasingly bleached out. It's more likely that you will want to decrease the brightness a little. The colors will often become richer and more saturated.

Unfortunately, as you decrease the brightness, a photograph takes on an ominous darkness. In combination with increased contrast, however, a photograph can take on a rich look that's full of life.

Consequently, you will probably find, as I have, that you must use both of these controls to improve the look of photographs. More times than not, I reduce the brightness a little and boost the contrast to get a substantially improved photograph. Indeed, it's amazing how much you can improve the look of a dull photograph by changing only contrast and brightness.

For IrfanView go *Image, Enhance colors*. The contrast, brightness, and gamma controls are conveniently together.

Gamma

Gamma is the light intensity of the monitor. It is another way to adjust the brightness and works a little differently than the brightness control. It wouldn't be mentioned here except that in some graphics editors the contrast and brightness controls, which are often displayed together, are displayed along with the gamma control too. If the control for gamma is not displayed with contrast and brightness controls, you can find it elsewhere in a graphics program.

For IrfanView go *Image, Enhance colors*. The contrast, brightness, and gamma controls are together for your convenience.

How Do You Do It?

Again, as you adjust the brightness, contrast, and gamma controls, the photograph will change before your eyes. Play with the controls (systematically). Have some fun. When you get a look that you like, it's time to save the photograph. The photograph is now the image that you adjusted it to be.

What if you want to go back to the original? That's OK. You haven't altered the original photograph until you save your work. That brings up an important point. You might want to keep all your original photographs somewhere special on your hard disk. When you decide to adjust one, make a copy first. Adjust the copy and save it. That way you'll always have the original.

Sharpen

Some image editors have a hybrid control called *sharpen*. Use this instead of using contrast, brightness, and gamma. It's quicker and easier, and it works well. For IrfanView, go *Image, Sharpen*.

This has become an increasingly popular feature of image editors because it's so handy. You will find this a time-saver for your eBay business should you choose to improve your photographs for your auction ads. See Figure A7.1 for the original photograph and Figure A7.2 for the IrfanView sharpen control.

Figure A7.1   Original photograph.

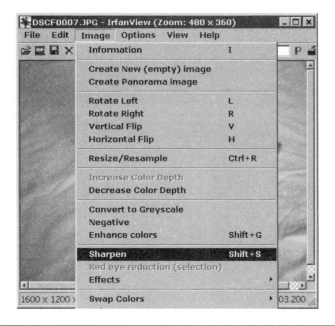

Figure A7.2   Sharpen control.

Resizing and Cropping

If you have the software to crop a digital photograph, you don't have to frame as carefully in your viewfinder when you take photographs. In fact, most inexpensive digital cameras take a 640 × 480 image, which is too large for an eBay ad. Anything larger that 400 × 300 will take too long to download, might be too large for your HTML work, and is more than you need. That means that you have to shrink your digital photographs to 400 × 300 (or smaller), or crop them to 400 × 300 (or smaller). Virtually every graphics editor has a resizer and cropper.

IrfanView has a resizer wherein you enter the numbers (the dimensions) you want. For IrfanView, go *Image*, *Resize/Resample* (see Figure A7.3).

IrfanView also has a visual cropper, go *Edit*, *Crop selection* (see Figure A7.4).

File Formats

There are many graphics file formats. Whatever you start with, you must eventually convert your photograph to a GIF (.gif) or JPEG (.jpg) format. You can also use PNG (.png) format, but it doesn't work in early Web browsers. Most graphics editors will convert photographs from one file format to another. Simply use Save As to save a photograph in the file format you want.

GIF

GIF files are compressed as much as 2:1 without loss of quality. However, they are only 8-bit files, that is, 256 colors. You need at least 256 colors to make a photograph look real, so GIFs work OK.

JPEG

JPEG files can be compressed a little or a lot. JPEG compression is "lossy," which means that quality diminishes during the compression process. The greater the compression, the smaller the file and the greater the loss of quality. But JPEGs are 24-bit files, that is, 16 million colors. Consequently, JPEG files can look good, particularly when they're not compressed much. JPEGs work better than GIFs for photographs because they have more colors.

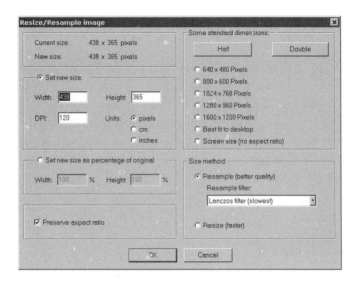

Figure A7.3   Resizing by the numbers.

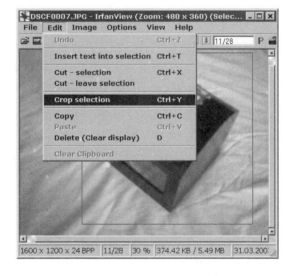

Figure A7.4   The cropped image.

There's More

Graphics editors offer a lot more than this chapter covers. Some offer much more than others. Color is highly technical as is the digital technology that makes color possible on a computer. Then too, in order to make good graphics, whether photographs or anything else, you have to have some artistic skills. It's not much fun to get bogged down in digital technology just to create something seemingly simple (i.e., an auction ad photograph). Therefore, a good strategy is to stick with a simple approach.

Summary

The procedure this book recommends for processing your photographs is simple:

1. Take a photograph.

2. Digitize it. (If already in digital form, transfer it to your hard drive.)

3. Crop it and resize it to a suitable size.

4. Adjust it (i.e., brightness, contrast, and perhaps gamma). This step is optional.

5. Upload it to your storage place on the Web for your eBay photographs.

6. Put it in your auction ad. Or, if you're using your own HTML template, put an image markup in your eBay auction ad to pull it in.

This is a simple strategy and an easy one that will accomplish your goal of posting photographs to get more bids and, therefore, higher bids on your eBay auction items.

Index